Secular Theories on Religion

Secular Theories on Religion

Current Perspectives

Edited by

Tim Jensen
Associate Professor, Department of Religious Studies
University of Southern Denmark
Odense, Denmark

&

Mikael Rothstein
Assistant Professor, Department of History of Religions
University of Copenhagen
Copenhagen, Denmark

Museum Tusculanum Press
2000

Secular Theories on Religion
© Museum Tusculanum Press, 2000
Cover design by Bente Jarlhøj
Set in AGaramond
Printed in Denmark by Special-Trykkeriet Viborg a-s
ISBN 87 7289 572 1

The publication has been made possible through a grant from
The Danish Research Council for the Humanities
Unibank-fonden

Museum Tusculanum Press
University of Copenhagen
Njalsgade 92
DK-2300 Copenhagen S
Denmark
www.mtp.dk

Contents

Preface

On our way home from a conference, we discussed the position of the scientific study of religion and the role of the scholar of religion in a cultural and academic environment which is not as secular as one might imagine – and the idea for this volume was conceived.

We have to recognise that the academic study of religion – be it history of religions, sociology of religion, anthropological studies of religion or something else – is not at all as emancipated from religion, not least Christian theology, as one might think. As a matter of fact religious approaches and agendas have been extremely dominant throughout the history of the study of religion. In many cases the notion of "religion", theories of religion and methods used to study what we normally term religion are seriously delimited by theological traditions. Furthermore, from an institutional point of view, many university departments in this area are intimately linked with theological faculties or even churches. Consequently, scholars of religion frequently have to explain and justify their academic, non-religious or secular approach. Such an approach should "confine itself to analytical models grounded in a view of the world based on the insights and achievements of the natural sciences [...] and apply methods, theories and models developed in the human and social sciences", as stated by Armin W. Geertz in the opening remarks of his article in this book. In so far as the present volume puts an emphasis on this issue, one of our goals is reached.

The authors have been asked to present their ideas of what a secular study of religion should be like, what methods it should apply, what aims, and what kind of scientific thinking that should be pursued. The result is a broad pattern of approaches, some wholly theoretical, some also based on case studies. All in all the texts offer a comprehensive account of modern scholarly positions and summarises much of the ongoing theoretical debate and the effort to further emancipate the study of religion from theological biases.

We have also asked the authors to touch upon the issue of the scholar of religion as "a public intellectual". The scholar is not placed outside society, he or she is not isolated from general societal developments, and we therefore need to discuss the position of the academic study of religion in the public sphere. Contextualizing the academic study of religion is one thing, but discussing the scholar's situation in his or her cultural environment is equally necessary.

Although we have asked the authors to address the same issues, we have not aimed at uniformity. On the contrary we have allowed everyone to compose a text of his or her own choice in order to demonstrate the rich academic variety in the field. A few contributors have based their papers on already existing articles, but in each cases they have added new comments to it or reedited it altogether. The rest of the texts are published in this volume for the first time.

Finally a few words regarding the book's title: The editors are aware that not every contributor is in favour of the title chosen. "Secular" may be too intimately connected to specific historical conditions and Christian notions, and consequently signal the opposite of what is intended. In this connection, though, we simply use the term to designate the academic study of religion as defined in opposition to religious thinking about religion.

We would like to extend our sincere thanks to all contributors. Everyone responded positively to our initial invitation, and soon the manuscripts started to arrive. We, the editors, as well as the authors, hope that the book will find its way to a wide readership, but our primary aim is to reach students and educators who are struggling with the premises of modern scholarship in the fields of humanistic and social scientific studies of religion.

We would also like to thank *The Danish Research Council for the Humanities* and *Unibank-fonden* whose financial support has made this publication possible.

Tim Jensen & Mikael Rothstein
Copenhagen, March 2000

Pragmatic Theory

Catherine Bell

Bernhard J. Hanley Professor, Department of Religious Studies
Santa Clara University, Santa Clara, CA, USA

The study of religion today is more firmly established institutionally and more broadly pursued in multiple disciplines than ever before. For participants and observers alike, the sheer diversity of ways of studying religion can give one pause. For those concerned with disciplinary integrity and clear standards, this is worrisome period of challenge and even chaos. For those concerned with generating fresh perspectives, it is a welcome time for one hundred flowers to bloom. Both perspectives have real justifications. There are, of course, many reasons for this diversity, with demographic ones among them, but the result is a large-scale shift in the ethos of the field and various reorganizations of its internal groupings. History of religions, for example, which for many years was most concerned with the methodological issues surrounding cross-cultural comparison, is now primarily struggling with the postcolonial concerns involved in 'writing culture' (Clifford & Marcus 1986). Meanwhile, perhaps in place of the fading philosopher of religion and the broad world religions comparativist, a new style of methodological studies has emerged – so far partly historiographical, partly general gadfly – to question the theological underpinnings of the history of religions and to try to ground the study of religion in general more scientifically. In this essay, I would like to address how I conceive the theoretical task of studying religion in the current context. If the 'voice' used in the discussion that follows sounds more candid than professional, it is because this essay attempts to speak from the existential experience of trying to be professional about so much that is so vigorously contested.

The formulation of an explicitly secular theory of religion at the close of the 20th century is a project that evokes historical echoes and fresh conundrums. Many secular and scientific approaches to religion have been formulated in the last few centuries by carefully differentiating the emerging practices of objective empiricism from the assumptions of religious belief and the practices of theological reasoning. In the process of differentiating themselves, these secular approaches to religion not only helped to articulate a modern scientific perspective, they also helped to shape new forms of theology and new styles of religious commitment. Even today what we mean by the secular, objective, and scientific is defined in great part by the foil of seeing religion as the subjective and partisan. Eighteenth and nineteenth century scientists cast religion as a matter of belief in revelation in contrast to which science explicitly shunned the creedal in favor of the empirical; today we tend to cast religion as the epitome of a cultural-bound world view in contrast to how secular and scientific objectivity is thought to transcend the constraints of culture. Even modern religious thought – that is, the self-conscious reflections of religious traditions living in close proximity to advanced technology, scientific ways of knowing, and secular institutions – has also tended to define itself in terms of its tensions with science and secularism.

Focusing on how science and religion have helped define each other can make the rhetoric of a secular science sharply opposed to religious belief appear ideologically exaggerated. When the secular and scientific study of religion is examined up close, irony abounds. The professional career of a scholar of religion today continues to be directly shaped by an overarching view of a radical polarization between religion and science, while on the ground the situation is full of ambiguities. For example, on the level of the personal and anecdotal, in the same month that I began this essay on non-theological approaches to religion, I also attended a conference of religious studies scholars, mostly theologians but also others hard to classify, who wanted to explore more effective strategies for teaching world religions. Their concern was to do objective justice to other religions without undermining the subjective faith experiences of their students or the religious missions of their institutions. On the level of national discourse in the field of religious studies, religiously-affiliated or theologically-inclined participants claim to feel marginalized by the secular assumptions, frameworks, and style of the field, while avowedly secular scholars argue that we must be on the defensive with regard to the overt theological agendas and covert habits of thought that still threaten the field (see Bell 1996:180). There are other levels of ambiguity as well. Although it appears that the vast majority of religious studies scholars teaching in higher education today have religious backgrounds that influenced their studies and that most of these scholars maintain religious affiliations of some kind, few of them would regard themselves as deviating from professional standards of secular and objective inquiry into religion. The secular and the religious are conjoined and conflicted at every turn.

Several recent studies remind us that the emergence of the terminology of "religion" to describe a pan-human phenomenon amenable to study was driven by two sets of concerns – on the one hand, to elaborate a non-sectarian style of universal religion that could replace divisive traditions and, on the other hand, to elaborate a scientific methodology ultimately able to explain religion and religiosity itself (Preus 1987; Asad 1993; McCutcheon 1995). At times both concerns have been united in the vision of particular scholars; just as often perhaps they have been demarcated or set at cross-purposes. It is clear today that neither concern has been able to seize the day and banish the other from the field. Many scholars continue to see their work as contributing, however indirectly, to the articulation of a more universal, less culturally particularistic, spirituality.[1] At the same time, there are fresh attempts nearly every decade to construct a more strictly scientific analysis of religion – despite on-going critiques of science, objectivity, and all forms of Western hegemonic discourse. Indeed, one can conclude that the field of religious studies *insists* on locating itself within a tense field defined by both the clash and the confusion between believers and non-believers. Attempts to create a theoretical middle ground have been little more than precarious bridges readily destabilized by the logical extremes to which they are pegged. Whatever the reasons for this pathology, it may be the single greatest obstacle to playing a larger role as public intellectuals. The wrangling of advocates for secular or theological approaches to religion appear to contribute little to the concerns of citizens, policymakers, international diplomats or business people.

A totally different framework for imagining religion, one free of this historical determinism, remains conceptually out of reach. I certainly do not have answers to the questions at the heart of these theoretical dilemmas. Indeed, I fear I am sufficiently shaped by post-1950 forms of the ambivalent dependency of science and religion that there are limits to what I can contribute to transcending the well-established framework. Nonetheless, while without an answer, I am not without a position. I am in favor of extricating the study of religion from recognizable theological and more

11

subtle teleological projects, and in doing so I hope to learn about the theological inheritance underlying many models and practices of scholarship. But I have no dispute with or fear of contagion from theological agendas and colleagues. Neither do I harbor any convictions about a superior rationality. I am not a 'believer' in the scientific study of religion. I am aware that the study of religion is as historically and culturally defined as any religious pantheon or doctrine, despite the peculiar type of cultural community that is seeking to generate a more abstract and general language with which to discuss multiple religious cultures. And while I naturally worry about the real cognitive value of my work and the field of religious studies in general, I usually conclude that they have a short-term contribution to make and a long-term fate to explore.

Ultimately, I see myself as a pragmatic theoretician, which is perhaps a bit different from scholars who are simply – and quite understandably – pragmatic about theory. While the latter employ just enough theoretical baggage to get the job done, the pragmatic theoretician enlists theory in such a way as to learn about theory-making in the process. If the study of religion today appears to be in something of a tight spot, hemmed in by various movements to dis-establish and re-establish the certainties of science and scholarly writing, then theory is the way to map the corner into which we have backed ourselves: I am under no illusions that theory knows how to find a way out of the corner, usually it appears to argue for redrawing the whole room. While the stance of the pragmatic theorist makes it hard to rise to those occasions when simple, clear and prescriptive scholarly advice is requested, it may have some redeeming virtues of its own to which I will return.

As a scholar and teacher, my theoretical approach to religion very much parallels what I have sketched out elsewhere as a type of three-stage method of critical-historical analysis for the study of ritual (Bell 1992:5). The first stage involves a analysis of the historical definitions of the problem or issue – in this case, what we mean by religion but also why the issue of religion has become an object of study for us in the first place and how current frameworks may render some analyses of the issue more meaningful than others. The second stage is the proposal of an interpretive perspective, hopefully a fresh one, which will seriously enable the issues that concern us, including our cultural categories, to engage and be engaged by the material. Our categories and framing of issues should allow difference and similarity to unfold rather than be dismissed or subsumed. Finally, the last stage should develop applications of the new perspective to appropriate case studies or pre-existing dilemmas so as to demonstrate its more effective interpretation of them.

Let me identify and illustrate more fully some of the premises built into this approach. In general, my theoretical approach to religion reflects a postmodern 'take' on the modernist enterprise, but certainly not an abandonment of it. That is, I attempt to take the history, politics, and sociology of discourse on religion into account even while contributing to this discourse. Other premises include the heuristic nature of all conceptual tools, sociological interpretation of meaningful theories, and the value of the persistent, open-ended debate about the goal of creating a body of knowledge about religion. I will briefly address each of these in turn.

The historicity of discourse on religion. It does not seem useful to talk formally about religion without repeatedly acknowledging that the term represents an idea that has its roots in particular historical and cultural circumstances even if we cannot grasp or articulate all of them. Hence, one must admit that ideas of religion are not obvious, fixed, or natural; they are historically located, debated, and slippery. The fact that the history of discussions about religion has been shaped by interests that can be identified as social and political among others does not reduce scholarly discourse to 'nothing but politics'; it is simply recognizing political dimensions and ramifications to our interest in Buddhist art, Christian history, or Dogon ritual. In doing so, we want to illuminate something of how we are working within cultural institutions of scholarly practice when we define an issue, a method of interrogation, and a working body of information. The historicity of our interest in religion is so basic that it cannot come as a given or an afterthought to any particular project in religious studies. I have tried to integrate this basic orientation into even the most introductory undergraduate course on religion that I teach.

The heuristic use of conceptual tools. Because what is best meant by religion is far from obvious and has been subject to historical shifts and endless formal debate, the use of religion as terminology is always heuristic. Terms afford a useful focus on some things at the expense of other things. Their insights and oversights are based on explicit and implicit premises that require self-conscious tracking in order to appreciate. Those approaches that begin with a clear and delimited definition of what is to be meant by religion will focus on only the data that seems to fit such constraints; they are forced to put aside data that does not fit but may still be intrinsically relevant – especially to reflecting on how another culture experiences and expresses the sort of thing we think we mean by religion. In contrast, those approaches that refuse to define religion face the problem of so much material that their process of attention and selection might well be less intellectually responsible than a narrower, more definition-driven approach.

Terminology should provide a focus and a rationale for the selection of materials that are sufficiently clear and systematic as to be subject to debate, replication, and modification. Yet terminology should not close off difference too early or foster a closed, circular system of reasoning. Terminology can be a valuable map to how we came to ask our current questions; if we prematurely discard terms as useless or misleading, we may lose our sense of where we are standing and why. Ultimately, good terms are tools that enable us to create a trail; they leave marks behind us so we know the exact course we have taken, allowing others to follow or veer off, and facilitating logical projections and, of course, formal challenges, etc. However, terms should not predetermine where we will end up. Terms should be flexible enough to open a real dialog with whatever challenges the very terms themselves.

Perhaps Ninian Smith is correct when he suggests that we should be able to use other cultural terms in our scholarly studies, such as the Chinese concept of *li*, with its ethos of decorum and etiquette, when we discuss ritual (McCutcheon 1995: 300). Certainly we have seen Azande notions of sorcery come, via Evans-Pritchard, to help shape larger discussions of magic. Likewise, Polynesian notions of *mana* and African notions of the fetish have shaped discussions of object-exchange and entered into our analytic language.[2] We routinely use terms like ritual or religion to survey activities that might enlarge the sense of these terms. Yet allowing enlargement does not always in itself afford a real challenge to the meanings of such terms. It is easy to let *mana* shape our notions of gift-exchange for that is exactly how we create an abstract formal language of key terms that purport to illuminate particular practices. But formal language, as well as the sociology of the field of religious studies, pushes for one main term, rather than a loose family of terms.[3] A full analysis of this dimension of terms is beyond the scope of this discussion, but my own investigations of an appropriate formal language for examining and analyzing ritual-like practices across cultures suggests that the privileging of a single term, which is instrumental in the creation of a field of knowledge, raises problems but it is not always an indefensible act of hegemony. More studies are needed to explore the social and political dimensions of the organization of knowledge in the modern academy[4]

Ultimately, the usefulness of a particular approach to defining religion, god, ritual, belief, or spirit, will greatly depend on the goal of the particular analysis. A narrower *a priori* definition of religion has traditionally served projects that use tightly comparable data to generalize about a human propensity to believe in a supernatural reality. More open categories tend to facilitate more in-depth exploration of particular concepts and practices. I have argued elsewhere that the focus of an analysis of the simple daily ritual of offering incense at a Chinese domestic altar will vary dramatically according to whether the analysis is being used to talk about religion in general, the underlying unity of Chinese culture, the way Cantonese women deal with lineage authority, or how one particular person makes sense of the forces shaping her life (Bell 1998).

As a field that is not theology and not anthropology, among others, religious studies has struggled to differentiate "religion" as a worthy focus of study-that is, as a widespread (if not universal) and irreducible phenomenon in its own right. This has meant that many definitions and analytic projects are interested in broad generalizations that indicate the clarity and legitimacy of religion as a category and focus of a field. At the same time, the field is often deeply involved in tracking cultural specifics that require more open-ended terminology. It is important to realize that we do both *not* because the field is incoherent, but because it embraces a variety of questions and discourse communities – with Sinologists and Judaica scholars talking to each other within the academy, as well as to groups outside the academy, such as government funding agencies and state legislatures. The early years in the founding of a discipline tend to see projects that aim to prove the legitimacy of the discipline's key categories and distinctive method. With more acceptance, there is less concern to define and defend disciplinary boundaries.

Communities of discourse. Traditionally, scholarship on religion has been constituted by a community of people that engaged in formal and informal dialog. The dialog that constitutes the community also sets up intrinsic differentiations that define relationships with those outside the academic community and with those people and materials that are the focus of the academic community. It is easy to forget that theorizing and scholarship are activities that make us members of certain types of self-regulating communities; the meaningfulness and value of what is done and said in scholarly theorizing depends on this community context. Even though scholarship is dedicated to the development of terms and meanings able to transcend particular cultural contexts and communicate across multiple regional and historical differences, this happens because a new sort of community is being defined at such a level. The power of religion as a abstract category that can inform the use of incense sticks in Beijing and Sabbath candles in Jerusalem does not reside in the term, but in the community of scholars who use the term to see through these particular actions to something such actions are deemed to have in common. Abstract categories may have little or no meaning outside the discourse community that uses them, while the discourse community clearly creates itself through the development of its distinct language.

Sometimes we imagine that the more abstract a term, the less it is constrained by particular cultural premises and interests. But this is to misunderstand just what a culture is and can be. As an abstraction, the term religion can do a decent job of transcending many of the cultural premises of a Lutheran talking about Catholics or an Hasid talking about Muslims, although biases can be found in the best of such studies.[5] But users of the category of religion constitute a community that has its own sort of culture. It may be a community that abjures specific theological commitments such as those seen in Christian or Islamic cultural communities, among others, and it may be a community that enables international dialog – but it is a culture nonetheless. As a community, it may involve a rather small group of individuals in classrooms and at computer terminals across many nations and linguistic groups. This social organization enables the community of people interested in religion to be very powerful in some circumstances and very marginal in many others. What this community knows about 'religion' may determine curricula across the country *and* be judged irrelevant by American state legislatures debating doctor-assisted suicide or the Chinese government debating the degree of autonomy to be given Chinese Christian churches.

The conundrum of the scholarly community is that its efforts to develop an abstract and analytic language about religion in general, what enables it to talk somewhat systematically about a diversity of religions, can make it culturally irrelevant to communities articulating issues in very non-abstract terms. Committed Christians concerned about assisted suicide may have very little interest in the professional opinions of scholars of cross-cultural religion and ethics; what counts as meaningful knowledge will differ for both communities since they are culturally distinct groups engaged in different projects and talking different languages. The assumption that the scholarly community's expertise should give them authority and power in debates within "less informed" communities is probably best seen as dating from a period in which the scholar was not so much a denizen of another community as a type of upper class. That is not the case in America today. The sheer expansion of the system of higher education since the 1950s, the growth of disciplines and specialties that "network" scholars from Peoria to Pretoria, and the precarious dependence of higher education on tax-payers and politicians – all this has helped to break down the social class authority of the scholarly community on the one hand, while not facilitating any closer identification with mainstream American life on the other.

There is much irony here. The more differences theoretical language must cross and account for, becoming more abstract and formal, the more unable it is to communicate directly with the particular. The self-consciously theoretical will subsume the particular, not address it or be addressed by it. This mechanism creates the discourse language of a professional culture. Yet if the professional culture has no real social authority, then its internal discourse – its concerns as well as its professional jargon – are not likely to be of much interest to those outside the community unless, that is, there is some demonstrable way in which its professional knowledge can be shown to work and produce tangible benefits. Current efforts to make scholars of religion more influential in public policy is a case in point. On the one hand, it is clearly a laudable goal: in a democracy, as many people and interest groups as possible should be involved and scholars may by nature tend to drift away from such involvement. On the other hand, such efforts seems naïve when they envision anything but the most modest tasks of providing more sources of diverse information.

The goal of the process. The goal of this sort of scholarship is still knowledge, although it is clearly culturally determined knowledge for a particu-

lar, if open-ended, community. The general applicability of this knowledge to concerns outside this community remains a very real question.
Some have suggested that the role of scholars of religion and their scholarship is to build bridges of understanding, especially in regard to cross-cultural issues (Berling 1993). Yet this formulation of purpose can be both
misleading and unsatisfactory. Naturally scholars of religion are concerned
with understanding and understanding certainly involves all sorts of
bridges, intellectual-theoretical ones as well as inter-personal, inter-insti-
tutional, and inter-cultural ones. Yet much in academic practice is not well
suited to real mediation of other groups. The more the field is concerned
to define terms and sharpen its language, the more it will fuss over internal
issues of method and jargon, and the more irrelevant it will be to particular concerns emanating from elsewhere.

Bodies of knowledge and discourse communities, however culturally
determined and self-reflexive, are certainly not neutral in the power politics
of social life. While we have much to learn about how these things work,
explorations of such power relationships should not make scholars yearn
for – much less claim – some ideal state of professional powerlessness!
Inevitably scholars of religion, like all members of the academy, must take
part in the verbal fray of a classless democracy. What do we bring to that task?

It is not fashionable among the more self-consciously scientific and secular methods for the study of religion to talk about humanist values in
scholarship. To do so has been identified as a carry over of theological
agendas, although such accusations seem to suggest an unfamiliarity with
standard practice in the hard and social sciences. Representatives of those
fields routinely talk about the congruence between their sense of their
field of study and key humanist values, ethical concerns, or moral issues.
Of course, such views are debated and opposed along with the science to
which they are linked. Few people today endorse "value-free" investigation
simply because it appears to be impossible and self-deluding; although we
may debate the values involved, there is some consensus that a failure to
make our values clear leaves us more subject to influence by underlying
and less laudable ones. Certainly, any teacher who has to hold the attention of an undergraduate class must strive to articulate some elements of a
humanistic vision. It does not need to be the one formulated over 35 years
ago by Mircea Eliade (Eliade 1961:1-11). It can be much more modest –
and pragmatic.

My professional experiences have convinced me that the practice of theory cannot be divorced from morality even as it pulls challenges to notions of "morality" into the welter of questions facing us. There are the basics, of course, such as striving for clarity and fairness, and working to ask real questions rather than just fabricating trendy constructions. Yet above all, it seems to me, scholars have the moral task of working to make complexity accessible. In theory, we are the ones with the skills and tools to make sure that very complicated situations and ideas can be put into words, thereby making it possible to have discussions about issues that can only be discussed if there is a language for reflexivity, nuance, counter-evidence, and doubt. Too often we appear to take complex realities and reduce them to impenetrably dense blocks of obfuscation rather than laying them open for a wider conversation. Dichotomies between popularizers and true scholars are often drawn in silly and destructive ways.

Our theories of religion and our expectations for theoretical scholarship will continue to have to negotiate the terrain we have created by differentiating science and religion in such a radically polarized way. I have no idea what this will mean for the field itself or even my own scholarship five years from now. I like to think I would write a different sort of essay after five more years of thought and experience, but maybe not. I do know that the pragmatic theorist of religion will need both humility and some faith in the process.

Notes

1. For one example, this purpose underlies many messages posted on the Buddhist Studies list on the Web.
2. For a more formal discussion of "unbounded analytic categories" and the use of "native categories," see Saler 1993.
3. For a discussion of a loose family of terms used in ritual studies, see Bell 1998.
4. For several provocative studies in this vein, see Latour 1993, Rabinow 1996, and Bourdieu 1988; more historically, see Shapin 1994 and Noble 1992.
5. For example, a Protestant bias in the study of religion is discussed by Douglas 1966: 18-19 and Smith 1990: 34.

References

Asad, Talal, *Genealogies of Religion: Discipline and Reasons of Power in Christianity and Islam*, Johns Hopkins Press, Baltimore, 1993.

Bell, Catherine, "Modernism and Postmodernism in the Study of Religion," *Religious Studies Review* 22, no. 3 (July): 179-90.

Bell, Catherine, "Performance", Taylor, Mark C. (Ed.), *Critical Terms in Religious Studies*, University of Chicago, Chicago, 1998: 205-224.

Bell, Catherine, *Ritual Theory, Ritual Practice,* Oxford University Press, New York, 1992.

Berling, Judith A., "Is Conversation about Religion Possible?" *Journal of the American Academy of Religion* 61, no. 1 (Spring 1993): 1-22.

Bourdieu, Pierre, *Homo Academicus*, translated by Peter Collier, Stanford University Press, Stanford, 1988.

Clifford, James and George E. Marcus, *Writing Culture: The Poetics and Politics of Ethnography*, University of California Press, Berkeley, 1986.

Douglas, Mary, *Purity and Danger: An Analysis of Concepts of Pollution and Taboo* , Praeger, New York, 1966.

Eliade, Mircea, "A New Humanism", in *The Quest: History and Meaning in Religion*, University of Chicago, Chicago, 1961.

Latour, Bruno, *We Have Never Been Modern*, translated by Catherine Porter, Harvard University Press, Cambridge, 1993.

McCutcheon, Russell T. "The Category 'Religion' in Recent Publications: A Critical Survey," *Numen* 42 (1995): 284-309.

Noble, David F., *World Without Women: The Christian Clerical Culture of Western Science*, Oxford University Press, New York, 1992.

Preus, J. Samuel, *Explaining Religion: Criticism and Theory from Bodin to Freud*, Yale University Press, New Haven, 1987.

Rabinow, Paul, *Essays on the Anthropology of Reason*, Princeton University Press, Princeton, 1996.

Saler, Benson, *Conceptualizing Religion: Immanent Anthropologists, Transcendent Natives, and Unbounded Categories*, E. J. Brill, 1993.

Shapin, Steven, *A Social History of Truth: Civility and Science in Seventeenth-Century England*, Chicago University Press, Chicago, 1994.

Smith, Jonathan Z., *Drudgery Divine: On the Comparison of Early Christianities and the Religion of Late Antiquity,* Chicago University Press, Chicago, 1990.

Smith, Jonathan Z., "Religion and Religious Studies: No Difference at All", *Soundings* 71 (1988): 231-44.

Analytical Theorizing in the Secular Study of Religion

Armin W. Geertz

Professor, Department of Religious Studies
University of Aarhus, Aarhus, Denmark

The secular study of religion is understood in this paper to mean the non-sectarian, non-religious study of religion.[1] It is not necessarily an atheistic approach. It simply chooses to interpret, understand and explain religion in non-religious terms. It confines itself to analytical models grounded in a view of the world based on the insights and achievements of the natural sciences. The study of religion, obviously, is not a natural science. It applies methods, theories and models developed in the human and social sciences: history, sociology, linguistics, psychology, anthropology, ethnography, and philosophy. It is further characterized by a comparative interest in all religions throughout human history. But its view of the world is secular and humanistic.

It is a common misconception that religious values should be employed in the study of religion. It is often pointed out that just as aesthetic values play a central role in the study of literature, music and art so should religious values play a role in the study of religion. But when applied to other human or social sciences, this assumption is not so obvious. Studies of politics are better conducted on the basis of scientific rather than political values, studies of French language on linguistic rather than aesthetic values, of an exotic culture on ethnographic rather than the particular culture's own values and so on.[2]

I have argued in several publications that the point of departure for a humanistic, secular study of religion must be an anthropological theory, i.e. a theory about the constitution of human beings, rather than a theological theory, i.e. a theory about the constitution of divinity.[3] Like any humanistic or social science discipline, the study of religion must reflect on its theoretical foundations. Any study of religion implies a series of primary assumptions, and it is very important that we clarify the primary theories that inform our general theories of religion and the subsequent definitions of religion and typological schemes that arise from those general theories. When we apply philosophical reflection to the study of religion, I would argue that we should use it to expose the deductive chain of premises that inform and nourish our typological schemes and our general claims, no matter what our individual stance on science may be. And, if possible, we should also try to establish a consensus for a rational and disciplined scholarly discourse on religion.

The study of religion is completely dependent on the basic theory that one has on religion. If one believes that religious claims are true in an absolute sense, then religious studies are used to provide primarily religious answers to scientific questions. The approach promoted here is that religion is a human and cultural product, a kind of overlay in relation to biological, psychological, cultural and social structures and mechanisms. I contend, therefore, that questions raised by religion must be answered in the secular study of religion by insights achieved in biology, cognitive and cultural psychology, cultural anthropology and sociology. In terms of this approach, religious answers, whatever their origin might be, are the scientific problem that a humanistic, secular and non-religious study of religion must address.

The Philosophy of Science

Philosophy has made significant contributions to the human and natural sciences. Not only has it developed intellectual tools such as various branches of logic and several approaches to semantic theory, it has also originated major topics that are now being taken on by other disciplines such as linguistics and cognitive psychology.

A central concern is, of course, philosophy as methodological criticism. What are the legitimate theoretical constructs of science, and what is their ontological status? What can we know, and how do we know it? These epistemological concerns have generated debates over internalism and externalism, foundationalism, coherentism, knowledge, the political implications of foundationalism, the maleness of reason, justification, truth, skepticism, the structure of knowledge, the politics of knowledge, etc., etc.

In dealing with the religions of living cultures and especially with cultures that have been subject to colonialism, students of culture and religion have been faced since the 1960's with a whole series of challenges that in part involved philosophical issues and in part require philosophical answers. Unfortunately, philosophers have not been all that helpful in handling the difficult issues of orientalism, the construction of the exotic, the representation or misrepresentation of other cultures, the politics of science, and feminist criticism. These criticisms have been collectively labelled "postmodern criticism". I have sketched out some of the antecedents of the postmodern challenge to the study of religion in earlier work and will only be brief here.[4] I venture three major antecedents, namely, the criticism of orientalism raised by former colonial subjects; the criticism of voice, raised by literary theorists and feminists, and the criticism of the epistemological foundations of science by philosophers of science.[5]

The basic argument of the orientalist critics is that anthropology and the cultural sciences grew out of and were instruments of colonialism.[6] Critic Edward Said noted that the problem is not so much that scholars have directly contributed to the political suppression of the people under study, but that their very activity elaborates and confirms the uneven exchange of various kinds of power, be they political, intellectual, cultural or moral.[7]

Another important area of concern is the fact that Europeans have been 'constructing' exotic peoples throughout their history. These peoples have all been objects of economical, political, or military interest: first the black African, then the American Indian, then the Oriental, and finally the Muslim. Western scholars have been deeply involved in representing, interpreting, and recreating non-Western cultures.[8]

The critical examination of voice is a central concern in feminist reflection, the second major source of postmodern criticism. Early feminists aligned themselves with the neo-Marxists in their critique of class and male bias and thus the original paradigm was emancipatory. By the early 1980's three significant streams of feminist scholarship had emerged. The first focussed on the social or cultural construction of gender,[9] the second on the historical construction of gender in relation to class, power, and changes in modes of production,[10] and the third on cross-cultural comparative analyses of the variables in women's status, role, authority, and power in various cultures.[11] Today feminist studies represent a wealth of new research and theoretical analysis in all fields of the human and social sciences.

The third major source of postmodern criticism comes from philosophers of science. From these quarters we find devastating attacks on one of the mainstays of the Enlightenment project, namely, rationality. In the first place attempts to use the natural sciences as models have been questioned since prediction, theory, results, and conclusions are all based on social conventions.[12] Second, it has been pointed out that human cognition is not capable enough to draw complicated conclusions.[13] Third, scientific language is no less metaphorical than any other language, indeed, metaphors and metonymical relations are intrinsic to the production of categories at the most basic cognitive level.[14] And, finally, not only is rationality culturally situated, but it is situated in a multi-paradigmatic and pluralistic situation in which science is essentially contestable.[15] As philosopher Paul A. Roth wrote:

> One task confronting a 'post-empiricist' epistemology is that of reforming the shattered consensus regarding the canons of rationality. In the post-positivist vacuum, a dispute has developed in the philosophy of social science which I refer to as the *Rationalitätstreit*. This 'dispute about rationality' also draws arguments and inspiration from the critics of positivism. The substance of the dispute concerns which set or sets of canons of justification qualify as rational. The sides in the dispute are determined by how each party responds to the demise of the positivists' project. One side wants to redo that project; the other side wants to *undo* the unity-of-method thesis. Those who would redo the project seek a single set of justificatory canons; the hope is that philosophers of science will specify these. Those who would undo the original program maintain that the unity-of-method [i.e., the positivist stance] thesis fails because, for one reason or another, there can be no *science* of society. The redoers view the term 'rational' as denoting forms of reasoning which are independent of the vagaries of cultural practices; the undoers take the term 'rational' as an honorific label bestowed by people upon their favored fashion of reasoning.[16]

It is not my goal in this paper to provide solutions to these problems. I have attempted to promote an approach called ethnohermeneutics as one way of dealing with several of the above-mentioned problems.[17] In agreement with Paul A. Roth, I reject methodological exclusivism for a methodological pluralism, in other words, "we cannot make sense of the notion of 'one proper set of rules' that defines the study of human behavior". As Roth wrote:

[A] methodological pluralist is able to respect what ought to be respected regarding canons of inquiry ... but need not insist that just one particular set of methodological canons or normative assumptions defines the rational pursuit of social inquiry.[18]

Analytical Theorizing

In this paper, I want to point out how extremely important philosophical reflection is to the secular study of religion, indeed, to any human or social science. One of the primary goals, I think, in using philosophy in the study of religion is to promote and clarify analytical theorizing. This is, in part, a necessary and definitive step away from the former text positivism that has characterized much of the history of religions. It is essential for a scientific study of religion to formalize definitions and typologies in relation to the explicit chain of theorizing that informs them, in other words, a theoretically informed study of religion.

Social philosopher Jonathan H. Turner understands 'analytical theorizing' as an attempt to isolate the universal generic properties of the human social universe and understand their operation. As he wrote:

[W]e can develop abstract laws of invariant properties of the universe, but such laws will need to be supplemented by scenarios (models, descriptions, analogies) of the underlying processes of these properties. Moreover, explanation is in most cases not going to involve precise predictions and deductions, primarily because experimental controls are not possible in the tests of most theories. Explanation will consist, instead, of a more discursive use of abstract propositions and models to understand specific events. Deduction will be loose, and even metaphorical. And it will naturally be subject to argument and debate. But, sociology is not unique here; most sciences operate this way.... [W]e do not need to abandon our search for invariant properties any more than physics has after recognizing that many formulations are stated, initially at least, rather loosely and that they are subject to political negotiation within a scientific community (Turner 1987: 159).

It is important to distinguish between what Jonathan H. Turner calls the varying strategies of analytical theorizing, namely, metatheoretical schemes, analytical schemes, propositional schemes, and modelling schemes.

Metatheoretical schemes address fundamental philosophical questions like what is the nature of human activity, what are appropriate procedures for developing theory, and so on. Turner is skeptical concerning the usefulness of such schemes because:

> They embroil theory in unresolvable philosophical issues and they easily become scholastic treatises that lose sight of the goal of all theory: to explain how the social universe works. Thus, metatheorizing is interesting philosophy and, at times, a fascinating history of ideas, but it is not theory and it is not easily used in analytical theorizing (162).

Analytical schemes consist of the construction of abstract systems of categories "that presumably denote key properties of the universe and crucial relations among these properties" (162). There are two contradictory approaches: 'naturalistic analytical schemes' and 'sensitizing analytical schemes'. The problem with the former is that it is similar to metatheorizing, and the problem with the latter is that it often rejects the search for universal laws.

Propositional schemes are statements that connect variables to one another. There are three general types of propositional schemes: 'axiomatic schemes', 'formal schemes', and 'empirical schemes'. Axiomatic schemes involve deductions from abstract axioms containing precisely defined concepts to an empirical event. But such schemes require laboratory controls, concepts defined in exact classes and a formal logical or mathematical calculus (163). Formal schemes are 'watered-down' axiomatic schemes:

> Abstract laws are articulated and, in what is often a rough and discursive manner, 'deductions' to empirical events are made. Explanation consists of visualizing an empirical event as an instance or manifestation of the more abstract law. The goal of theorizing is thus to develop elementary laws or principles about basic properties of the universe (163).

Empirical schemes are not really theory at all, but many theorists and researchers consider them to be so:

> [T]here is a tendency to confuse what is to be explained (the empirical gener-
> alization) with what is to explain (the abstract law). This confusion takes sev-
> eral forms. One is to elevate the humble empirical generalization to the status
> of a 'law', as is the case with 'Golden's law', which merely reports that industri-
> alization and literacy are positively correlated. Another is to follow Robert
> Merton's famous advocacy for 'theories of the middle range' where the goal is
> to develop some generalizations for a substantive area–say, urbanization, orga-
> nizational con trol, deviance, socialization or some other substantive topic [he
> refers to Merton 1968 here]. Such 'theories' are, in fact, empirical generaliza-
> tions whose regularities require a more abstract formulation to explain them.
> Yet a good many sociologists believe that these 'middle range' propositions are
> theories, despite their empirical character (163-164).

Turner believes that formal theory is the most useful approach to analytical theorizing.

Modelling schemes consist of two types, namely 'abstract-analytical
models' and 'empirical-causal models'. Abstract-analytical models develop
context-free concepts and then represent their relations in a visual picture.
These relations are usually expressed in causal terms. Empirical-causal
models "are usually statements of correlation among measured variables,
ordered in a linear and temporal sequence", but they are in effect empirical descriptions because the variables are restricted to a particular empirical case (164-165). Thus, the former type of model is the most effective in
analytical theorizing.

In conclusion, Turner summarizes that:

> ... analytical theory must be abstract; it must denote generic properties of the
> universe; it must be testable or capable of generating testable propositions; and
> it cannot ignore causality, process and operative mechanisms. The best
> approach to theory-building in sociology is thus a combination of sensitizing
> analytical schemes, abstract formal propositions and analytical models ... [I]t is
> the *simultaneous* use of all three approaches that offers the most potential for
> developing a 'natural science of society' (166).

Students of religion should, in my opinion, address and identify viable
strategies of analytical theorizing. Turner's procedure is to "start with sensitizing schemes, propositions and models, and only then move on to the

formal collection of data or to metatheorizing and scheme-building"
(167). This seems to be a sensible approach.

My approach to the study of religion is basically similar to Turner's
approach to the study of social behavior. His is a kind of positivism, mine
is what is called unrepresentative realism. It is a *realist* position in two
senses: 1) that the physical world is independent of our knowledge of it,
and 2) to the extent that theories are applicable to the world, they are so
inside and outside of experimental situations. Second, it is *unrepresentative*
because it does not incorporate a correspondence theory of truth. As
philosopher A. F. Chalmers argued:

> We can appraise our theories from the point of view of the extent to which
> they successfully come to grips with some aspect of the world, but we cannot
> go further to appraise them from the point of view of the extent to which they
> describe the world as it really is, simply because we do not have access to the
> world independently of our theories in a way that would enable us to assess the
> adequacy of those descriptions.[19]

Theory understood in this manner is much more than propositional statements purportedly subjected to falsifiability or confirmation by the facts.
Theory in the sense proposed here becomes the basic framework for con-
ceiving of the object of study. And this is why our object must be defined.
And, furthermore, a definition must be a compact version of the theory or
sets of theories informing the definition.

This latter statement brings me back to my point of departure. A scientific theory of religion must be deductively derived from an overall anthropological theory if it is to qualify as a humanistic rather than a theological
theory. My argument is that the claims we make should be scientific claims.
And by that I do not mean absolute claims, nor claims that must of necessity be true representations of what is out there in the real world. Scientific
claims are scientific because they are theoretically informed claims. We are,
in fact, completely dependent on our theories about the world and about
the object of our study whether explicit or not. Our explanations and interpretations of religion and particular religions must of necessity be loose deductions based on a discursive use of abstract propositions and models and
all of it subject to argument, debate and negotiation. This approach is an
essential requirement to the pursuit of a secular study of religion.

Notes

1. This paper is based on a paper read at a roundtable on "Science, Philosophy and the Study of Religion" during the Twentieth World Congress of Philosophy in Boston, August 11, 1998 hosted by the International Association for the History of Religions and the North American Association for the Study of Religion. The paper was entitled "How Does Philosophy Affect the Study of Religion? An Introduction to the Issues".
2. See Jensen 1997: 14.
3. Geertz 1994c, 1997b, 1999b.
4. Geertz n.d.1. and n.d.2.
5. See the excellent introduction to the whole range of issues in Pels & Nencel 1991. The next few paragraphs are based on Geertz 1997a: 60-67.
6. Asad 1973.
7. Said 1978: 12.
8. Wagner 1975.
9. Two main collections here are MacCormack & Strathern 1980 and Ortner & Whitehead 1981.
10. Two important works are Sacks 1979, and Etienne & Leacock 1980.
11. Three examples of this are Martin & Voorhies 1975; Schlegel 1977; and Sanday 1981.
12. Pinch 1985.
13. Faust 1984.
14. See Lakoff 1987; Lakoff & Johnson 1980; Lakoff & Turner 1989; Keesing 1985 & 1989; and Sweetser 1990.
15. Shweder 1986.
16. Roth 1987: 2-3.
17. See Geertz 1994a, 1994b, 1994d, n.d.1., and 1999a.
18. Roth 1987: 6.
19. Chalmers 1994: 163.

References

Asad, Talal, 1973, "Introduction", in *Anthropology & the Colonnial Encounter*, edited by Talal Asad, Atlantic Highlands: Humanities Press 1973, 1990, 9-19.

Chalmers, A. F., 1994, *What Is This Thing Called Science? An Assessment of the Nature and Status of Science and Its Methods*, Buckingham: Open University Press, 2nd ed.

Etienne, Mona & Eleanor Leacock, eds., 1980, *Women and Colonization*, New York: Praeger.

Faust, David, 1984, *The Limits of Scientific Reasoning*, Minneapolis.

Geertz, Armin W., 1994a, "On Reciprocity and Mutual Reflection in the Study of Native American Religions", *Religion. An International Journal* 24 (1), 1994, 1-7.

– 1994b, "Critical Reflections on the Postmodern Study of Religion", *Religion. An International Journal* 24 (1), 1994, 16-22.

– 1994c, "On Dendrolatry and Definitions: Perspectives from the Study of Oral Traditions", in *The Notion of "Religion" in Comparative Research: Proceedings of the XVIth Congress of the International Association for the History of Religions, Rome 3rd-8th September, 1990*, edited by Ugo Bianchi, Rome: "L'Erma" di Bretschneider 1994, 661-665.

– 1994d, *The Invention of Prophecy: Continuity and Meaning in Hopi Indian Religion*, Knebel: Brunbakke Publications 1992, Los Angeles: University of California Press, rev. and abridged edition, 1994

– 1997a, "Hermeneutics in Ethnography: Lessons for the Study of Religion", in *Vergleichen und Verstehen in der Religionswissenschaft*, edited by Hans-Joachim Klimkeit, Wiesbaden: Harrassowitz Verlag 1997, 53-70.

– 1997b, "Theory, Definition, and Typology: Reflections on Generalities and Unrepresentative Realism", *Temenos. Studies in Comparative Religion Presented by Scholars in Denmark, Finland, Norway and Sweden* 33, 1997, 29-47.

– 1999a, "Ethnohermeneutics in a Postmodern World", in *Approaching Religion. Part I*, edited by Tore Ahlbäck, Åbo: The Donner Institute 1999, 73-86.

– 1999b, "Definition as Analytical Strategy in the Study of Religion", *Historical Reflections/Reflexions historique* 25(3), 1999, 445-475.

– n.d.1., "Can We Move Beyond Primitivism? On Recovering the Indigenes of Indigenous Reli gions in the Academic Study of Religion", in *Beyond "Primitivism": Indigenous Religious Traditions and Modernity*, edited by Jacob Olupona, (in press).

– n.d.2., "Global Perspectives on Methodology in the Study of Religion", in *Perspectives on Method and Theory in the Study of Religion: Collected Essays from the XVIIth Congress of the International Association for the History of Religions, Mexico City, 1995*, edited by Armin W. Geertz & Russell T. McCutcheon, Leiden: E. J. Brill (in press).

Jensen, Jeppe Sinding, 1997, "Rationality and the Study of Religion: Introduction," in *Rationality and the Study of Religion*, edited by Jeppe Sinding Jensen & Luther H. Martin, Aarhus: Aarhus University Press.

Keesing, Roger M., 1985, "Conventional Metaphors and Anthropological Metaphysics: the Problematic of Cultural Translation", *Journal of Anthropological Research* 41 (2), 1985, 201-217.

– 1989, "Exotic Readings of Cultural Texts", *Current Anthropology* 30 (4), 1989, 459-479.

Lakoff, George, 1987, *Women, Fire and Dangerous Things: What Categories Reveal about the Mind*, Chicago: University of Chicago Press.

Lakoff, George & Mark Johnson, 1980, *Metaphors We Live By*, Chicago: University of Chicago Press.

Lakoff, George & Mark Turner, 1989, *More Than Cool Reason: A Field Guide to Poetic Metaphor*, Chicago: University of Chicago Press.

MacCormack, Carol P. & Marilyn Strathern, eds., 1980, *Nature, Culture and Gender*, Cambridge: Cambridge University Press.

Martin, Kay & Barbara Voorhies, eds., 1975, *Female of the Species*, New York: Columbia University Press.

Merton, Robert K., 1968, *Social Theory and Social Structure*, New York: Free Press.

Ortner, Sherry & Harriet Whitehead, eds., 1981, *Sexual Meanings*, Cambridge: Cambridge University Press.

Pels, Peter & Lorraine Nencel, 1991, "Introduction: Critique and the Deconstruction of Anthropological Authority" in *Constructing Knowledge: Authority and Critique in Social Science* edited by Lorraine Nencel & Peter Pels, London: Sage Publications 1991, 1-21.

Pinch, Trevor, 1985, "Theory Testing in Science – The Case of Solar Neutrinos: Do Crucial Experiments Test Theories or Theorists?" *Philosophy of the Social Sciences* 15 (2) 1985, 167-187.

Roth, Paul A., 1987, *Meaning and Method in the Social Sciences: A Case for Methodological Pluralism*, Ithaca & London: Cornell University Press.

Sacks, Karen, 1979, *Sisters and Wives: The Past and Future of Sexual Equality*, Westport: Greenwood Press.

Said, Edward, 1978, *Orientalism: Western Conceptions of the Orient*, London: Routledge & Kegan Paul 1978, Penguin Books 1991.

Sanday, Peggy Reeves, ed., 1981, *Female Power and Male Dominance*, Cambridge: Cambridge University Press.

Schlegel, Alice, ed., 1977, *Sexual Stratification: A Cross-Cultural View*, New York: Columbia University Press.

Shweder, Richard A., 1986, "Divergent Rationalities", in *Metatheory in Social Sciences: Pluralisms and Subjectivities*, edited by Donald W. Fiske & Richard A. Shweder, Chicago: University of Chicago Press 1986, 163-196.

Sweetser, Eve, 1990, *From Etymology to Pragmatics. Metaphorical and Cultural Aspects of Semantic Structure*, Cambridge: Cambridge University Press.

Turner, Jonathan H., 1987, "Analytical Theorizing," in *Social Theory Today*, edited by Anthony Giddens & Jonathan H. Turner, Oxford: Polity Press 1987, 156-194.

Wagner, Roy, 1975, *The Invention of Culture*, Chicago: University of Chicago Press 1975, 1981.

Reason without Consolation:
Theological Misappropriations of the Discourse Theory of Jürgen Habermas and their Implications for the Study of Religion[1]

Marsha Hewitt

Professor, Trinity College
University of Toronto, Toronto, Canada

More than a decade ago, the late British-born Canadian theologian Charles Davis declared that the student of religion is "unavoidably concerned with the experience of faith. Those with no taste for the divine are not in a position to analyze the ingredients of religious experience nor to distinguish good religion from bad." (Davis 1984: 394) This statement crystallizes an issue that is central to the ongoing controversy about what constitutes the proper study of religion. For many scholars in the field, the study of religion is a religious act whose chief aim is to validate religious experience and contribute to the cultivation of religious faith. From this perspective faith, religious experience and religious activity are necessary components in the study of religion. Religion is understood to possess a *sui generis* quality that suggests the indisputable reality of a transcendent Truth. Scholars of religion who do not share this perspective, who bring no personal religious or faith experience to the study of religion, are capable only of discussing "husks empty of that kernel of meaning which alone constitutes religious faith and its phenomena as distinctive, intelligible objects of discourse." (Davis 1984: 394) The implication here is that direct, personal religious experience is a non-negotiable requisite of good scholarship in the field of religious studies.

Academics in religious studies who hold to this view are described by Donald Wiebe as 'scholar-devotees,' as contrasted with what he calls 'scholar-scientists.' (Wiebe 1984: 401) According to Wiebe, the scholar-scientist rejects the claim that religion is a "*sui generis* phenomenon," the study of which does not need the external justification of being involved in a "realization of transcendent truth." (Wiebe 1984: 407) I do not intend here to enter into the details of the Davis-Wiebe debate, nor do I wish to delve into the intricacies of the wide range of definitions of what might constitute the study of religion as a 'science,' nor even the appropriateness (or not) of the term 'science' as applied to the academic study of religion. What is most important about the controversy that transpired between Charles Davis and Donald Wiebe is that it encapsulates a continuing debate about what the study of religion is, or rather *should* be.

Rather than wading into this controversy head-on by adopting one position or another, my purpose here is to explore the theoretical and conceptual problems that arise when the study of religion proceeds as a theological or religious activity whose main interest is to promote or illuminate faith. I have long been interested in the truth claims made by Christian 'scholar-devotees,' about non-religious theories and disciplines and the ways in which they are perceived as contradictory or inadequate due to their lack of interest in religion and its substantive contents. For some decades many Christian theologians have been engaged in various attempts at appropriation, dialogue and direct critique of non-religious disciplines which they recognize as being of some importance to their efforts to 'modernize' religion. This was particularly true with respect to liberation theology, which for a time embraced Marxian social theory as part of its efforts to address the poverty and widespread oppression in Latin America. (Hewitt 1990) Most often the aim of the scholar-devotee with respect to other disciplines is to demonstrate the need of the non-religious theory for a religious/theological perspective and content, on the premise that without theology, most fields of thought are substantively inadequate to their own subject.

This last point is especially true with respect to the recent Christian theological revision known as "public theology." Those scholar-devotees who are engaged in formulating public theology are attempting to fashion a new role for theologians as public intellectuals or "religious critics" whose task is to elaborate the "ultimate meanings" and "spiritual culture" of a society (Dean 1994: xiv) in order to inspire a revitalization of spiritual culture in the contemporary modern age. They perceive a breakdown of spiritual culture that involves the loss of meaning and fragmentation of communities, the loss of public credibility of Christian values and beliefs as well as a general sense of vague despair that results from the complexities and uncertainties of pluralistic societies. The role of the religious critic or public theologian is to help restore a sense of wholeness and meaning within society that would arise from a restoration of Christian values which are seen as the guarantor of democratic processes and peaceful resolutions of conflict.

In an important sense, public theology represents an intellectual and spiritual missionizing movement whose aim is to convince Christians and non-Christians of the innate compatibility of Christianity, democratic values and the good life. By making such universal truth claims, public theology seeks to re-establish a hegemonic place for Christianity that will provide the ethical and spiritual axis of democratic, pluralistic societies. The construction of a Christian public will be able to "significantly contribute to an understanding not only of human nature and society, but also of rationality and modernity." (F. Schüssler Fiorenza 1992: 3) These claims regarding rationality and modernity are what I wish particularly to examine here, because they are central to evaluating the intellectual credibility and coherence of public theology which insists that its religious rationality is entirely appropriate to modernity.

One of the main avenues that most of the public theologians use to establish their place within modernity involves an attempted appropriation and critique of Jürgen Habermas' theory of communicative rationality. By turning to Habermas these public theologians-mainly Francis Schüssler Fiorenza, David Tracy, Ronald Thiemann, and Helmut Peukert-seek to secure a central place in modernity for theological reason. By partially grafting Habermas' concept of communicative rationality on to theological rationality, public theology hopes to address a variety of ethical, political and philosophical issues in ways that are relevant, revitalizing and convincing in pluralist societies. One thing the public theologians do not address is how to make a credible case for the supremacy of Christian values in societies that include a wide range of non-Christian traditions that may be directly opposed to Christian ideas.

Concern for the "spiritual culture" of a society motivates public theologians such as Thiemann to argue for the *necessary* role of (Christian) religion to generate convictions and develop "public policies" that are shaped by (Christian) religious values. (Thiemann 1996: 15) For Thiemann, public theology is "faith seeking to understand the relation between Christian convictions and broader social and cultural context," with a view to find-

35

ing ways in which Christian theology may "play a role in forming the reality out of which American public policy might be formed." In a critical assessment of David Tracy, Thiemann declares that the issue of "whether theological arguments are available for public examination and whether theological assertions are intelligible beyond the confines of a particular religious community" are of secondary importance to questions concerning the "salutary influence" of Christian theology in the development of public policy. (Thiemann 1991: 21; 38; 42-3) The overriding premise of Thiemann's notion of public theology is that Christian values are the true bedrock of democratic values in pluralistic societies. The formation of religious identity undertaken by the public theologian is a political and social task that serves the work of democratic processes in heterogeneous contexts. An observation of Robert Wuthnow concerning the pragmatic universalism of Christians in civil society is pertinent to Thiemann, who, like many theologians, ignores the fact that "some people may want to be loved but not in the name of Christ." (Wuthnow 1996: 90)

Thiemann is not concerned with the philosophical and theoretical assumptions of public theology. While they may be "intellectually interesting," they do not address what he considers to be the "far more important questions" concerning public theology.(Thiemann 1991: 43) Thiemann's understanding of public theology is relevant to this discussion because he explicitly articulates the political aims of public theology, which are to direct and shape both public values and public policy. In this respect Thiemann's work illuminates the implicit political and Christian 'missiological' undercurrents in the work of more philosophically and hermeneutically-oriented public theologians such as David Tracy.

In only apparent contradiction to Thiemann, Tracy declares that the theologian, no more than philosophers, historians and social scientists may not "allow his own-or his tradition's-beliefs to serve as warrants for his arguments." (Tracy 1978: 7; 1981: 64) A closer examination of Tracy's work largely dissolves the contradiction between him and Thiemann. Thiemann only finds himself in opposition to Tracy (Thiemann 1991: 20-1) because he does not confront the theoretical foundations of Tracy's public theology. Tracy doesn't need to be explicit about the political interest of public theology, which is to establish a Christian set of values that will form the normative standards for social and political processes. The theologian's task is to render Christianity publicly credible and acceptable to Christians and non-Christians, and thus reestablish its hegemonic place in modernity. For Tracy, a public theology capable of addressing and potentially resolving many of the normative conflicts that arise in pluralistic societies is one which is a product of a revised Christian theology that is able to 'correlate' an updated and reinterpreted Christianity to the ultimate meaning and totality of a "common human experience." Tracy's revisionist theological model seeks to construct a "philosophical reflection upon the meanings present in common human experience and language, and upon the meanings present in the *Christian fact.*" (Tracy 1978: 43) (Italics added) For Tracy, there is a pregiven "universal meaningfulness" that organizes a "common human experience" (Tracy 1978: 206) which can be discovered through critical theological reflection and discursive "conversation" practices. Strangely, he looks to the philosophical programme of Habermas, which he finds "promising" for "any theology concerned with the public realm." (Tracy 1992: 22)

Tracy not only sees in Habermas "a natural conversation partner for theology," he also declares his fundamental agreement with Habermas' philosophy. (Tracy 1992: 27;31) It is difficult to imagine how this could be the case, given Tracy's assumption of the existence of a common human experience or "ultimate reality" to which a revised "modern" theology might correlate and disclose. Tracy's foundational concept, upon which his entire revisionist theology depends, is both metaphysical and premodern, with its appeal to a transcendent totality that is accessible to human consciousness through theological interpretation. The directing concepts of Tracy's theology could not be farther from Habermas. Consider this statement by Habermas: "Philosophy can no longer refer to the whole of the world, of nature, of history, of society, in the sense of a totalizing knowledge ... All attempts at discovering ultimate foundations, in which the intentions of First Philosophy live on, have broken down." For Habermas, "philosophical thought" in modernity has irrevocably "surrendered the relation to totality." (Habermas 1984: Vol. 1: 1-2).

Habermas' theory of communicative rationality regards "determinate theological affirmations" as "meaningless." (Habermas 1985: 12) They are meaningless because they operate from a completely different mode and concept of rationality than that of communicative rationality. For Habermas, reason is constituted through intersubjective communication, without recourse to heteronomous sources of validity, since the sphere of validity in discursive action is identical with the sphere of human speech. (Wellmer 1985: 53) In this sense, theology is not communicative; it can only be assertive, and mere assertion is insufficient to guarantee its truth or rationality. Communicative rationality requires that all truth claims be subject to critical scrutiny through argumentation, with the result that competing truth claims are adjudicated through the force of the better argument. While Tracy agrees that "the validity claims of the religious demand, in modernity, the kind of critical reflection, dialogue, and argument on their claims that are accorded all other claims," he *simultaneously* pleads for special exemption for theological truth claims from such scrutiny. He accounts for this startling move by invoking the "peculiar logic" of religious claims which is necessary to their function of disclosing "the whole of reality." Since religious claims are "exceptionally difficult to analyze in modern, critical terms," it seems to follow for Tracy that they remain protected from the kind of argumentative justification required in communicative action while somehow formally subject to the same standard of critical scrutiny that attaches to any other truth claims. Tracy seems oblivious to the glaring contradiction in his own thinking. Nonetheless, he still insists that modern theology-his "public correlational theology"-is a "fully modern critical discipline." (Tracy 1992: 35-6)

Despite Tracy's efforts to construct a correlational, revisionist theological model without recourse to myth or cosmology, he cannot break through the metaphysical boundaries that bind theology to a premodern era. Not only Tracy, but public theology itself works with a concept of rationality that has little in common with Habermas' concept of communicative rationality. For Habermas there is a "unity of reason," rooted in the structure of speech acts, that is perceptible only in "the plurality of its voices." (Habermas 1992: 117) It is this notion of reason that he identifies as most adequate to peaceful and noncoercive modes of life in modern, pluralistic societies. The reliance of public theology on a metaphysical totality with a corresponding ultimate meaning that gives form and coherence to the public realm deploys the rhetoric of homiletics rather than philosophical argument. Despite its claims to universal relevance in pluralistic societies, public theology can only be interesting to already convinced Christians.

That Tracy privileges theological rhetoric over philosophical or even hermeneutical argument is further indicated in his criticism of Habermas' position that contested norms and truth claims must be redeemed in argumentative speech, where each speaker is called upon to give reasons for his/her argument such that one's discourse partners, through the communicative process, may demand increasingly better reasons until the force of the superiour argument prevails. In this way, the rationality of a decision is generated through the intersubjective, discursive action of all those affected or potentially affected by the outcome. The issue of consent in discursive action is less important than the "rationality of the procedure for attaining agreement" which in turn helps cultivate "normative practices and moral relationships within which reasoned agreement as a way of life can flourish and continue." (Benhabib 1990: 345; 346) Argumentation is a "problem-solving procedure that generates *convictions*" where the distinction between the norm's validity and its mere "social currency" may be established. (Habermas 1993: 158; 160) Tracy, however, rejects argumentation as a means for resolving contested truth claims, preferring in its place 'conversation' or 'dialogue' (argumentation *is* a form of dialogue) because dialogue "opens beyond dialectical argument to the *equally rational* realm of these disclosure possibilities for the true, the good". (Tracy 1992: 41) Conversation is a "looser," (Tracy 1987: 118 n. 28) less demanding and rigorous mode of discourse which inevitably implies a less critical interrogation of truth claims than that required by argumentation. Conversation is perhaps more suitable to the "peculiar logic" of religious claims, insulating and protecting them from the kind of critical scrutiny required by argumentation in communicative action.

What Tracy is thus asking for, and in direct opposition to Habermas, is that the background beliefs of a specific community or group be exempt from discursive justification in terms that echo Thiemann's assertion that their "axiomatic status" renders their "explicit justification unnecessary." In Thiemann's view, such "defining characteristics are resistant to change, because they provide the community's essential identity." (Thiemann 1996: 134) Habermas' concept of argumentation on the other hand requires that all such background beliefs become "expressly thematized" and open to discursive scrutiny based on the accepted understanding that if a better argument against them occurs, these background beliefs will be discarded. The insistence from the outset, that in theological discourse, certain basic beliefs are non-negotiable pregivens reinforces public theology's rhetorical nature.

The rationality of public theology is utterly incompatible with the communicative rationality of Habermas because it is motivated by faith rather than reason. The primacy of faith accounts for many of the incoherent and contradictory concepts that are central to public theology, which ultimately abandons reasoned argument in favour of homiletic rhetoric. For Habermas, communicative rationality is more suited to the postmetaphysical condition of modernity which "can and will no longer borrow the criteria by which it takes its orientation from the models supplied by another epoch; it has to create its normativity out of itself." (Habermas 1990: 7) In modern, complex and pluralistic societies, it is no longer sufficient to appeal, as theologians do, to a "premodern certainty" meant to inspire confidence (Habermas 1992: 240) in an epoch where the "truly convincing grounds" of traditions have long "gone by the boards" with the "collapse of religious and metaphysical worldviews." (Habermas 1990: 72) While Habermas understands that the intent of public theology is to find a common ground where the basic ethical contents of Christianity are widely accepted as in agreement with "the basic principles of a universalist morality," (Habermas 1992: 229) he also sees the impossibility of making this claim if theology is to insist on its own incorrigible faith assertions. The attempt to establish universalizability with respect to moral principles through communicative action is not possible in theological discourse because of its embeddedness in a "specific religious tradition" (233) that necessarily limits the degree of its freedom of communication and thus forms a barrier against the general interweaving of all "linguistic functions and aspects of validity" (234) that occur in daily praxis. Theological discourses, rooted in specific religious traditions with their 'axiomatic,' non-negotiable beliefs, cannot enter into any meaningful dialogue with philosophy or politics, since such an encounter merely juxtaposes rhetorical assertion and citation with sustained self-reflexive argumentation. Religious authorship and religious experiences cannot supply a common ground where theology could meet Habermas in any kind of collaborative partnership. Whatever insights into the human condition or moral principles that theology has to offer can only be theoretically deployed, according to Habermas, when they are "uncoupled from the event of revelation." (233).

However, the public theologians persist in their refusal to submit theological validity claims to the critique and sustained scrutiny that Habermas argues is necessary for all segments of the lifeworld. In the absence of argumentative justification, the public theologians offer unquestionable assertion based on divine warrant. As Helmut Peukert perhaps prophetically observes, if theology "does not want to abandon itself, [it] obviously cannot renounce making a claim to truth." (Peukert 1992: 55) Public theology nonetheless tries to maintain the impossible position of both refusing either to abandon itself or its interest in appropriating Habermas' theories to its own ends. Certainly to maintain the latter would inevitably involve the former. Habermas realizes this himself when he asks "what still constitutes the distinctiveness of theological discourse" in the light of its insistence that it shares a "*common ground*" with philosophy and even science. (Habermas 1992: 231; 230).

Peukert offers another illustrative example of the unresolvable contradiction generated by public theology's efforts to maintain the dichotomous position outlined above. The problems involved in theology's attempt even "critically" to appropriate Habermas are clearly demonstrated in Peukert's critique of Habermas' notion of the communication community. Taking his cue from Habermas' claim that communicative action has a "stubbornly transcending power" (Habermas 1982: 221), Peukert tries to show that Habermas fails to account sufficiently for that "transcendent power" by refusing to acknowledge the limitations in his thinking concerning the necessity of including the dead of past generations in the communication community. According to Peukert, the notion of solidarity that is presupposed in speech acts must be "illimitable" (Peukert 1992: 61) if the concept of a communication community is to have true coherence, something which he claims Habermas does not allow for, which in turn renders communicative rationality aporetic. Habermas' 'restriction' of the communication community to those who are actually living participants undermines, in Peukert's view, the very possibility of human solidarity and freedom, since the fact of death extinguishes these possibilities and renders them futile. He writes:

> For communicative action, which in the face of the annihilated victims still anticipates the communicative realization of possible freedom in a practical way and in this exposes itself to the risk of failure, the question of the salvation of the annihilated victims arises: the quest for an absolute freedom, saving even in death. The analytics and dialectics of communicative action point beyond themselves to the question of the foundation of theology.

Peukert's assertion that communicative action somehow relates inevitably to theology and that it must account for the victims of history recycles an older controversy that took place between Max Horkheimer and Walter Benjamin some sixty years ago, and to which Peukert refers.(Peukert 1986: 206-10) Benjamin was concerned with the redemption of history through a solidarity of remembrance between present and past generations, so that the innocent victims of history, from whose efforts subsequent generations benefit, would not have died and suffered in vain. (Lenhardt 1975; Hewitt 1995: 147-70) Horkheimer's response to Benjamin was:

> The thought that the prayers of the persecuted in direst need, that those of the innocents who must die without clarification of their situation, that the final hopes for a superhuman authority, are to no avail, and that in the night in which no human light shines is also devoid of any divine light, is monstrous. Without God, eternal truth has just as little a foothold as infinite love-indeed they become unthinkable concepts. But is atrocity ever a cogent argument against the assertion or denial of a state of affairs? Does logic contain a law to the effect that a judgement is false when its consequence would be despair? (In Habermas 1982:238)

Habermas adopts Horkheimer's reply to Benjamin in his response to Peukert, pointing out that Peukert's critique only finds coherence within the context of religious language upon which it is dependent-without it, his argument "loses its evidence." Peukert "resorts to an experience accessible only in the language of the Christian tradition" and in doing so, relies on rhetorical assertion rather than argumentation. In this sense, Peukert's position is contrary to communicative action, not an elaboration of it. That human beings are dependent upon "those rare constellations in which their own powers are able to be joined with the favourableness of the historical moment...is still no license for the assumption of a divine promise of salvation." (Habermas 1192: 238)

To conclude that Habermas merely rejects theology or bears it any hostility would be as simplistic a reading of his responses to the public theologians as theirs often is regarding his theory of communicative rationality. Neither does Habermas deny that religion has any role to play in public and political discourses or even in communicative action. Habermas is well aware that the participants in a discourse situation bring a complex web of traditions, cultures, norms, worldviews, beliefs and values to any discussion. These elements, including religious views, constitute the social, cultural and psychological identities of individuals. Where Habermas questions theology concerns the status of those identity forming elements and the procedures for their justification. Habermas disagrees that the most cherished religious beliefs of communities and individuals hold an "axiomatic" status that immunizes them from the argumentative justification that is required of all other claims to validity. Insofar as it is possible in any discourse situation, all such beliefs must be explicitly thematized as part of the process of argumentation and all are equally vulnerable to being abandoned in the face of a better argument. Thiemann would assert that since the background beliefs of a community "provide the community's essential identity," that in itself makes their "explicit justification [is] unnecessary." (Thiemann 1996: 134) Tracy, as has been seen, appeals to the "peculiar logic" of religious beliefs as grounds for insulating them from the rigorous critique that must be accorded all other claims to validity. Peukert takes a somewhat different tack by resorting to the strictly homiletical plea for turning to God's salvific power as a means of extending membership in communication communities to include the past victims of suffering and injustice. However genuine the wish that public theology may appropriate Habermas or the conviction that it has something vital to add to his theories, it inevitably stops short at the key element before which theology dissolves: the demand for argumentative justification of validity claims that all participants in a discussion can accept as rational.

Habermas' lack of serious interest in religion is rooted in his concept of reason in modernity which is procedural and formal, oriented to questions of justice in ethical deliberations. In a discursive reformulation of the Kantian imperative, Habermas outlines the conditions necessary for the acceptance of contested norms by the participants in a practical discourse:

> Unless all affected can *freely* accept the consequences and the side effects that the *general* observance of a controversial norm can be expected to have for the satisfaction of the interests of *each individual*. (U)

and,

> Only those norms can claim to be valid that meet (or could meet) with the
> approval of all affected in their capacity as participants in a practical discourse.
> (D) (Habermas 1990: 93)

'U' is not to be confused with "substantive principles" or "normative content"; 'U' refers to the logic of argumentation, the formal procedure
deployed in communicative action. It is a "rule of argumentation only"
that is not to be confused with "substantive legal and moral principles."
(94) 'U' is the 'transcendental-pragmatic' part of the discursive process.
Although the claim to reason within discourse ethics contains what
Richard Bernstein reiterates as a "stubbornly transcending power, because
it is renewed with each act of unconstrained understanding," (Bernstein
1982: 32) any reference to transcendence cannot be understood theologically, nor can it be driven in a theological direction, i.e. the appeal to God
as the absolute guarantor of the truly unlimited communication community. Nor can the admitted "utopian perspective" (Habermas 1982: 227)
of communicative rationality be shaped to fit a theological agenda. The
utopia of a society where conflicts are resolved through unrestrained discourse, where mutual understanding takes precedence over agreement,
where social and personal relations are structured in terms of intersubjec-
tivity rather than domination and manipulation, is a real possibility for
Habermas that derives from his theory of the nature of speech acts.
(Habermas 1979) The possibility for solidarity, reciprocity and mutual
understanding are ingrained in the linguistic medium itself. In communicative action, "the structures of action oriented toward reaching understanding always already presuppose those very relationships of reciprocity
and mutual recognition around which *all* moral ideas revolve in everyday
life no less than in philosophical ethics." (Habermas 1990: 130) As solidarity and justice "have one and the same root," (200) communicative
action is always already both oriented and mobilized toward them.

The critique of Habermas mounted by the public theologians is misdirected partly because it is limited by the interests of religious faith, and
partly because of its presupposition that Habermas is uncritically hostile
to religion. It is simply misguided to insist that if Habermas took the truth
claims of theology seriously, his theory of communicative rationality and
discourse ethics would be strengthened and expanded. From the perspective of Habermas' theory of rationality, theology simply has no place in

modernity because it operates out of a premodern, metaphysical and totalizing concept of rationality that resorts to divine warrant for its credibility.
David Tracy may assert that "public correlational theologies" such as his
own are "fully modern critical disciplines," (Tracy 1992: 36) but, in the
spirit of Horkheimer to Benjamin, assertions alone do not guarantee
truth. Tracy complains that there is "no *argument* in Habermas that disal-
lows" (37) the validity claims of religion. What Tracy fails to appreciate is
that there is no *need* for such an argument in Habermas' theories. This
kind of theological critique of Habermas mounted by the public theologians replays the standard theological condemnation of the alleged 'atheism' of Karl Marx. Marx's perspective on theological accounts of the creation of nature and humanity is relevant to Habermas. For Marx, (and for
Habermas) the very question of theology presupposes theoretical reliance
on an abstraction that is both incoherent and irrelevant with respect to his
thinking:

> When you ask about the creation of nature and man, you are abstracting, and
> in so doing, from man and nature. You postulate them as *non-existent*, and yet
> you want me to prove them to you as *existing*...Give up your abstraction and
> you will also give up your question. (Marx 1978: 92)

However, despite the fact that Habermas' theories are based upon a concept
of reason that is entirely different from that assumed by public theology, he
does not deny that religious discourses may have some place in modernity.
This place exists, however, more by default than necessity. Recalling his
idea that postmetaphysical philosophy and ethics critically appropriate
some of the contents of religion without taking over its theological foundations or incorporating its metaphysical consolations, Habermas concedes,

> Viewed from without, religion, which has largely been deprived of its world-
> view functions, is still indispensable in ordinary life for normalizing inter-
> course with the extraordinary. For this reason, even postmetaphysical thinking
> continues to coexist with religious practice-and not merely in the sense of the
> contemporaneity of the noncontemporaneous ... As long as no better words
> for what religion can say are found in the medium of rational discourse, it will
> even coexist abstemiously with the former, neither supporting it nor combat-
> ting it. (Habermas 1992: 51; 145)

45

Habermas' position with respect to religion is similar here to Hork-heimer's view that despite the movement from "religious longing to con-scious social practice," religion continues to "leave its mark behind. Part of the drives and desires which religious belief preserved and kept alive are detached from the inhibiting religious form and become productive forces in social practice." (Horkheimer 1972: 129-31)

Both Habermas and Horkheimer accept that the ethical contents and utopian visions of religion may persist into modernity although their the-ological forms and consolations have long since passed away. Religion may well be "the record of the wishes, desires and accusations" (Horkheimer 1972: 129) of past generations, but that does not mean that those same wishes, desires and accusations require divine warrant for their moral jus-tification in the arena of emancipation struggles. For Habermas, moral principles and ethical decisions find their justification in an entirely differ-ent concept of a procedural rationality that emerges out of communicative action. Such procedural rationality promotes self-determination and self-realization in a "rigorously intersubjective sense." Participants in commu-nicative action understand themselves as "autonomously acting and indi-viduated being[s]" who are capable of cooperatively making moral deci-sions in their unconstrained effort to seek the truth that is relevant to them. The concept of rationality central to discourse ethics could not be farther from either theology or theodicy, no matter how persistent reli-gious language may be.

From the perspective of communicative rationality, religious language is an expressive discourse that perhaps belongs more to the realm of aesthet-ics, although Habermas does not explore this possibility. Theology, like most artistic forms, may be approached as a possible aesthetic vehicle whose symbolic language belongs to the "mytho-poetic" power of lan-guage. As with all symbols, theological symbols arise "when language pro-duces signs of composite degree, in which the meaning, not satisfied with designating some one thing, designates another meaning attainable only in and through the first intentionality." (Ricoeur 1970: 551; 16) This is one reason why religious language persists alongside other discourses, such as philosophical ones. It cannot however be concluded from this that reli-gious language is a superiour discourse to others by virtue of its self-asserted ability to disclose 'total reality.'

One of public theology's main goals is to create a deprivatized, public and socially aware theology capable of transforming the world into a more just and humane place. It believes that such a transformation is finally possible only through the rehabilitation of Christian values and convictions. Habermas describes its aim in terms of a pursuit of "this-worldly goals of human dignity and social emancipation" where theology "interprets the self-understanding of [its engagement] in such a way that it helps express our best moral intentions without tearing down the bridges to secular languages and cultures." (Habermas 1992: 228) If this is indeed the self-understanding and intent of public theology, then the question remains as to how it can preserve its distinctively theological character. The effort to connect with non-religious theories and disciplines is evidence in itself that theology is insufficient to adequately address the complexities of complex, pluralist societies. This insufficiency is compounded further as theologians seek to impose their faith commitments on non-religious theories under the guise of critical dialogue. It would be more fruitful, and certainly more honest, if scholars interested in understanding religion and its role in society and culture tried to examine those marks and traces spoken of by Horkheimer and alluded to by Habermas that are left behind by religion in fields such as ethics, philosophy and social theory. Then theology runs into the problem indicated by Habermas of preserving its own identity. From the discussion of public theology presented here, it is apparent that its ultimate concern is with rehabilitating its identity and claims to truth rather than establishing genuine dialogue with other theories. If theology wishes to make good its claim to be a thoroughly modern discipline, it must immediately abandon the 'peculiar logic' used to support its truth claims to universal, public relevance in modernity. It must, as Peukert unintentionally acknowledged, abandon itself.

Note

1. This essay is dedicated to the memory of Charles Davis, mentor and supervisor of my doctoral work.

References

Benhabib, Seyla, "Afterword", in *The Communicative Ethics Controversy*, (eds.) Seyla Benhabib and Fred Dallmayr, The MIT Press, Cambridge, 1990.

Bernstein, Richard J., in *Habermas and Modernity,* (ed.) Richard J. Bernstein, The MIT Press, Cambridge, 1985.

Davis, Charles, "'Wherein there is no Ecstasy'", *Studies in Religion/Sciences Religieuses*, Vol. 13, no. 4, 1984.

Dean, William, *The Religious Critic in American Culture*, State University of New York Press, New York, 1994.

Habermas, Jürgen, "What is a Universal Pragmatics?" in *Communication and the Evolution of Society,* trans. Thomas McCarthy, Beacon Press, Boston, 1979.

–, "A Reply to my Critics, in *Habermas and Modernity*.

–, *The Theory of Communicative Action,* trans. Thomas McCarthy, Beacon Press, Boston, Vol. 1, 1984.

–, *Philosophical-Political Profiles*, trans. Frederick G. Lawrence, The MIT Press, Cambridge, 1985.

–, *The Philosophical Discourse of Modernity*, trans. Frederick G. Lawrence, The MIT Press, Cambridge, 1990.

–, *Moral Consciousness and Communicative Action,* trans. Christian Lenhardt and Shierry Weber Nicholsen, The MIT Press, 1990.

–, *Postmetaphysical Thinking: Philosophical Essays*, trans. William Mark Hohengarten, The MIT Press, Cambridge, 1992.

–, "Transcendence from within, Transcendence in this World," in *Habermas, Modernity and Public Theology,* (eds.) Don S. Browning and Francis Schüssler Fiorenza, Crossroad, New York, 1992.

–, *Justification and Application: Remarks on Discourse Ethics,* trans. Ciaran P. Cronin, The MIT Press, Cambridge, 1993.

Hewitt, Marsha Aileen, *From Theology to Social Theory: Juan Luis Segundo and the Theology of Liberation,* Peter Lang Publishing, Bern, 1990.

–, *Critical Theory of Religion: A Feminist Analysis,* Fortress Press, Minneapolis, 1995.

Horkheimer, Max, "Thoughts on Religion," in *Critical Theory: Selected Essays*, trans. Matthew J. O'Connell, Continuum, New York, 1972.

Lenhardt, Christian, "Anamnestic Solidarity: The Proletariat and Its Manes," *Telos*, no. 25, Fall, 1975.

Marx, Karl, "Economic and Philosophic Manuscripts, 1844," in *The Marx-Engels Reader,* (ed.) Robert C. Tucker, W.W. Norton & Co., New York, 1978.

Peukert, Helmut, *Science, Action and Fundamental Theology: Toward a Theology of Communicative Action,* trans. James Bohman, The MIT Press, Cambridge, 1986.

–, "Enlightenment and Theology as Unfinished Projects," In *Habermas, Modernity and Public Theology*.

Ricoeur, Paul, *Freud and Philosophy: An Essay on Interpretation,* trans. Denis Savage, Yale University Press, New Haven, 1970.

Schüssler Fiorenza, Francis, "Introduction: A Critical Reception for a Practical Public Theology," in *Habermas, Modernity and Public Theology*.

Thiemann, Ronald F., *Constructing a Public Theology: The Church in a Pluralistic Culture,* John Knox Press, Louisville, 1991.

–, *Religion in Public Life: A Dilemma for Democracy,* Georgetown University Press, Washington D.C., 1996.

Tracy, David, *Blessed Rage for Order: The New Pluralism in Theology,* The Seabury Press, New York, 1978.

–, *The Analogical Imagination: Christian Theology and the Culture of Pluralism,* New York, Crossroad, 1981.

–, *Plurality and Ambiguity: Hermeneutics, Religion, Hope,* Harper and Row, San Francisco, 1987.

–, "Theology, Critical Social Theory, and the Public Realm," in *Habermas, Modernity and Public Theology,* 1992.

Wellmer, Albrecht, "Reason, Utopia, and the *Dialectic of Enlightenment,*" in *Habermas and Modernity.*

Wiebe, Donald, "The Failure of Nerve in the Academic Study of Religion," *Studies in Religion/Sciences Religieuses,* Vol. 13, No. 4, 1984.

On Universals in the Study of Religion

Jeppe Sinding Jensen

Senior Lecturer, Department of Religious Studies
University of Aarhus, Aarhus, Denmark

In this essay I shall defend the idea of ontological universals in religion – as well as their epistemological necessity in the study of religion. This is a controversial stance and likely to be confused with theological and universalist notions about a transcendent 'essence' of religion or with universalist psychological assumptions about unique 'sui generis' religious experience. The argument here is different and, although explicitly not theological, it is debatable to what extent it qualifies as a 'secular theory'. It does not contain a theory in any interesting sense of that term, such as when speaking of a semantic, a cognitive or a socio-biological theory, where 'theory' denotes a consistent set of conceptions which motivate and guide research strategies. It is emphatically not a 'theory' in the more colloquial sense, that is, a hypothesis to be proven true or false. It is rather a set of considerations concerning some metaphysical and epistemological conditions that must necessarily underwrite the study of religion for it to be theoretical and scientific, and thus also, inevitably, secular. I shall propose that we reconsider the possibility of the existence of (some) cross-cultural ontological universals in religions and that these are not simply epistemological, that is, that they exist not only as part of our scholarly conceptual complexes, but also, somehow, in the things themselves. This is not a statement about the purported reality of transcendental referents of religions, but rather about certain properties of religious systems, such as, for instance, their semantics and their inclusion of counter-intuitive notions. Although scholars in the study of religion tend to work mainly from what they perceive to be innocently nominalist perspectives when they construct analytical categories and frameworks, there are – or must be – *speci-*

51

fiable conditions for including some forms and modes of social practice in the category religion and some not. It is worth considering whether such conditions appear in the eyes of the beholder only or whether they are salient features of the objects of study. Without unduly pressing for an 'eternal return' of metaphysical realism, they are probably both.

To be honest, I am so much in favour of universals that I suggest we must *invent* them where we do not find them and this ought not be controversial, because it is what happens in many a good science. It is, of course, a normative statement, one that it is important to recognize for the study of religion. Both in terms of its activities of theoretical construction, in relation to the ensuing objects, and in terms of the operative value of those constructions. There is no doubt that scholars construct religion as what is often called a 'second-order' concept and most agree with Jonathan Z. Smith's well-known dictum that 'Religion is solely the creation of the scholar's study. It is created for the scholar's analytic purposes by his imaginative acts of comparison and generalization. Religion has no independent existence apart from the academy' (Smith 1982: xi). We may add, however, that it is also a very powerful 'folk-model' and that as scholars of religion reside, precisely, in the academy, they should not yet toss the concept of religion on to just any heap of conceptual rubbish. If religion is a fiction it is still a useful fiction, although the day may come when it will be relegated to the realm of discarded notions, such as 'phlogiston', 'ether', 'phrenology' or, in what concerns the study of religion, such terms as 'dendrolatry', 'nagualism', and 'Pan-Babylonialism'.

Scholars of religion notoriously have a deep distrust of matters general, philosophical and so forth. Their training often consist in rigourous philological and historical erudition, which emphasizes the importance of the empirical and the particular. To this may be added, in the prevailing intellectual climate, a dosis of postmodernism and deconstruction, of anthropological cultural relativism, and of anti-ethnocentric political correctness (or religious sensibility), so that upon hearing, and being persuaded, that religion is but a Western academic construction some react with relief and feel justified in theis own questioning and criticism of all modes of theory, generalization and comparison. Historicist particularism then goes hand in hand with deconstructivists' dismantling of grand schemes and metaphysics – strange bedfellows indeed. But, when so doing, one also questions the validity of the study of religion as an academical enterprise. If 'religion' is but a scholarly fiction, then, so are the fictions 'society', 'culture', 'economy' in other academic fields. For all the things that humans construct we have but names that are also human constructions. It should come as no surprise that it is humans who create social and institutional facts, and what is interesting, then, is what makes something 'count as' something (Searle 1995: 31-57). The constructed nature of social reality does not entail that such reality does not exist, on the contrary – and scholars of religion should be the first to recognize this.

A perennial problem of terminology, taxonomy, 'label'-ology and definition has haunted the study of religion and continues to do so – and, as it seems, even increasingly. If a scholarly field cannot agree on some common conception of an object it does not hold much promise as an undertaking in the academy – there simply remains to little to talk about.[1] However, some of these qualms are unnecessary: that a common object may be said to be a construction is not a problem particular to the study of religion. In comparison to departments of art, literature, history and others in the humanities or the social sciences, scholars of religion are not really in any worse position than they are. After all, what *is* 'art', or 'literature'? The problem is not so much the names we give things, it is more that the process of naming is not duly recognized as a theoretical project, which it is because names are relative to our theories *more* than to the objects to which they refer (anyone in doubt may refer to the history of any science). That names change is no cause for alarm, we should worry more about so many becoming so worried when names change. The idea that names could or should not change is a positivist and inductivist one. Thus only positivists should worry about the universe not furnishing its own labelling. And if things have more than one name it is because labelling may be the result of theoretical plurality – also not a cause for alarm. Methodological promiscuity can be virtuous and theoretical polytheism need not be a sin, both may help us get things 'as right as we can' (Jensen 1997: 126-129). There might well be a possiblity for nominalism 'without dispair' – that is, a form of nominalism that does not land us in total relativism or particularist skepticism. The question is whether it is possible to uphold nominalism at some levels of reality and universalism at others? In order to probe this possibility, we need to exorcize some ghosts from the past. That can be done because the study of religion is a collective enterprise – a scholarly endeavour is warranted by its intersubjective nature.

The referentiality of religion

If we allow for the use our construction 'Religion' as a descriptive term, then it certainly is a widespread social phenomenon. It is also persistent – it may have been with the human species since the Neolithic, at least. There is, all terminological skepticism aside, a lot to interpret and explain for the study of religion. Considering the 'amount of religion' in the world something suggests that university departments for such studies are grossly underpopulated, also because religions can be many 'things': social realities, cultural systems, semantic universes, collective representations, cognitive models; patterns and complexes of actions and socio-cultural institutions (that should cover most of it). My particular view of religion is non-essentialist, that is, religions do not partake in some common numinous essence; it is non-referentialist, that is, religions do not refer to – or are true – in terms of some reference to the world (or a 'beyond'); this view is constructionist, that is, religion is something that humans make up. This view is fundamentally semantic and semiotic, that is, religion has to do with the production, organization and manipulation of ideology, of meaning (Jensen 1993). Such a holistic semantic approach, because that is what this amounts to, sees religions as reflexive systems of meaning that are inherently rational as self-referential entities – because their elements are not true or false by virtue of reference to the 'real' phenomenal world. That lack of reference does not entail, however, as some would think, that religion becomes meaningless, which would be a blatantly erroneous conclusion (Godlove 1989, Penner 1994, 1995). On the contrary, they become very powerful semantic engines in spite, and because, of their lack of reference. On this issue Lawson and McCauley state:

> ... no possible empirical consideration can defeat a model [: religion] whose several material commitments do not need to *refer* to the phenomenal world. If such models' particular symbolic claims did rigorously refer, then these systems would be subject to empirical assessment and their limitless flexibil-

54

ity would be curtailed ... after all, if they can include every possible experience within their purview, then they cannot help but be reflexive (1990: 156-7).

This does not mean that a semantic approach is idealist. Religious meanings (in the semantic sense of propositional contents) are embodied and manifested in ritual objects, temples, dress codes, settlement layouts, in political power relations, in forms of economic transactions, in modes of sexuality, dietary restrictions and so on – all such manifestations reveal that the locus of religion is manifold and may be found anywhere in human sociality. Such a view of religion is therefore also totalitarian, in that it sees religion as a social entity which may encompass all that humans do. Religions are preeminent instruments of control – of mind, body, and environment. Religions may even claim that they can control the invisible 'other world'. In fact, most of them do! But, we do not have to take their word for it, because from the view of a theory of semantic reflexivity religions' claims to transcendence are the very signs of the self-referential immanence of those forms of discourse.

Theories and constructions

Critics might object that the just mentioned examples of universals: 'holistic reflexivity', 'semantic engine', and 'symbol system' are 'theoretical universals' only, and not real 'object universals'. That would, however, mean reviving precisely the forms of empiricism and inductivism which have caused so much trouble in the business of defining religion. Religions are not 'real class' objects in the world, religion is not a 'natural kind' – nor is religion some 'primitive' term in metaphysics. As it turns out, not only is the scholars' term 'religion' a construction, but those aspects of social reality it is meant to describe are also constructions. But there is still something there; languages, politics, money, buildings and all the other things that humans construct are real enough, no doubt about that. There is, however, a double aspect to constructionism, because scholars also construct, e.g. second-order scientific classifications of first-order human behaviour. If humanly constructed religions make sense, then the constructed study of religion should, preferably, also make some sense. But, because the study of religion is a construction at different level it should

55

make a different sort of sense at a different level, and therefore religion is, when practiced, entirely different from what it is as an object of science. The boundary conditions of religious practice are not the same as the boundary conditions of scholarly inquiry (e.g., Wiebe 1998).

Theories and their objects *come* together – and they *go* together.[2] Things disappear when words disappear, because 'The reality of an object is inseparable from the methods given for its description', as Émile Benveniste once said on methodology in linguistics. It is true that it is *we* who decide to call a certain spectrum of human social activity 'religion', but linguists also have decided to call certain kinds of phonetic noise 'language'. And they speak freely about grammatical 'case', for instance – yet no one ever saw a 'case', but only instantiations of it. It is a theoretical construct through which you can explain certain relations between words. But those relations are real, however metaphysical is a 'relation'. It is plausible that some of the confusion around, and the frequent collapse of, concepts and phenomena is due to the fact that both universals and particulars are named by concrete singular terms. For instance, when you say 'sacrifice', as a universal and metaphysical concept, some say 'what sacrifice?' – referring to a particular empirical entity. Or, if we have a theory about physical objects in the world we demonstrate their existence by that theory – without it they would not be there – for us to know about. In that sense, the theory has both ontological and epistemological consequences. However, theories do not cause physical objects; no theory-change ever changed the shape of the planet Earth, as something tells (most of) us that the planet existed long before it became an object of human knowledge.

Theories not only label things that are already there, they also cause the existence of new social and cultural phenomena, such as for instance, new knowledge of things that were already there; only, now they have been appropriated by humans in the form of 'cultural posits'. Theory, in this context, is more than another word for 'hypothesis' – one which you prove in relation to empirical findings. Rather, it is that whole conceptual idiom within which we ask our questions and state our claims. Among the main epistemic virtues of a theory is that its concepts provide useful explanations of phenomena, that it be 'simple' and able to explain or cover much in terms of a restricted number of entities. And, it should allow for generalizations and deductions that are empirically adequate, also in the study of religion, because such a study should preferably present claims that are testable, somewhere down the line. Too many studies of religion do not – and that is precisely what we find is at fault with them. So, constructivism, as a theoretical position, does not mean that *we* invent things that have no relation to *those* invented things that most of us (still) call 'religion'. If that were so we would have a real case of the 'inscrutability of reference' – refined theory indeed, but totally detached from the world of human action.

Therefore, the idea that there should be concrete 'object universals' – similar things lying about in the world – before we may legitimately speak of theoretically posited or produced universals is putting the matter the wrong way around. But such is the presumption of an inductivist methodology, one which is detectable in much of the current critique of the 'notion of religion', as in the oft repeated assertion among historians of religions that 'there is no religion, only religions'! That fear of 'religion' in the singular was (is?) an example of involuntary Platonism: as if admitting that there be a universally valid concept of 'religion' implied that mundane religions must partake in some transcendent religion 'an sich' – a theological claim as historians would see it. Therefore, many attempts at generalizing and universalizing about religion have been seen as covert theological operations, which, in fact, they often were and still are (McCutcheon 1997: 101-157). If we agree that observations are theory-laden then we could of course find theories that do not allow for universals in religion, and not even for 'religion', and then dismiss the issue. But, it is equally, if not more, plausible that there are theories that can account for the opposite, and that we may insist with credibility that there are such entities as religions in the world, that they resemble each other in many aspects, and that the reason for those resemblances is that they share a number of features and that it is thus fair to say that there are universals *'in them'*, bearing in mind that these universals are only available to us by means of specific theoretical idioms.

Tool-kits and terminologies

Religions are the subject matter on which we use our terminologies, conceptual apparatuses, theories and models as a 'tool-kit'. Without a tool-kit, we cannot work. But, equally, without theoretical knowledge we cannot use our tools. The tool-kits of many studies on religion resemble the 'bricoleur's' – that Lévi-Straussian 'do-it-yourself' type – in that all kinds of concepts, models and theories have been dumped into it for when it might come in handy. With some more rigorously defined and designed theory we might be in a better position to develop the tools that could help us construct religion, religions and things religious in such ways that some measure of comparativity, comparability, generality and universality becomes plausible and defendable. This problem is not confined to the study of religion, but maybe, for instance, art historians and literary critics do not perceive the problem to be as urgent as do scholars of religion, probably because religion appears to be a more 'universal' object and because the vices of ethnocentrism are a major issue in the history of the field. Modesty is a virtue, also in the academy, but if a theory of religion only covers about three-and-a-half religions, then that is a poor theory. Literary critics and art historians seem to be involved in the study of a limited portion of all the art and literature there is – or can be said to be – in the world. In principle, scholars of religion study any and all religions, but they are stuck with the problem that the 'tool-kit' stocks only instruments applicable, as it seems, to the study of about three-and-a-half religions. That is rather poor. If the ambition is global, then it must be because scholars have a 'robust intuition' that all religions, without any priviledges awarded, could be studied, through concepts and terminologies that are theoretically validated and have global coverage.

The current situation in the study of religion resembles that of linguistics when it was primarily inductivist, historical-philological and worked from the basis of a terminology supplied by Greek and Roman philology. The study of religion has problems related to the heritage from these philologies and Christian theology, because these disciplines were self-supplying in terms of terminologies. That is, it was the subject matter of their fields of investigation supplied the scholars with the terms considered relevant. To make matters more complicated, terms that could be supplied from outside those same fields were often considered irrelevant and suspect. The end result was a circularity of conceptualizing (this is a topic worthy of genuine debate and investigation). It is well known, that the terms most commonly employed in the study of religion have a European, or Western, background. That is not new, but the genealogy of that enclosed epistemological reflexivity is revealing. It is also related to a particular form of a-theoretical textual positivism and logocentrism that thrives so well in the study of religion: The idea that the right terms for an analysis of, for instance, 8th.century Buddhist texts are Buddhist terms etc., and that all we could ever want to know leaps right out of the texts – by virtue of its immanent essence and our own empathetic understanding: 'not being biased by theory', 'keeping an open mind', 'not being preju- diced', and taking into account only 'that which appears' etc.. Therefore, it is commonly advocated that we should 'speak the same language' as the text. That is, not only philologically, which is but one necessary condition, but we should use the same 'indigenous' concepts as the texts themselves do or, according to the argument, we fail to understand. To the propo- nents of those methods, or attitudes, the tragedy of being an 'outsider' car- ries all the connotations of depressive anxiety, because only 'insiders get it right'. These views are not only known to scholars of religion, they also proliferate in anthropology (Spiro 1987: 56-57).

The priviledging of insiders' religious intuitions is based upon relin- quished modes of subjectivist hermeneutics of 'Einfühlung' and 'Nacher- lebnis'. In defense of this mode of hermeneutics we often encounter the truism that the scholar of religion also works from within a 'world', per- haps even a religious one. That is undeniable, but the differences between scientific and religious practice, quite perceptible to most, do undermine the impact of that comparison. The distanced analytic position is not by necessity a tragic one. There are quite a few things in the world of which one would prefer to obtain knowledge *without* participating. And although participation, observation and interpretation are the necessary conditions for the gathering of information it is, equally undeniably, through the scholars' lenses and by means of their tools, e.g. scholarly con- cepts, that such information is transformed into knowledge. The termi- nologies of research in cultural analysis depend upon the standards of research and not upon those of the objects studied. I can only concur with Bruce Lincoln whose observations in this respect are that:

> When one permits those whom one studies to define the terms in which they will be understood, suspends one's interest in the temporal and contingent, or fails to distinguish between "truths", "truth-claims", and "regimes of truth", one has ceased to function as historian or scholar. In that moment, a variety of roles are available: some perfectly respectable (amanuensis, collector, friend and advocate), and some less appealiing (cheerleader, voyeur, retailer of import goods). None, however should be confused with scholarship (1996: 277).

Scholarly concepts are scholars' tools and as such they are meta-formations and 'experience-distant'. They are, of course, also culture-bound – not to the culture of origin, but to the culture of reception. That may be lamented, but so be it. All there is to say is that this is where critical and reflexive rationality is called for.

On the translation of religion

If the study of religion had been invented in Buddhist lands, as it might well have been, then Christianity, Islam and Judaism could have been described, not as monotheistic, but as *'non-karmic'* religions, because that difference could have been more interesting from a Buddhist perspective than the number of gods involved. It is my contention here that this would not, however, make scholars with a Buddhist cultural background see similarities and differences between religions in a radically different manner. Similarly, a study of religion based on a terminology of New Zealand Maori-terms is not impossible: Maori scholars of religion, the 'tohungas', would find a lot of things in western religions that could make sense in a Maori universe. From fieldwork experience I know that Old Norse religion makes good sense in a traditional African discursive universe – to mention but one example.[3]

The issue here is the translatability of religious systems or 'worlds'. In Donald Davidsson's philosophy of language translatability is one fundamental characteristic of semantic systems: a non-translateable language is simply not a language; nor is a *radically different*, non-translatable conceptual scheme a scheme at all, for as he says: 'we could not be in a position to judge that others had concepts or beliefs radically different from our own' (1984: 197). Consider his statement about conceptual schemes, and translate these 'into religion': '... we have found no intelligible basis on which it can be said that schemes are different' and 'if we cannot intelligibly say that schemes are different, neither can we intelligibly say they are one.' The alternatives for religion are then: 1) either we can translate religions and they are not radically different schemes, or 2) we wouldn't know. My positions is clear, I do not endorse the delusions of epistemological relativists who simultaneously claim that cultures are radically different and that they (the relativists) understand them.

There must be something without which language would cease to be language, culture culture, and religion religion. On the track of universals the 'Big Question' becomes: What are the indispensable constituents of religious semantic systems? What are the necessary forms and structures of conceptualizations that a religious semantic system needs in order to operate? The conditions indispensable and necessary are not so by reference to some eternal realm of Truth, but because they constitute the possibility of the existence of a given community of communication – in its historical particularity different from all others, but at the same time like them, because they are subjected to those same necessary and indispensable conditions. These questions are philosophical – but they are also scientific and they may be given both philosophical and scientific answers.

On the track of religious universals

In a scholarly, and thus secular, perspective, religion is a human phenomenon. Consequently, religious universals must somehow be human universals. Thus, it is not a question here of transcendent ontological universals, nor about 'religio universalis', nor is it an argument of the kind suggested by Joachim Wach that the phenomenology of religion should: 'inquire into the nature of the Divine' or 'provide a theory of revelation' (1958: 24). However, although I disagree with Mircea Eliade and Friedrich Heiler on many points, I do consider it necessary for the study of religion to analyze the 'morphologies of the sacred' (Eliade) and 'zum Wesen vorzustossen' (Heiler) – stripped, of course, of all transcendental assumptions and religious aspirations. In fact, I do think that religion has an essence, perhaps even more, and that at least one of them is communication. Other candidates could be semantic and cognitive modelling and self-reflexivity. And a science of religion that is unable to analyze, interpret and explain the modes of such phenomena would be in a poor state. All this cannot be done without involving acts of comparison. Comparison implies the possibility of generalization, or, as it turns out upon closer inspection, generalization is the precondition of comparison.

On the plight of generalization and universalization in cultural analysis Melford Spiro has attributed, in a commendable essay on cultural relativism, two claims to the many relativists in anthropology: '(1) panhuman generalizations and theories (cultural, social, and psychological) are either false – because ethnocentric – or trivial and vacuous. Hence, anthropology neither is nor can it in principle become an explanatory – a scientific – discipline. Rather, (2) it is ... an interpretive – hermeneutic – discipline' (1992: 134). Spiro counters these opinions by arguing that generalization has been possible 'precisely because of wide range of human diversity' (ibid.). This is so because: 'A scientific generalization... is a statement, not to the effect that some object or event is universal – but that the world being lawful, its occurrence ... is governed by a *principle* that is universal' (135). Spiro goes on to apply this to religion and says that 'a nonvacuous generalization regarding religion is a generalization not about religion in general, but about concrete types of religious-belief systems: monotheism, polytheism, and the like' (ibid.). Therefore 'scientific generalizations regarding society and culture are statements not of frequencies but of *regularities ...*' that 'pertain not to universals but to differences' (ibid.). Somehow Spiro manages to contradict himself here, because it might well be that religion *in general* is governed by a range of universal principles. And that is quite enough. Between the trivial particularist recording of the variability of religions on the one hand and the just as trivial universal surface definition of religion as a cultural system lies a much more interesting field of generative cognitive *and* semantic mechanisms or principles that account for religions having been made into what they are: different but comparable. Consequently, we are not simply looking for surface regularities and uniformities, nor are we concerned with referential convergence to some 'great mystery beyond'. Social and religious universes are constantly changing – but their fundamental structures and dynamics are not so much. Therefore, without pretending to disclose sets of strict laws, there may still be discernible sets of rule-making and rule-following. It is not so much universals in form that the study of religions seeks, but regularities of functions and structures. However puzzling it may sound, the universals could, first and foremost, pertain to the making of differences.

Therefore, saying that there are universals in religion, is not the same as saying that religion is universal in the sense that every human individual or group has it or that they should have. What I *am* saying is that in spite of all the surface variations there may lie, in those socio-cultural complexes which we choose to call religion, some commonalities, generalities, or universals of forms, functions, structures or, most controversially, of meanings, that is, of semantic contents. However, as religion is a highly complex category, it is plausible to suggest that these 'mechanisms' lie at different levels. It is also plausible that not all of those items that we may insert in a global catalogue as a result of our 'etic' endeavours should be evenly distributed, have the same frequence or intensity, but that would not detract from our 'intuition' that religions display results of rule-governed operations and generative principles. The critical question is: 'Why should religion be *that* singular case of human cultural products which does *not* depend upon any sort of regularity'? That singularity is often taken for given, but the case for it has not been argued convincingly. And, until it is, it remains a sound thesis to hold that there are, if not common denominators, then some common operators that produce similarities under conditions that are necessary or inescapable when semantic systems become religious – that is when they are tied to conceptualizations of supernatural entities. If religions are somehow like languages or games, then there must be rules, and operations of these rules must be accountable for, either causally or structurally.

Multiple levels of universals

The level of universals most obvious when speaking of humans is the biological. All humans are biological phenomena (as long as they live), but to make religion, therefore, a biological phenomenon to best be explained by biologists is to commit 'the fallacy of partial description' (as philosopher of science Larry Laudan has dubbed it). Of course, at some level, our genetic makeup is involved, but I do not consider biological theorizing very informative (in its present state): It may account for our species' ability to have religion, but it is more doubtful whether it may account for *why* we have or *how* we have it. Ecology may come under this category, but as far as bio-ecological relations are mediated by cognitive and cultural factors there are reasons to consider the direct causally explanatory potential of bio-ecological theories of religious universals to be limited.

Cognitive universals are a fact, also in religion. The limits of human cognition are also the limits of religion. However, that deceptively simple rubric 'cognitive' covers in fact a very vast range of phenomena: from species-specific biologically grounded properties to high-level complex cultural representations. If the term cognitive covers all that which pertains to our mental life it really covers a lot, perhaps too much for the term to be significant: We have low-level cognitive abilities tied to the perception of objects, processes and properties but we also have high-level cognitive abilities connected to the processing of complex semantic information, where the cognitive mediates between the biological and the sociocultural. And so far none seem to have convincingly answered the question of what cognitive representations consist of. That non-withstanding, there is 'high-level' cognitive research available that can account for certain regulatory principles and processes in religious conceptual systems, that would count as universals (e.g, Lawson and McCauley 1990).

Social universals are involved in the formation of social entities. In the study of religion, the protagonists of symbolist or projectionist theories posit universal mechanisms and processes in the formation of religions as dependent variables of the social. This is, however, not possible, without including universals concerning the relations between modes of production, or subsistence and ideologies (in the broadest sense) in the explanatory schemes. Social universals will also be found in 'elementary forms of kinship': there are limits as to what can be considered a human society and there are rules as to their composition if they are to function and be recognizable as societies. But, what is social involves a combination of the biological, the cognitive and the cultural.

The level of cultural universals is as wide as it is contested. However, as culture must fundamentally be viewed as the production and organization of meaning and the foundation, in language, of human sociality, there are bound to be such things as cultural universals. For instance in 'the logic by which symbols are connected' (Leach 1976). Cultural universals may be subdivided into: First, linguistic universals. Although these days more often linked to the cognitive, linguistic universals are also eminently cultural. The grammars of languages are certainly different but there is no language without grammar or syntax, or if not, would we call it a language then? All languages process and transmit semantic propositional contents (Leech 1990: 231-254). Any language can, in principle, be translated into any other language. It is only fair to assume that there are universals in operation – although these may be of a very complex nature (Overing 1985: xx). These universals pertain not only to the properties of cognitive processing in the human mind but also to the logics of the semantic representational systems themselves as has been so amply demonstrated by Claude Lévi-Strauss. At higher-order emergent levels narratological theory and discourse analysis suggest universals in the formations of narratives and discourses. Even the strangest of myths start somewhere and finish somewhere and they all evolve within universes of modalities of thought, speech and action. Second, symbolic universals need not be tied to, or validate, theories of universal contents or referents as in the theories of C.G. Jung or Mircea Eliade. Research on metaphoric association and processing demonstrates the existence of universals in the processes of symbolization. Although often heavily emphasizing the cognitive aspects such theories do consider and include the semantic as cultural-representational in the form of schemata, models and category-formation. There is no language, no society and no culture without classification, briefly stated: culture *is* classification. The forms of classificatory schemes are vastly different, but their translatability is a fact – as even epistemological relativists recognize – wherefore there must be universals involved at some level of their construction. Third, religious, including mythological, universals are a combination of linguistic and symbolic universals. Religions are systems of difference and the production of differences is nothing but a universal. Where religions differ from other conceptual schemes is in their constructions of 'other worlds' of super-natural entities with counter-intuitive properties.

Now, if it could be said that only a few of the world's societies have religions, and only three-and-a-half of these include counter-intuitive supernatural entities, then I would be convinced that I am wasting my time looking for universals, but that is not the case. What has just been outlined is what can be found *anywhere*. That is one good reason for considering universals at least as interesting as the particulars. Why, if humans have to inhibit worlds of meaning, such remarkable constructions? That question may not be answered by particularistic, empirical research, however minutely detailed. It is a theoretical question. Ritual practice is probably the field where it is 'easier' to convince sceptics that there are universals in religion, because it demonstrates what religious competence consists in. But again, not at the simple level of resemblance; the tracking of universals requires theorizing.

The study of religion is a truly interesting field in the study of humanity and humanness. Its scope is so broad that it simply needs generalization, comparison and theory; because the sheer mass of empirical material is too overwhelming. It has to tackle the problems of generalization, comparison and universals of forms, functions, structures, and, as the most problematic, of 'meaning' – still in the semantic sense of propositional content. And, then it would be possible to demonstrate how religions, as modalities of the theoretical object 'religion', contain universals which are functions of universals of cognition, universals of sociality, and universals of semantics. As it happens, I am primarily occupied with the latter, but since religion is an 'impure subject' that comprises just so many aspects there is no need for monopolizing. Theories of universals often come with an associated power-game, but that is unnecessary. The only point I must insist on is that, *if* we want to have theories about religion and religions, then we cannot bypass the issue of universals. No theory can be about particulars only. Therefore, although it has often been assumed that the issue of universals in religions must be a theological or ideological affair, the arguments set forth above should contain enough persuasive power to lead to the conviction that this need not be so. In fact, talking about universals is a methodologically and theoretically legitimate business – indeed, it is a prerequisite for doing theory, and thus also for scholarly practice.

Notes

1. Cf. e.g. the contributions to the symposium on 'new comparativism' in *Method and Theory in the Study of Religion*, 8-1, 1996, 1-49, and Smith 1990.
2. In my department we are, so to speak, 're-inventing magic' because there are now theories about metaphors and cognition that allow for new models on that vexed subject (remember that the little dolls with pins in them were there all time ...).
3. 'Native' or local translations of imported (e.g., missionary) religious discourse is an underrated subject in the study of religion.

References

Davidson, Donald, 'On the Very Idea of a Conceptual Scheme', in idem, *Inquiries into Truth and Interpretation*, Oxford Univ. Press, New York, 1984: 183-198.

Godlove, Terry F., *Religion, interpretation, and the diversity of belief. The framework model from Kant to Durkheim to Davidson*. Cambridge Univ. Press, Cambridge, 1989.

Jensen, Jeppe Sinding, 'What Sort of "Reality" is Religion?', in Martin, Luther (ed.), *Religious Transformations and Socio-Political Change*, Mouton, Berlin and New York, 1993: 357-379.

Jensen, Jeppe Sinding, 'Social Facts, Metaphysics and Rationality in the Human Sciences', in Jensen, Jeppe Sinding and Martin, Luther H. (eds.), *Rationality and the Study of Religion*, Aarhus University Press, Aarhus, 1997: 117-135.

Lawson, E. Thomas and McCauley, Robert N., *Rethinking religion: Connecting cognition and culture*. Cambridge Univ. Press, Cambridge, 1990.

Leach, Edmund, *Culture and Communication. The Logic by which Symbols are Connected*. Cambridge Univ. Press, Cambridge, 1976.

Leech, Geoffrey, *Semantics. The Study of Meaning*, Penguin Books, Harmondsworth, 1990 (rpd.).

Lincoln, Bruce, 'Theses on Method', *Method and Theory in the Study of Religion*, 1996, 8, 225-227.

McCutcheon, Russell T. *Manufacturing Religion. The Discourse on Sui Generis Religion and the Politics of Nostalgia*, Oxford Univ. Press, New York, 1997.

Overing, Joanna, 'Introduction', in Overing, Joanna (ed.), *Reason and Morality*, Tavistock, London, 1985: 1-28.

Penner, Hans H., 'Holistic Analysis. Conjectures and Refutations', *Journal of the American Academy of Religion*, 1994, 62 (4): 977-996.

Penner, Hans H., 'Why does semantics matter to the study of religion?', *Method and Theory in the Study of Religion*, 1995, 7-3: 221-249.

Searle, John, *The Construction of Social Reality*, The Free Press, New York 1995.

Smith, Jonathan Z., *Imagining Religion. From Babylon to Jonestown*, The University of Chicago Press, Chicago and London, 1982.

Smith, Jonathan Z., 'Connections', *Journal of the American Academy of Religion*, 1990, 58 (1): 1-15.

Spiro, Melford, *Culture and Human Nature: Theoretical Papers of Melford E. Spiro*, B. Kilborn and L. Langness (eds.), University of Chicago Press, Chicago, 1987.

Spiro, Melford, 'Cultural Relativism and the Future of Anthropology', in Marcus, George E. (ed.), *Rereading Cultural Anthropology*, Duke Univ. Press, Durham and London, 1992: 124-151.

Wach, Joachim, *The Comparative Study of Religion*, Columbia Univ. Press, New York, 1958.

Wiebe, Donald, *The Politics of Religious Studies*, St. Martin's Press, New York, 1998.

Beyond Essence and Intuition:

A Reconsideration of Understanding in Religious Studies

Morny Joy

Professor, Department of Religious Studies
University of Calgary, Calgary, Canada

From its inception, Religious Studies has been something of a hybrid discipline. As a result, its nomenclature,[1] definition, methodology, and even subject matter have provided causes for contention. Initially, this could be ascribed to growing pains, but more recently this has escalated into a debate between those who wish to rid the discipline of any ontological, not just theological, remnants, and those who would support a pluralist paradigm that is not hostile to ontological topics. This could be depicted as just one more battle between realists who favour a cognitive, strictly (social-)scientific, approach and idealists whose orientation allows for philosophically based insights, but this would be a false dichotomy that does not take into account the complexities of late twentieth-century thought where reflexive hermeneutics and postmodernism has challenged such absolutist positions and definitions. Nor does it acknowledge the critiques of dominant Western epistemological frameworks by women, indigenous people, people of colour and postcolonial scholars who have found their ideologically laden presuppositions both exclusionary and inaccurate.[2] The question of otherness has always loomed large in Religious Studies, a discipline that was introduced initially to better understand religions other than Christianity – though this was not without, in some cases, a not-so-covert missiological intent. Today, however, otherness or difference has far more extensive implications, for it need not necessarily be confined to whatever lies beyond the Eurocentric pale. Otherness delineates any difference – be it textual or personal – that is encountered, but it is not, as in a proto-Hegelian model, simply something to be assimilated into an existing system of knowledge. Rather, otherness can provide a challenge that encourages an evaluation of the culturally based norms which both foster and reinforce a worldview and its concomitant scholarly methods.

As a discipline, Religious Studies has not developed very much beyond a Hegelian incorporative mode, yet it has the potential to be one of the areas of study that, in an increasingly multicultural world, could be an exemplar of a non-exploitative encounter with otherness. But a change is needed, with regard to attitudes towards difference, both internal and external to the discipline.

The opposition between understanding and explanation, as respectively representative of the human and natural sciences underlies much of the contemporary wrangling. It would seem that unless it is possible to bring these two approaches into dialogue, if not to reconcile them, then mainstream Religious Studies will continue to be beset by a type of internecine theoretical warfare. In contrast, those groups, listed above, that have conventionally been located on the periphery of the field, will, in their critical and constructive contributions, be the source of more dynamic and creative scholarship. Indeed, other human sciences, such as Anthropology, would seem to have been more versatile and self-reflexive in their methodological responses to the changing conditions of research in today's world than Religious Studies.[3] What follows is a modest proposal for a revision of the methodological impasse that hampers Religious Studies today, so that it might not lag behind other disciplines. This is by no means a defence of any established theory or method, but an attempt to expand and explore a form of methodology that takes into account historical and material conditions of knowledge and a critical assessment of those conditions. What is required to support such an endeavor is a careful scrutiny of the philosophical underpinnings of the various methodological approaches.

But first to a working or functional definition of religion.[4] In a series of works, Ninian Smart (1976; 1983; 1996) has modified his appreciation of the non-normative study of religion, situating it within the perspective of a worldview where, rather than defining religion *per se*, he characterizes it as an aspect of human life whereby one orients oneself in the cosmos so as to give expression to "the exigencies of our own nature and existence." Religious Studies is thus a

"Worldview analysis" – the attempt to describe and understand human worldviews, especially those that have had widespread influence – ranging from varieties of Christianity and Buddhism to the more politically oriented systems of

70

Islam and Marxism, and from ancient religions and philosophies such as Platonism and Confucianism to modern new religions in Africa and America ... (1983: 5).

In order to describe religion so as to illustrate how subjective elements and objective practices interact, Smart has refined and expanded a list of diverse dimensions: doctrinal, mythic, ethical, ritual, experiential, social, material and political. These categories establish a provisional structure that permits a systematic approach of either a historical or thematic nature. Such categories also encourage the type of polymethodic studies that alone can negotiate the multifaceted and interwoven elements of religion considered as a worldview. As Smart states:

> The modern study of religion takes religion as an aspect of life and tries to understand it historically and crossculturally. It applies the insights of various disciplines – such as psychology, anthropology, sociology, linguistics – to illuminate its dynamics. It is parallel to, and sometimes overlaps with, political science and economics ... But whether we have spelled it out to ourselves or not, each one of us has a worldview, which forms a background to the lives we lead. The modern study of religion has as one main focus the exploration of such worldviews (1983: 3-4).

While Smart's descriptive categories do provide a helpful initial orientation, they do not take into account the interpretive factor involved. Also, there is a major and problematic gap between such an objective description and the implied subsequent act of understanding. Understanding is not automatic, nor is it immediately evident what understanding entails. Indeed, the word "understanding" is a term that has provoked much discussion concerning the correct methodological approach in Religious Studies. Yet what the word actually means is today left imprecise. Somehow it has been consigned to a heritage of German idealist and Romantic thought, with strong subjectivist overtones. On such grounds, it is dismissed – its meaning self-evident – as by R. J. Zwi Werblonsky:

> Little need be said here on the history of the concept of *Verstehen* and the philosophical discussions around it. The literature on the subject is by now classical (1975: 146).

It is also often aligned with a somewhat facile notion of empathy or intuition and regarded as inferior to the more cognitive or science-based approach, characterized by explanation. It is time, I believe, to make a more detailed examination of understanding and move beyond the rather naive way it is employed both by its supporters and detractors in Religious Studies. I would like to explore, in particular, how the concept of understanding (*Verstehen*) has been developed in the work of Paul Ricoeur, and how its subtle interplay with the mode of explanation could help alleviate some of the methodological squabbles that prevail. This is a selective account as there will not be sufficient space to undertake a detailed critical history of the influence of the term from the time of Kant and Hegel, to its present role in the influence of phenomenology and hermeneutics on Religious Studies. With regard to phenomenology, this has been done to some extent, though not in depth (Capps, 1995: 105-156; Allen, 1987: 272-285). But the influence of hermeneutics, except with reference to its more narrow focus in biblical exegesis, has not received extensive treatment. What is particularly relevant is Ricoeur's qualification of the excessive claims made by proponents of Husserlian phenomenology to objectivity by bracketing (*epoche*), and to the subsequent intuition of an essence (*eidos*). What is required instead is a discerning contextualization that tempers the resultant ahistorical idealizations or theological aspirations. Ricoeur's hermeneutic phenomenology regards any understanding as historically conditioned and, as such, requiring to be subjected to a rigorous examination of any personal or social distortions – a "hermeneutics of suspicion."[5] Such a modification would permit a more chastened estimation of what can be achieved by adopting an approach that does not subscribe to an unrestricted subjective sympathy or to its reactive opposite, a reductive objectivist exposition. Understanding is thus relieved of the burden it has borne within a purely phenomenological framework and allowed a more modest scope of activity, though it does not thereby concede authority to explanation.

It is noteworthy that Smart, although his own relationship with the term is ambivalent, warns against the use of the term "phenomenology" (1983: 16). Partly this is because of the rather superficial employment of the word in the study or classification of religious phenomena (Allen, 1987: 273), and partly because of the harsh criticism levelled at those, such as Geradus van der Leeuw, who had adapted Husserl's philosophical phenomenology so as to constitute a distinct and intrinsic approach within the wider study of religion.

It is perhaps van der Leeuw (1890-1950) who is principally responsible for the problematic status of the term "understanding" in Religious Studies. In his classic work, *Religion in Essence and Manifestation* (1963), van der Leeuw expounded his confessional stance:

> The more deeply comprehension penetrates any event, and the better it "understands" it, the clearer it becomes to the understanding mind that the ultimate ground of understanding lies not within itself, but in some "other" by which it is comprehended from beyond the frontier. Without this absolutely valid and decisive understanding, indeed, there would be no understanding whatsoever ... In other terms, all understanding, irrespective of whatever object it refers to, is ultimately religious (1963: 683-4).

But van der Leeuw is not the only guilty party,[6] as many other early scholars in Religious Studies, while not equally Christian apologists, resorted to similar terminology in the service of ontological ideals.[7] Whether primordial or essential, such a core of religion was most often reached by an intuitive or speculative act of understanding.

Joachim Wach (1898-1955) who was largely responsible for bringing the discipline of Religious Studies (as *Religionswissenschaft*) to North America, employed a composite definition of understanding. It was influenced variously by the ideas of Dilthey, Husserl, Otto and Weber. He accepted the fact that though religious experience was manifold, in its genuine form, Ultimate Reality was revealed. Understanding then situated itself as a means of appreciating the essence of these "genuine experiences," and in discovering (by induction) the structures that operate according to "strictly spiritual laws" and their own "phenomenological rules" (1961: 25). Mircea Eliade, Wach's successor at the University of Chicago, has also been criticized for his similar imposition on phenomena of ontological presuppositions which predetermine exactly what understanding will discern (Penner 1989). Unfortunately, none of these scholars employ either the term "phenomenology" or "understanding" in a consistent way. As Douglas Allen observes:

> Controversies arise from criticisms that the Phenomenology of Religion is highly normative and subjective because it makes non-empirical, non-historical, *a priori*, theological, and other normative assumptions and because it grants an ontologically privileged status to religious phenomena and to special kinds of religious experience (1987: 283).

In all of the above mentioned scholars, the mode of understanding is given priority over the mode of explanation. It is also presented as a virtually self-explanatory term, exhibiting an idiosyncratic adaptation of Husserl's phenomenology.

A certain amount of blame for this development can also be assigned to Wilhelm Dilthey (1833-1911), though Dilthey is more remembered for his influence on hermeneutics than for any connection with phenomenology. His project of finding an appropriate method for the human sciences (*Geisteswissenshaften*), as distinct from that of the natural sciences (*Naturwissenschaften*), introduced the bifurcation of understanding from explanation. Richard Palmer describes Dilthey's approach:

> The key word for the human studies, Dilthey believed, was "understanding." Explaining is for the sciences, but the approach to phenomena which unites the inner and outer is understanding. The sciences explain nature, the human studies understand expressions of life. Understanding can grasp the individual entity, but science must always see the individual as a means of arriving at the general, the type (1969: 105).

Yet while Dilthey has certain affinities with aspects of Schleiermacher, who saw understanding as involving a re-experience of the author's mental processes of creation, as well as with Husserl's intuitive grasp of essences, he did introduce one basic concept that distinguishes his work – historicality (*Geschichtlichkeit*). Historicality, which acknowledges the contextual nature of all knowledge and the finitude of human knowing by situating the knower in an intersection of past cultural influences with present contingencies and future aspirations, became henceforth a central tenet of hermeneutics. There was an inevitable tension in Dilthey's work between his effort to establish ahistorical epistemological foundations for the human sciences (his major goal) and his insight regarding the inevitable contextualization of life which is not easily amenable to fixed structures and categories. As Jean Grondin observes:

> Nowhere does he show how interpretative psychology would validate the objectivity of propositions in the human sciences. In these respects ... Dilthey's project could not get beyond the merely programmatic stage (1991: 86).

Yet it is on these three basic ideas bequeathed by Dilthey – understanding, explanation, and historicality – that the contemporary hermeneutic scholar will focus as s/he attempts to revise hermeneutics so as to eliminate the dubious legacy of subjectivist psychological tendencies and claims to universal knowledge. In their stead, a phenomenological hermeneutic scholar such as Ricoeur will promote a productive dialectic between the distinct modes of understanding and explanation (which he sees as placed in a false antinomy). He locates this interaction against a historical background which also requires a hermeneutics of suspicion, e.g., an emancipatory critique such as that of Habermas.

My choice of Ricoeur in preference to Hans-Georg Gadamer as representative of the contemporary field of hermeneutics depends largely on his adamant inclusion of this moment of suspicion or critique. While Gadamer, because of his notion of dialogue and fusion of horizons (1994: 302-307; 366-79), is frequently cited as a model of decenteredness that would promote a non-reductive encounter with otherness (Halbfass 1988: 164-7; Dallmayr 1996: 49-58), his views of tradition as legitimating authority have been taken to task by Habermas (1977: 243-276).[8] In an essay "Hermeneutics and the Critique of Ideology," Ricoeur himself effects a mediation between Gadamer and Habermas. In this essay, he begins by acknowledging the contribution of tradition:

> The interest in emancipation would be quite empty and abstract if it were not situated on the same plane as the historical-hermeneutical sciences, that is, on the plane of communicative action ... The task of the hermeneutics of tradition is to remind the critique of ideology that man can project his emancipation and anticipate an unlimited and unconstrained communication only on the basis of the creative reinterpretation of cultural heritage (1981:97).

This view, however, must not be mistaken for an unqualified endorsement of tradition, for Ricoeur is equally insistent on the role of critique:

> However, on its side, a hermeneutic which would cut itself off from the regulative idea of emancipation would be no more than a hermeneutic of traditions and in these terms a form of philosophical restoration. Nostalgia for the past would drive it unpityingly toward the positions of Romanticism which it started out to surpass (1973: 165).

The question, of course, remains as to whether phenomenological hermeneutics, in Ricoeur's version, has thrown off the vestiges of Romanticism and can provide the basis for a methodology in religion that concerns itself as much with material conditions as it does with the understanding of meaning. Ricoeur, in his hermeneutical theory, does not have a vested interest in the maintenance of any ideal of religion as having a *sui generis* nature. Ricoeur's interactive model is nonetheless influenced by Hegel, though it is not in the service of *Geist*. Ricoeur has referred to Hegel's philosophy as the tricks of a magician that no longer work. There is also a very strong critical Kantian component in his philosophical make-up. Insofar as his work has an ontological flavour, Ricoeur's allegiance is to modes of being-in-the world that influence meaning in ways which could have either secular or religious implications, e.g. emancipation or justice. Thus, while he would agree with Dilthey that human beings can only be understood by way of their cultural productions, for Ricoeur these objectifications have psychological connotations that are different from those of Dilthey. These have to do with the notion of prejudice, and it is this attitude that also leads him to be critical of Gadamer, and by implication, Heidegger.

> Thus Gadamer, speaking of the texts of our culture, repeatedly insists that these texts signify by themselves, that there is a "matter of the text" which addresses us. But how can the "matter of the text" be left to speak without confronting the critical question of the way in which preunderstanding and prejudice are mixed? (1981: 89-90).

Ricoeur's own response, then, is not to espouse the other extreme and privilege critique, but to formulate a vital exchange between expanded definitions of understanding and explanation (particularly at the level of texts). At the same time, he incorporates a further level of productive interaction between the modes of subjective appropriation and objective distanciation (which have reference to a dynamic of existential extrapolation). Ricoeur's intention is not simply to perpetuate a bifurcation between the terms, but to foster a system of mutual checks and balances.

> It is indeed my concern to avoid the pitfall of an opposition between an "understanding" which would be reserved for the "human sciences" and an "explanation" which would be common to the latter and to the nomological sciences, primarily the physical sciences. The search for a flexible articulation and a continual to and fro between the investigator's personal engagement with the matter of the text, and the disengagement which the objective explanation by causes, laws, functions or structures demands, is the guiding thread [of my work] (1981: 36).

In this interplay, Ricoeur's own revised understanding of the concept of "understanding" is crucial. As one illustration, at the textual level, of the relation of understanding to explanation (where structuralism provides the grid of an explanatory method), Ricoeur explains:

> Understanding has less than ever to do with the author and his situation ... To understand a text is to follow its movement from sense to reference, from what it says to what it talks about. In this process the *mediating* role played by structural analysis constitutes both the justification of this objective approach and the rectification of the subjective approach. We are definitively prevented from identifying understanding with some kind of intuitive grasping of the intention underlying the text (1981: 218).

This leads to further reflection on understanding, which, for Ricoeur, although it will finally effect an augmentation in knowledge of a personal nature, it will always be refined by an objective assessment that determines its validation (or lack thereof). Ricoeur's criteria for the acceptance incorporates procedures of establishing probability by argumentation which, given his hermeneutic bias, would be more mediatory and dialogical than antagonistic. The following quote exemplifies this process:

To the procedures of validation also belong procedures of invalidation similar to the criteria of falsifiability emphasized by Karl Popper in his *Logic of Scientific Discovery*. The role of falsification is played here by the conflict between competing interpretations. An interpretation must not only be probable, but more probable than another ... The logic of validation allows us to move between the two limits of dogmatism and scepticism. It is always possible to argue for or against an interpretation, to confront interpretations, to arbitrate between them, and to seek for agreement, even if this agreement remains beyond our reach (1981: 213).

While initially Ricoeur's work seemed to be directed primarily to textual interpretation, in a key essay, "The Model of the Text: Meaningful Action Considered as a Text," Ricoeur allows that this procedure can also be applied to the analysis and interpretation of human behaviour.

That the meaning of human actions, of historical events, and of social phenomena may be *construed* in several different ways is well known by all experts in the human sciences ... What seems to legitimate this extension from guessing the meaning of a text to guessing the meaning of an action is that in arguing about the meaning of an action I put my wants and my beliefs at a distance and submit them to a concrete dialectic of confrontation with opposite points of view (1981: 213-4).

Such a move has distinct and important implications for methodology in Religious Studies. Firstly, it supports a move of hermeneutics from being simplistically applied to texts and to human behaviour and productions. Secondly, it does not immediately propose meaning as deriving solely from empirical evidence according to predetermined formulas or doctrines. Thus while any explanatory method of a logical or scientifically based nature can be employed, its findings are not automatically acceptable. As a result, neither personal authority nor scholarly dogmatism is endorsed. Both are recognized as limited perspectives, and it is only by a process of trial and error that human constructs which attempt to make the world comprehensible can stake a claim to a form of knowledge. This claim is then subjected to public debate and exchange which constitutes a process of ultimate validation by consensus. In this procedure religion does not hold any special status or prerogative that would distinguish it from other human constructs. It is one worldview among others, and within the polymethodological framework of the discipline of Religious Studies, many different explanatory methods could be employed – be they philosophical, psychological, sociological, or anthropological – to help clarify the mechanisms that contribute to the construction of religious worldviews.

However, Ricoeur does not stop at the stage of critical textual response and empirical analysis. He also introduces another level of interaction that occurs between the modes of appropriation and distanciation at an existential level. In point of fact, this is parallel to, if not intimately related to the exchange of understanding and explanation but, for purposes of exposition, Ricoeur separates them out as if they belonged to further ordering in a progression of knowledge. As Ricoeur observes: "The dialectic of distanciation and appropriation is the final figure which the dialectic of explanation and understanding must assume" (1981: 183). Initially, within a context of textual interpretation, Ricoeur depicted appropriation as the moment when readers take from a text new capacities for knowing themselves and their world. But Ricoeur was only too aware of the possibility of personal illusions or distortions that could colour such arrogations. As he states:

> Our understanding is based on prejudices which are linked to our position in the relations of force of society, a position which is partially unknown to us. Moreover, we are propelled to act by hidden interests. Whence the falsification of reality. Thus the critique of "false consciousness" becomes an integral part of hermeneutics. Here I see a place for a necessary dialogue between hermeneutics and the theory of ideology as developed by Habermas (1981: 191).

Such a dialogue can take place by means of the movement of distanciation. "Distanciation, in all its forms and figures, constitutes *par excellence* the critical moment in understanding" (1981: 113). And while the critique of ideology has been noted as one example of the strategies of suspicion that constitute distanciation, Ricoeur does not hesitate to employ other modes. What this implies is that the desires and interests that are either embedded in tradition as prejudices or in the psyche as projections are submitted to careful evaluation. Set within the parameters of historicality, with finely attuned awareness as to the attendant circumstances of any encounter, there can be no easy imposition by the scholar of a personal agenda. Ideally, one becomes conscious of what Ricoeur calls the imperialistic ego and its need for control. In its place, there needs to be an acknowledgement of the finite capacities of understanding on the part of the scholar. This does not prevent the rigorous work of evaluation from being undertaken, nor an intense critique, but it set it in a perspective where facile totalizations or false universals cannot flourish. As Ricoeur observes, within a hermeneutic rubric, these prerequisites of interpretation signify

> that philosophy mourns the loss of absolute knowledge. It is because absolute knowledge is impossible that the conflict of interpretations is insurmountable and inescapable (1981: 193).

Ricoeur then continues, "Between absolute knowledge and hermeneutics, it is necessary to choose" (1981: 193). Yet while a resultant conflict of interpretations is inevitable, such conflicts need not be hostile. With the hermeneutic principles as guidelines, and with appropriate criteria of validation and legitimation, discussion and argument can be conducted in ways that lead to further insight rather than intransigence. Understanding and explanation need thus no longer be regarded as mutually exclusive, but as critical, mutually reinforcing modes in the quest for knowledge. And while this approach does not demand that all scholars of religion be trained philosophers, it demonstrates the need for honest reflection of a philosophical nature. As Ricoeur remarks:

> [I]t is the task of philosophical reflection to eliminate deceptive antinomies which would oppose the interest in the reinterpretation of cultural heritages received from the past and the interest in the futuristic projections of a liberated humanity (1981: 100).

Ricoeur has thus clarified and expanded the notion of understanding (from its former quasi-psychological perspective) both with regard to its application to texts and the self-reflective expansion of knowledge.[9] Ricoeur acknowledges his indebtedness, both to the reflective philosophy of Kant and the speculative philosophy of Hegel, for their obvious influences on hermeneutic philosophy. But he spells out his differences, particularly with reference to the impossibility of an unqualified notion of the cogito, and to the importance of context – both linguistic and historical. I believe that Ricoeur's mediatory approach could help to clarify the substance of the various limited claims that are the causes of contention in Religious Studies. It could also lead to a more productive exchange that acknowledges diversification and difference, and that provides grounds for their critical evaluation without capitulating to subjectivism or relativism.

In Religious Studies, perhaps the area where such attitudes, particularly with reference to a revised notion of understanding within a hermeneutic phenomenology could have their most lasting and important impact, will be in the encounter with otherness. This is because Ricoeur believes that such encounters present the paradigmatic situation for the application of the hermeneutic template. Initially, Ricoeur described this with reference to a textual or personal modes:

> The relation between the self and the other gives the concept of prejudice its final dialectical touch: only insofar as I place myself in the other's point of view do I confront myself with my present horizon, and with my prejudices (1981: 76).

Too often, Religious Studies, particularly in its studies of other religions, has been content to stay within the confines of its own horizon, with the presuppositions or prejudices endemic to the historical constellation of ideas that led to its foundation. The voice of the other has rarely been acknowledged or respected in its own right. The work of Armin Geertz (1994) and his postulate of ethnohermeneutics is an endeavour to allow the indigenous interpreter/scholar a voice. Such an interactive model, should not be inferred (as it has been by some) to be a total surrender to the position of the other. Nor does it imply a solipsistic guilt trip where the only voice is that of a conscience stricken researcher castigating his/her own cultural or scholarly indoctrination. Instead it is an honest recognition that knowledge, in ideal circumstances, is a reciprocal venture, where the other's horizon brings to the association some information that may require not just rearrangement of priorities on the part of the scholar, but a radical revision of the worldview that has informed his/her categories or epistemology. Ultimately, Ricoeur would also hold that there could be an ontological alteration as well. By this he means simply a change in our mode of being-in-the-world, of our conduct and attitude towards the other.[10] This is no simplistic recipe for benign solicitude nor an appeal to a rarefied ethics of the exotic, but rather a charge of responsiveness and responsibility so that academic study no longer believes that it alone can prescribe with impunity the precepts and practices of dealing with subjects that it deems alien or extrinsic to its customary terms of reference.

Such an approach to the discipline, within the domain of a "worldview," with a clarified philosophical orientation, would allow Religious Studies to take its place as a field of study within the human sciences. It is not beholden to any theological agenda, though philosophical discussions of ethics and value, and traditional questions, such as those concerning the problem of evil and the existence of God, could still be included. What would be paramount in any course that is taught within Religious Studies is that both professor and student engage in a process of learning that includes a self-reflexive component, though this will vary from course to course, (depending on whether the basic approach is anthropological, historical-critical, psychological, philosophical, sociological). In this process, the tenets of context and historicality, involving the unstated premises of the approach, as well as the presuppositions of both teacher and learner, need to be foregrounded. And this foregrounding is not simply an acknowledgement of possible technical obstacles, but of inherent human limitations. What results is a more modest, yet perhaps more honest evaluation of the promise and contribution of Religious Studies to contemporary knowledge.

Today this is something of a delicate manoeuvre, perhaps intensified by the statements of public accountability that are now being required of all departments (not just Religious Studies), particularly in North American universities. And it is against this backdrop of the increasing commodification and service-oriented rationale that is informing the administrative levels of many universities, that defining the role of the scholar of religion as a public intellectual has ambiguous implications. For while there needs to be public self-justification if the discipline is to remain extant while other departments are closed down as irrelevant, the public intellectual needs to be extremely discerning in his/her portrayal of the contribution that a keen intelligence, honed in the study of religion, can offer. For if a religious scholar publicly disputes the credentials of fellow scholars, the situation is fraught with difficulty. This is because there is a widespread public misunderstanding of just what Religious Studies is, though it is not just the public that is at fault – many fellow academics have a similar misapprehension. Most often it is voiced in a question – such as that posed to the late president of my university by the good citizens of the city – as to why Religious Studies departments need to exist at all. Surely, the opinion goes, that is what churches and bible colleges take care of? Perhaps the situation and solution are not as grim as that depicted by the late Bill Readings in his book *The University in Ruins*:

> If we are not to make the situation of the professor into an analogy for the waning power of the priesthood – faced by unbelief on the one hand and television evangelism on the other – this requires us to be very clear about our relation to the institution, to give up being priests altogether. In other words, the ruins of the University must not be, for students and professors, the ruins of a Greco-Roman temple within which we practice our rites as if oblivious to their role in animating tourist activities and lining the purses of the unscrupulous administrators of the site (1996: 175).

Nonetheless, there are grave dangers today that have to be carefully weighed, firstly in telling the public what they may or may not want to hear on religious topics, and secondly, in packaging oneself both to the public and to an administration that may have rather particular ideas about what a public intellectual can or cannot say (academic freedom notwithstanding). I am thoroughly in agreement with the majority of the points made by Russell McCutcheon, in his article "A Default of Critical Intelligence? The Scholar of Religion as Public Intellectual" (1997), especially the following:

> I am recommending that scholars of religion as public intellectuals should not simply repeat or merely translate uncritically religious claims; instead, they are the ones who accept the challenge of generating critical, scholarly theories *about* normative discourses; they recognize the critical potential of the tools at their disposal ... Our scholarship is not constrained by whether or not devotees recognize its value; it is not intended to celebrate or enhance normative, dehistoricized discourses but, rather, to contextualize and explain them as human constructs (1997: 458).

But, informed by a hermeneutics of suspicion as I am, I would want to place such a statement in the context of what I have just described. There is a sea change happening with regard to the constitution and role of the university. Such a change may not be palatable, and dealing with difference in this situation is not always conducive to establishing the desirable conditions of reciprocal recognition. The public intellectual, specifically as a representative of the discipline of Religious Studies, has thus a demanding and sensitive task, judiciously balancing the roles of educator and critic if s/he is not to provoke the type of hostile or dismissive response from her/his ersatz "constituents" or "shareholders" (to use the current jargon) that may signal the demise of the discipline. Perhaps an equal emphasis could be placed on the constructive as well as the critical role of the scholar of religion. For the scholar of religion is uniquely placed to help explain the worldviews of those belonging to religions other than Christianity. In our increasingly multicultural environments such a task would no longer be undertaken with the aim of conversion, or self-validation, but rather to promote communication and, in addition, that much maligned term, understanding.

Notes

1. In this paper, I will leave the debate concerning the translation of *Religionswissenschaft* to one side. I will use Religious Studies simply because it is the term I am most familiar with, though I realize that there are supporters of other translations.
2. In my essay "Beyond a God's Eyeview: Alternative Perspectives in the Study of Religion" (forthcoming), I surveyed innovative scholarship that has been undertaken in Religious Studies by women, people of colour, and postcolonial scholars.
3. In "Beyond a God's Eyeview" (Joy forthcoming), my main focus was the self-critical and other-responsive work of male and female theorists, especially anthropologists and sociologists – Talal Asad, Chandra Talpede Mohanty, James Clifford, Kalpana Ram, Kamala Visweswaran – whose work moves beyond the narrow confines of Eurocentric thought.
4. I am assuming a functionalist definition to be one that is both general and non-normative. It makes no claims to be universal or exhaustive. It is basically a heuristic device that serves as a guiding principle for research.
5. Ricoeur introduced this notion in his work, *Freud: An Essay of Interpretation*, New Haven: Yale University press (1970). Here he referred to Nietzsche, Marx and Freud as the "masters of suspicion." By this term Ricoeur wished to indicate that these thinkers alerted us to the possibility that we may not be fully in control, because of external or unconscious influences, of what we say or do.
6. Donald Wiebe (1989) also has published a critical analysis of the work of van der Leeuw, but his approach has different implications from mine.

7. For example, Cornelius Petrus Tiele (1830-1902) looked for religion's inner core by way of phenomenology, and C.J. Bleeker (1898-1983) sought the essence of religion by means of the *entelechia* – which he proposed as a mode of phenomenology.
8. Dallmayr (1996) discusses more recent work of Gadamer (as yet to be translated) where he elaborates in more detail what he believes are the critical elements in his own position.
9. In his more recent three volume work, *Time and Narrative*, Ricoeur has further refined these positions by a detailed recasting of the term *mimesis*.
10. There will be some who will object to the use of the term "ontological." I would argue that this is a perfectly acceptable term within a humanistic setting that does not necessarily entail any implication of religious foundations or paraphernalia. Because of its metaphysical associations, there will be others – either for reasons of faith, or because of professional or personal distaste of mixing faith and scholarship – who will automatically make such a connection.

References

Allen, Douglas. "Phenomenology of Religion," *Encyclopedia of Religion*, Mircea Eliade (ed.), Macmillan, New York, Vol. 11, 1987: 272-285.

Capps, Walter, *Religious Studies: The Making of a Discipline*, Fortress Press, Minneapolis, 1995.

Dallmayr, Fred, *Beyond Orientalism: Essays on Cross-Cultural Encounter*, State University of New York Press, Albany, 1996.

Gadamer, Hans-Georg, *Truth and Method*, Continuum, New York, 1994.

Geertz, Armin, "On Reciprocity and Mutual Reflection in the Study of Native American Religions," *Religion* 24, 1994: 1-22.

Grondin, Jean, *Introduction to Philosophical Hermeneutics*, Yale University Press, New Haven, 1994.

Habermas, Jürgen, "A Review of Gadamer's *Truth and Method*," Fred Dallmayr and Thomas McCarthy (Eds.), *Understanding and Social Inquiry*, University of Notre Dame Press, Notre Dame, 1977.

Halbfass, Wilhelm, *India and Europe: An Essay in Understanding*, State University of New York Press, Albany, 1996.

Joy, Morny, "Beyond a God's Eyeview: Alternative Perspectives in the Study of Religion. To be published in *Method and Theory in the IAHR: Collected Essays from the XVIIth Congress of the International Association for the History of Religions, Mexico City, 1995*, Armin Geertz and Russell T. McCutcheon (Eds.), forthcoming.

McCutcheon, Russell T., "A Default of Critical Intelligence? The Scholar of Religion as Public Intellectual," *Journal of the American Academy of Religion*, 65/2, 1997: 443-468.

Palmer, Richard, *Hermeneutics*, Northwestern University Press, Evanston, 1969.

Penner, Hans, *Impasse and Resolution: A Critique of the Study of Religion*, Peter Lang, New York, 1989.

Readings, Bill, *The University in Ruins*, Harvard University Press, Cambridge, 1996.

Ricoeur, Paul, *Time and Narrative*, Vols. 1-3, trans. Kathleen Blamey and David Pellauer, University of Chicago Press, Chicago, 1983-8.

Ricoeur, Paul, *Paul Ricoeur: Hermeneutics and the Human Sciences*, John B. Thompson (Ed. and trans.), Cambridge University Press, Cambridge, 1981.

Ricoeur, Paul, "Ethics and Culture: Habermas and Gadamer in Dialogue," *Philosophy Today*, 17/2, 1973: 153-165.

Smart, Ninian, *The Religion Experience of Mankind*, Charles Scribner's Sons, New York, 1976.

Smart, Ninian, *Worldviews: Crosscultural Explorations of Human Beliefs*, Charles Scribner's Sons, New York, 1983.

Smart, Ninian, *Dimensions of the Sacred: An Anatomy of the World's Beliefs*, University of California Press, Berkeley, 1996.

Van der Leeuw, Geradus, *Religion in Essence and Manifestation*, Vol. 1 and 2, Harper and Row, New York, 1963.

Wach, Joachim, *The Comparative Study of Religion*, Joseph Kitagawa (Ed.), Columbia University Press, New York, 1961.

Wiebe, Donald, "Phenomenology of Religion as Religio-Cultural Quest: Geradus van der Leeuw and the Subversion of the Scientific Study of Religion," *Religionswissenschaft und Kulturkritik: die Zeit des Geradus van der Leeuw*, Hans G. Klippenberg and Brigitte Luchesi (Eds.), Diagonal-Verlag, Marburg, 1991.

Zwi Werblonsky, R. J., "On Studying Comparative Religion: Some Naive Reflections of a Simple-minded Non-philosopher," *Religious Studies*, 11, 1975: 145-156.

Community and Locality in the Study of Religions

Kim Knott

Professor, Department of Theology and Religious Studies
University of Leeds, Leeds, England

I. A metaphorical introduction

A workshop was set up for William in a disused saddle-room, next to the stables. This was half-full of the tin boxes, the wooden crates, the tea-chests of things Harald had purchased – apparently with no clear priority of interest – from all over the world. Here were monkey skins and delicate parrot skins, preserved lizards and monstrous snakes, box upon box of dead beetles, brilliant green, iridescent purple, swarthy demons with monstrous horned heards. Here too were crates of geological specimens, and packs of varied mosses, fruits and flowers, from the Tropics and the ice-caps, bears' teeth and rhinoceros horns, the skeletons of sharks and clumps of coral. Some packages proved to have been reduced to drifting dust by the action of termites, or compacted to viscous dough by the operation of mould. William asked his benefactor on what principle he was required to proceed, and Harald told him, 'Set it all in order, don't you know? Make sense of it, lay it all out in some order or other.' William came to see that Harald had not carried out this task himself partly at least because he had no real idea of how to set about it. He felt moments of real irritability that treasures for which men like himself had risked life and health should lie here higgledy-piggledy, and decay in an English stable. He procured a trestle-table and several ledgers, a series of collecting cabinets and some cupboards for specimens that would not lie flat and slide conveniently in and out of drawers. He set up his microscope, and began to make labels. He moved things from day to day from drawer to drawer as he found himself with a plethora of beetles or a sudden plague of frogs. He could not devise an organising principle, but went on doggedly making labels, setting up, examining (Byatt, 1993: 24-5)

In this story told by A. S. Byatt, set in the second half of the 19th century, William Adamson, explorer, naturalist, journal writer, and soul searcher wrestles with the problem of how to do the work of science with integrity. His questions are both methodological and ethical: What scientific process should he devise for understanding and explaining the plethora of data collected by his patron Harald Alabaster? How may the data best be allowed to speak for themselves, and how and where may he find his own satisfaction as a creative investigator and naturalist? Quite apart from his patron, he has three masters – his subject (science, the study of the natural world), the data, and his own life. All hunter-gatherer scientists, including those who work on religion, are pulled in similar ways, by similar forces.[1]

Imagine the undergraduate student of religious studies, given Ninian Smart's *The World's Religions* or *A New Handbook of Living Religions*, edited by John Hinnells. Imagine the postgraduate researcher at the beginning of her studies, free from the pressures of undergraduate essay deadlines, roaming between the Amish and the Zoroastrians in the University library, or Buddhist ethics and Spiritweb on the Internet. How do these students respond in the face of such religious riches? Many will yearn for an organising principle, a grand theory which gives a satisfying unity to such diversity. A simple theory of religions as comparable systems displaying the same dimensions (as in the work of Joachim Wach, Ninian Smart, or Michael Pye) or a functionalist theory (such as those of Emile Durkheim, Thomas Luckmann, or Mary Douglas) might suffice. But do they not also notice, on the edge of their vision, that the data seem to have a life of their own, their own logic, drawing the student away from the general into the particular?

I return to William Adamson in order to take my next step. How does he proceed? First, let me begin parenthetically and mention what is often a tangent in many scholarly studies, sometimes not mentioned at all: the author's private, muddled life in which scholarly objectivity jostles with feelings, desires, prejudices, and hunches. In Byatt's account, William's leaky private life spills over into his science, calling it into question, testing it for integrity. Although grammar demands that I close the parenthesis before moving on to the matter-in-hand (and the phenomenological tradition of "epoché" invites such bracketing), I am aware that in this essay, as in William's story, and all other scholarly accounts, the private narrative runs alongside the scientific one, weaving in and out, visible then invisible, but ever present (Knott 1995).

How does William proceed? Despite fretting that he had lost his sense of purpose, his vocation, he buries himself in his work.

> He did go back to the cataloguing of Harald's collection, and put in hours and days and weeks of work in mounting specimens, inventing ingenious forms of storage, even comparing, under the microscope, African ants and spiders with those from Malaya and the Americas. But the collection was so random, so intermitted, that he was frequently discouraged. And such work was not what he had been made for. He wanted to observe *life*, not dead shells, he wanted to know the processes of living things. (73)

Then, out of his despair a chink of light, a possibility for creativity emerged. Encouraged by an intelligent, earthy governess and the children of his patron's household, he began an observation of a community of ants in the garden, an "ant-watch" of the Elm Copse Ant Colony:

> The city and its satellite suburbs were mapped and all their entrances and exits carefully recorded. Drawings were made of the way in which the gates of the city were closed at night with barricades of twigs behind which the watchers slept. Maps were made of the paths of the foraging ants, and judicious investigations were made of the nursery chambers, the eggs, grubs and cocoons which formed both the city's population and its living treasure. A kind of census was taken of guests and parasites in the community. (94)

The governess and children were the research assistants, observing, mapping, logging, asking questions. The following winter a book was compiled, *The Swarming City: A Natural History of a Woodland Society, its polity, its economy, its arms and defences, its origin, expansion and decline* (108).

William's answer to the deadening problems of data overload, abstraction, lack of organisation and failure to identify a working principle was to focus down on what was around him, on a community in his own midst. His approach was to observe and understand the particular in order to evaluate better the general. But he favoured the living particular, moving away from "the dead shells" of his patron's collection. The ant colony, unlike the desiccated beetles, butterflies, animal skins and bones, was organic and dynamic. His work grew to incorporate a study of the community's internal relationships, its ecology, its location, relations with its neighbours, its seasonal changes. His was a study akin to anthropology in its attention to the whole life of a society. Moreover, it was a case study based on community and locality.

II. Religions, community and locality at Leeds

A Department of Theology and Religious Studies has existed at the University of Leeds since the 1930s. Coaxed into being by religious professionals at local Christian Nonconformist colleges and by a supportive vice-Chancellor, it nevertheless emerged as a non-confessional department in a secular university (Hastings 1987-1988). Its first professor and head of department was an anthropologist on the religious studies side of the "Theology and Religious Studies" equation, despite also being a clergyman: E. O. James. Throughout its life, the Department has attempted to strike a balance between the two disciplines, not confusing them, but allowing both space. Since the 1960s, on the religious studies side, several of its scholars, including Trevor Ling, Michael Pye and Ursula King, have contributed to different aspects of the methodological debate in the subject: What is religious studies? How does it relate to other disciplines? How are religions best approached and studied?

A practical step to answering some of these questions was taken in the mid-1970s by the establishment of the Community Religions Project (CRP) within the Department.[2] One of its founders, Michael Pye, reflected on the value and interest of taking the religions of the locality as a starting point:

Since the writer himself is prone to study what lies thousands of miles away or hundreds of years ago it may seem odd for him to urge the study of what is near at hand. Yet it is the experience of observing and reflecting on real life phenomena the very existence of which is hardly known to one's contemporaries which sets up strain in the way one views the world ... By now the City of Leeds itself contains population elements from south and east of the Hindu Kush. In addition the hymns of Martin Luther are sung in German, the Catholic mass is celebrated by Poles, and Greek Orthodox perform their exits

90

and entrances in the Church of the Three Hierarchs directly beside the main West Indian and Sikh communities of Chapeltown. Moreover, Yorkshiremen are interesting too, and so is the Church of England in its mysterious empirical forms (1977: 1).

As one of the first cohort of students to study under the auspices of the CRP in my first year as an MA student, I undertook a study of ritual activity at a local Hindu temple, and also surveyed all the places of worship within my own neighbourhood in Leeds. This was a fine opportunity to learn first hand about the practice of those very religions I had previously studied only in books. I soon realised how different were the religious expressions of Hindus in Leeds to those of early Aryan migrants in North India or 19th century Bengali intellectuals, and how rich was the variety of forms of Christianity available in one small area of my own city. Other studies followed, my own on Hinduism (Knott 1986), others on Muslim, Sikh and Hindu communities in Bradford, and a pilot project on "Religion and religions in contemporary Leeds" (which led to a more wide-ranging quantitative study of conventional and common religion in the city).[3] In parallel, those of us involved in the project began the tasks of building up a computerized bibliographical and institutional database of religions in West Yorkshire, and developing an archive of publications and ephemera.[4] The discontinuation of funding and the information explosion of the 1980s and '90s made these impossible to maintain, but they were innovative for their time. The work of the Community Religions Project has continued steadily, however, focusing particularly on the religions of ethnic minority communities in Britain, but not forgetting contemporary manifestations of Christianity, nor neglecting Leeds and surrounding areas.[5] It has published the work of staff and students in monographs and research papers, and in the year of the centenary of the City of Leeds, it honoured the religious history of the city with a public lecture series and a book of essays (Mason, 1994). More recently, local funding has enabled further research to be undertaken in the city, on inter-religious social action.[6]

Research and publications have not been the CRP's only pursuits. Those involved saw its implications for teaching from the start. Courses on minority community religions, religion and locality, local approaches to Christian history, and on the study of local religions have all been offered. Most notable has been "The Religious Mapping of Leeds". With students working co-operatively with local religious and voluntary bodies to map the religious life of an area of the city, it aims to investigate local religious dynamics and the engagement of religion with, for example, social action and educational provision. Students are assessed on the report and directory they produce, and on the presentation of their work to people at an evening gathering in a local venue. In 1994 an ethnically mixed area in South Leeds known as Beeston was mapped; in 1996 the north Leeds area of Moortown, with its mix of synagogues and churches, was studied. In 1997, Leeds city centre was the focus of student investigation. In their initial induction students are introduced to the idea that religions and religious communities manifest differently in different contexts, whether it be in a socially disadvantaged area like Beeston or in the more wealthy suburb of Moortown. The Anglican churches of Beeston and Moortown are not simply reflections of the national church, but places of worship within unique communities, shaped by their location, its historical developments and contemporary socio-economic character.

III. Community and locality in the study of religions: Definitions and methodology

It often feels risky to concentrate on a single religious community and what is near at hand: the general and the exotic have seemed the more easily justifiable and of higher scholarly status, just as the study of the empirical has seemed to be of secondary importance to the theoretical. Accusations of parochialism, particularity, small-mindedness and mere descriptiveness have had to be challenged. The example of Miss Marple, the investigator of the criminal mind who appears in the novels of Agatha Christie, is instructive.[7] Miss Marple saw the broader canvas in and through her experience of the behaviour and relationships of her neighbours in the village of St. Mary Mead. Practising her investigative skills and honing her moral sense in the local domain, she was then able to extend her powers of critical analysis to comparable situations further afield, finally drawing out general characteristics and offering explanatory models.

Such studies in and of places, whether neighbourhoods of Leeds or villages like St. Mary Mead, are vital because of the primacy of "place" in human experience. Citing Archytas, Aristotle and Heidegger, Edward Casey reminds us that, "Place is the first of all things" (1996: 16), and, following Husserl and Merleau-Ponty, that we perceive and know in and through our place.[8] He turns on its head both the idea that existential "space" precedes place, and that space is general whereas place is particular. "Local knowledge", he writes,

> comes down to an intimate understanding of what is generally true in the locally obvious; it concerns what is true about place in general as manifested *in this place*. Standing in this place thanks to the absolute *here* of my body, I understand what is true of other places over *there* precisely because of what I comprehend to be the case for this place under and around me. This does not mean that I understand what is true of *all* places, but my grasp of one place does allow me to grasp what holds, for the most part, in other places of the same region. (1996: 45)

He might have been identifying Miss Marple's founding principle; he was certainly identifying the assumption of many anthropological subjects, that the wider world, the space beyond the village, is known and "culturized" by their experience of their own place.

When is the particular merely particular, and when is it indicative, a starting point for new ideas, a trigger for the imagination – not an example (as that would imply that one already knew what one was looking for), but a type, the examination of which leads beyond itself? The intellectual process which is predominant in such work is one of inductive rather than deductive reasoning, inferring from the particular to the general, though there will be some shifting back and forth from the one to the other, and from the descriptive to the theoretical. Many separate studies of different religious communities in West Yorkshire, or of the place of religion in different neighbourhoods in Leeds may allow a more general picture to be drawn. They allow comparative analysis to be undertaken, from which hypotheses may emerge suitable for transplantation to other geographical or religious fields or cases.

What do I mean by community and locality? My definitions are common sense ones, and other scholars would be at liberty to choose their own operational definitions. By community I mean a social group with

93

one or more common features or interests, which has a greater or lesser awareness of these, and thus a more or less conscious communal identity.[9] Examples might be local communities (people living in the same geographical area, often but not always with a sense of place), ethnic communities, caste communities, religious communities (residential, sectarian, denominational), or communities drawn together by political, leisure or other social interests. In late-modernity some of these groups, particularly the latter but also many ethnic communities, are not defined by what we normally think of as locality. Some may form loose networks, others segregated by migration and national boundaries.[10] I have written about a number of such communities, but the ones I want to concentrate on here are those embedded within particular localities. This notion of locality is well-elucidated by my colleague, Haddon Willmer, with reference to Leeds and its environs.

> All religion is local in some sense – it is in a place. But the study of religion in the world is not local as we intend it here. The locality is generally smaller. But can a size be specified, so that all localities larger are ruled out? That kind of measure is too rough and open to exceptions to be sufficient. We are concerned with localities which in themselves have more coherence, or are more manageable conceptually. A village can be overseen physically from a hill outside; a city can be grasped as a working system and set of communities by looking at its government, its media, its cultural activities and associations, all of which may proclaim themselves to be local – Leeds City Council, Leeds Chamber of Commerce, Leeds Churches Together etc. – and thus reflect a local if nebulous 'patriotism'. An ethnic group settled in a place can also be local in the same sense.
>
> Do we want to rule out the study of religion in larger localities, e.g. regions? It is more difficult, less efficient to present in one study, religion in Yorkshire – but it may be valuable. Such a study would be built up from many more local studies. How sound would it be to attempt to study religion in Yorkshire without studying religion in Bradford and Selby and Middleham as discrete cases?
>
> Perhaps one way of identifying the kind of localities we are concerned with is to say that they are of a size and character where we can discern in detail the interaction between the individual, the small group within the local setting and religion and other realities beyond the local setting which affect it, even intrude upon it. (Willmer, 1996; c.f. Knott and Willmer, forthcoming)

The stress here on the two aspects of coherence and conceptual manageability is critical. From the perspective of the inhabitants, communities and religions under investigation, the significance of locality lies in its capacity to be meaningful for those within it, to be important for individual and group identity, and to be a practical working environment. From the perspective of those studying it, it should be capable of study as an atomic unit, either by virtue of its small size or its coherent internal structure (whether geographical, political or social). To borrow a term used by the anthropologist Adrian Mayer (1960, for caste groups in India), our interest is in the "effective" locality, the arena in which interactions commonly take place and institutions recognise one another and engage meaningfully.[11]

The purpose of identifying such localities and the communities within them for the study of religions is to go beyond seeing such places as the accidental habitats of religious groups to recognising the human ecology of the place and the way in which its geography, social character, political and economic structures and religious life develop in dynamic engagement with one another. Religious studies scholars, irrespective of the methods they employ, place great emphasis on religious contexts. A further aim of studying religions in their localities is to work on areas which are sufficiently small and manageable to enable a researcher to investigate fully the relationship of religion and its context, the impact of aspects of that context on the religion and the active shaping of the locality by the religions within it.

The type of study I am commending is first and foremost anthropological. In *Small Places, Large Issues*, Thomas Hylland Eriksen informs us that "anthropology is concerned with accounting for the interrelationships between different aspects of human existence", and that usually "anthropologists investigate these interrelationships taking as their point of departure a detailed study of local life in a particular society or a delineated social environment" (1995: 2). Anthropology, he writes, asks large questions whilst drawing its insights from small places. It is also a field-science, in which cultures and societies are understood (and "written") through ethnographical studies in "the field".[12] It is this same approach that I commend here for students of religion, though in our case we place religion centre-stage in our examination of local interrelationships.[13]

Other disciplinary approaches are also vital for the success of such a study. Historical perspectives enable current manifestations to be understood, and invest contemporary studies with an appropriate temporal dynamic: what we describe must not be thought to be static. Social and cultural geography offers a concern with demography, the study of residential patterns and population movement, mapping, the meaning of landscape and place, all of which have a bearing on studying local religious communities.[14] Sociology offers perspectives on processes of globalization, institutionalisation, on social stratification, social interaction, gender, ethnicity and other social variables which are essential in providing a meaningful context for understanding religious activity and organisation in localised studies. It also provides some of the practical methods essential for the collection of data and necessary to the descriptive process: quantitative and qualitative methods, including surveys, structured and unstructured interviews and particant observation. Other methods come from humanities disciplines, particularly local history and folklore studies. They include the collection of data by means of oral history and the examination of material culture and printed ephemera.

So, our studies must be multi-disciplinary in character. Focusing on religious phenomena, we bring together anthropological, historical, geographical and sociological approaches in a localised study. But the study of religions offers more to such a investigation than this uniting of other approaches. It recognises the significance of the religious meanings, interpretations, and theologies at work in the community or communities under investigation, particularly those which are locally derived or pertain to the neighbourhood or area itself. Necessarily, there may be a number of these and they may be in conflict with one another. The religious studies scholar resists judging the authenticity or veracity of such meanings, interpretations, and theologies (though she might have to wrestle with and understand the place of her own situation, beliefs and ideas in her account).[15] Further, the religious studies scholar may employ an informed comparative approach in investigating different religious communities within a single locality. Finally, there is a special burden on such a scholar to make sense of the relationship between the general characterisations of religious traditions, their beliefs and practices, and actual, local manifestations. What we learn in textbooks of "World Religions" will be unlikely to match with what we observe of religions in small localities in Leeds, Nairobi, or Osaka, for example. This brings us back to induction and deduction. It is important in local studies not to import, deductively, general notions of how religions ought to operate, what religious people should believe or do. Our interest is in what they actually think and do, and, issuing from this, what the implications of such data might be for understanding broader religious issues, and for challenging notions of what religions are and how they operate.

IV. Case studies in religion, community and locality

There are many excellent case studies of religious communities in particular localities, by scholars from a variety of disciplines, offering us theoretical tools to employ and examples to compare in other contexts.[16] Three examples are discussed briefly below. They all take seriously the way in which religion functions in given local communities and demonstrate the way in which the locale creates the religion, giving it its particular character and concerns. They come from different disciplines, and consider different religions and types of localities. The first takes a sociological approach to religion, offering two snapshots from different decades in the twentieth century of a single, broadly Christian, American town. The second deals with the history of a place of worship in my own city, showing the multi-religious dynamism of the locality in which it is situated, and the complex community relationships which have emerged within it. The third is broadly anthropological (though the contributors hail from a range of scholarly backgrounds). It takes its starting point in a particular photographic image, but invites reflection on the recent development of one religion, Islam, in a variety of new locations in America and Europe. Between them they mention a wide range of approaches and methods – from the use of local archives and resources, to questionnaires and ethnographic studies -and raise many pertinent questions for the relationship between religions and their localities.

One locality which has produced two related sociological studies is "Gastonia" in North Carolina. Liston Pope first wrote about it in the 1940s, publishing his work, *Millhands and Preachers: A Study of Gastonia* in 1942. He focused particularly on developing a theory of church attendance from local data. Thirty years later, when Donald Shriver went there as a minister (and scholar of religion), he was asked by the managers of Gaston's textile plants to consider writing a sequel: "Gastonians ask many of the questions which sociologists and ethicists ask", Shriver reflected (Earle, Knudsen and Shriver, 1976: 346). With two other sociologists he published *Spindles and Spires: A Re-Study of Religion and Social Change in Gastonia* in 1976. Of Gastonians, they wrote,

> Here ... is a community whose elite believe that their local society hangs together, functions, and has its being partly in terms of a certain 'civic consciousness' shared by its citizens. Is there such a consciousness? If so, what is its content, who shapes it, and to what purposes? (14)

Like the managers, they were interested in whether the locality produced, through its mills and churches, labour, race and religious relations, a particular local consciousness, and whether such a consciousness had helped the community to adjust to the forces of rapid social change. Their study is a sociological examination which attempts to answer these questions, and which demonstrates the research potential of local actors and scholars working together.

The impact on local religious developments of social and economic change in an earlier period (and in the neighbourhood referred to by Pye above) is discussed by a historian of Christian Nonconformity, Clive Binfield. Using local sources – a souvenir brochure of Newton Park Church, its minute books, a school-girl's diary, and a novel by a congregant – Binfield accounts for the rise and fall of the unique "unity church" founded by Congregationalists and Baptists in a nineteenth century garden suburb of Leeds (now Chapeltown). He suggests that " the localized contribution has a national significance" (1994: 104). Looking back to nineteenth century, northern English Nonconformism, such contributions easily disappear from view, lost in the more general picture. However, when brought into focus, their "startling originality" emerges afresh.

Newton Park Church is also the chosen subject of scholars of religion charting religious developments among the Punjabi population of Leeds (Toon 1977; Kalsi 1992; Knott Kalsi 1994): following its closure in 1949 as a Nonconformist church, it was bought for use as a Sikh temple (in 1960).[17] They examine the ritual life of its *diwan* or congregation, the way in which different communities of Punjabis, separated by religion or caste, have contested its use and management, and the relationships between the *diwan* and its neighbours.[18] From their work, together with Binfield's, emerges a history of this place of worship, and the communities which created it and breathed life into it over the course of a century.

The final example is a cover-photograph and the collection of essays which it illustrates. It shows Pakistani Muslim men at prayer on the occasion of the laying of a foundation stone for a new mosque in Bradford in the north of England. The picture comes from an archive of interviews and photographs housed in the Bradford Historical Research Unit of the local library. As the cover of a book edited by Barbara Daly Metcalf, *Making Muslim Space in North America and Europe*, it signifies not only Islam's transnational character, but also its ability to transform local places into Muslim spaces. The act of transformation is taking place before viewers' eyes in the photograph as, to the right of the picture, a man sits in an earth-mover waiting to dig the foundations of the mosque-to-be. The surrounding buildings and vehicles show this to be twentieth century, inner-city Bradford; a nineteenth century church suggests that this was once a flourishing Christian neighbourhood.

Beneath the cover of the book, anthropologists, sociologists, historians, and specialists of religion, architecture, and music discuss new Muslim places and their relationship with traditional locations, in South Asia, Africa, Turkey, Saudi Arabia and Iran. But these new communities, their buildings and institutions, are not merely local projections of a global Islam; neither are they simply the outposts, for example, of South Asian or Iranian Islam. Several authors argue that the new locations have become sites of sacred power in their own right, through architectural and other material-cultural changes, and through such practices as oral rituals and processions. This process, of "stamping the earth with the name of Allah" (Werbner, 1996: 165), is not only a spiritualization or Islamicization of new spaces, of *dar al-Harb* (the house of war), it is the emergence of something novel and different as people, religion and place cohere and a new expression, an *Autgeist*, emerges.

V. The local monographer of religion

How is a particular, local religion formed by its context, and how does it grow and change as its context changes? How does it express itself through this context? This is not just a question of the effect of local demographic, social, economic and political factors upon religion. Religions and the institutions and individuals that constitute them do not arise passively from their local circumstances. They recruit and are built by local people with their own particular interests; they meet local needs. What, then, are the *local* forms and styles of these religious bodies, and how and why have they come about? How do local religions engage with one another and with other local agencies and institutions, meeting local needs and producing locally informed networks? To what extent do religions perceive their locales as sacred, or their people specially blessed or empowered? Do local religious bodies look outward to external national or global centres of activity and authority, or within to their own sources and resources? How do the local, national and global interact, and with what consequences?[19]

And how, as students and scholars, are we to study these local forms? What is our place, having stepped beyond the confines of the library into the community?

Many of the studies carried out by researchers or students working on local religions have been phenomenological, often describing aspects of the religious lives of particular communities for a wider public with little previous knowledge, thus bridging the gaps between different public groups, and, as Cady (1998: 37) suggests, between scholarly expertise and the life-world of outsiders. Such studies have often been underpinned by an empathetic approach in which the place and significance of the beliefs and practices of participants have been the starting point. The scholarly process, however, has then involved the techniques of historical, sociological, geographical and anthropological study, all of which have helped to build up a detailed local picture. Often criticised as mere description, such a picture may be profoundly challenging to a wider public (both academic and non-academic) whose ideas about religions and the people who live them may be limited and general, and who may start from a position of misunderstanding or bias.[20] They may cut through the universalised and reified notions of religions, their ideas and behaviour which are often held by an uninformed public.[21]

Phenomenological accounts of this kind do not, of course, avoid interpretation, as processes of data selection, identification of gatekeepers and spokespersons, contextualisation of religious phenomena, and writing up are all interpretative acts. The complex issues of insider/outsider and the ethics and politics of fieldwork come to the fore. Being a Sikh of a certain caste studying Sikhs of other castes with whom you have lived, worked, argued and joked cannot fail to invite self-reflection (Kalsi 1992). As a young, white, female, non-Hindu student living and studying among Gujarati Hindus (Knott 1986, 1995) or a Christian interfaith officer and researcher of Islam working among Bradford's South Asian Muslims (Lewis, 1994), one must face difficult questions of scholarly identity and role. The lines between private and public, participant and observer shift, disintegrate, and re-assert themselves.

Those who go beyond the university into a local community do not become invisible. Unlike William Adamson, they are not mere observers. They too are "ants" in the "colony", taking up space, and asking questions with evoke new answers and provoke new attitudes. They are often called upon to join in with rituals, to offer personal opinions, to speak with the authority of the academy, to represent the community to others, even to act as brokers for communities in their dealings with official agencies. Each of these is different, some stances being more overtly interventionist or political than others. They are all public stances, however. The researcher of a local religious community must engage with its members, and often with those beyond it, and, as such, cannot avoid working through his or her own position, considering such issues as honesty and deception, appearance, self-disclosure, representation, manipulation, and advocacy. In doing so, a researcher undoubtedly goes beyond the limited role of public "caretaker" (McCutcheon 1997), one who uncritically presents and maintains, without disturbance, the religious life of a community. All such research is profoundly disturbing, to the one who undertakes it, the community involved in it, and the wider public, because it requires a shift in how each sees both itself and the other.

In addition, such work, whether done in conjunction with research or teaching, involves actual, practical engagement with people who live and work nearby. As a result of this, scholars and students are required to make their studies accessible and relevant; they are invited to account for their views and their analyses of local situations. This provides an invaluable opportunity for them to test their work, to explain it, and to make it increasingly useful. They may even think it appropriate to develop projects from ideas arising within the locality itself (Burlet Reid 1998). Even if they do not, they may be assured of local interest, and an informed critique by people on whom the work has a direct bearing.

The dangers of this type of study include the tendency towards anecdotalism, an inability to see beyond the particular to the interesting questions raised by it, and the problem of universalising from what is local. However, when done with both rigour and imagination, such microcosmic studies are of great value in generating ideas for comparative analysis and larger scale study, and for viewing the bigger picture of religion from multiple, different local perspectives:

> He was ... impressed by the belief that every province should have its own monographer. The field of Nature being beyond the power of any one man to cultivate in full, let everyone begin with his own parish and till that area intensively.
> (Walter Johnson describing the work of Gilbert White, author of *The Natural History of Selbourne*, 1982, p. xxxvi)

Notes

1. A version of this essay was first delivered in "The Oxford Interdisciplinary Seminars in the Study of Religions" at Mansfield College, Oxford, in March 1998.
2. A version of this section appeared in my article, "Issues in the study of religions and locality", *Method and Theory in the Study of Religions*, 10:3, 1998. There is also a brief account of the early history of the Community Religions Project in Knott, 1984, and lists of publications and projects are obtainable from the Department of Theology and Religious Studies at the University of Leeds.
3. "Religion and religions in contemporary Leeds", 1979-80, funded by the Social Science Research Council, directed by Robert Towler and Michael Pye, researcher Richard Toon; "Conventional religion and common religion in Leeds", 1981-3, funded by the Social Science Research Council, directed by Robert Towler, researchers Richard Toon, Helen Krarup and others (Religious Research Papers, 1981-4).
4. Community Religions Working Papers from 1977 to 1980 discuss the schemes and methods used.
5. The directors of the Community Religions Project have been Michael Pye (1976-82), Ursula King (1982-89), and Kim Knott (1989-present). Other major related projects have included "A survey of ethnic minority religions in Britain", 1983-6, funded by the University of Leeds, researcher Kim Knott; "The changing character of the religions of the ethnic minorities of Asian origin in Britain", 1986-91, funded by the Leverhulme Trust, researchers Kim Knott and Sajda Khokher.
6. "Inter-religious social action: A Leeds-based study", 1996-8, funded by Leeds Church Institute and the Department of Theology and Religious Studies, University of Leeds, researchers Stacey Burlet and Helen Reid.
7. See *The Murder at the Vicarage* and other novels by Agatha Christie.

8. This is true of scholars as well as anthropological subjects. Feminist standpoint theory sees all scholars as located in an intellectual and personal space. Reflexively knowing and owning the place where they stand, they may then use it fruitfully to engage theoretically with other voices.

9. Focusing upon religious "communities" is not without its intellectual or political difficulties, and studies which do so should be aware of these. It is all too easy to depict "a community" in such a way as to silence those at its margins or boundaries, to over-solidify it, thus creating more of an impression of shared ideas and experience than actually exists, or to neglect membership of multiple communities. An interesting book which challenges the political reification of minority religious communities in Britain on feminist grounds is Sahgal and Yuval-Davis (1992).

10. Anderson's "imagined communities" are an illustration of this development (1983).

11. Definitions of "the local", "locality", and "location" are debated within anthropology (Geertz, 1983; Gupta and Ferguson, 1997).

12. "The field" as a location, "the field-worker", and her "field-practices" may be understood differently in various sub-disciplines within anthropology, e.g. historical anthropology, contemporary anthropologies of science or the internet, urban anthropology, and in post-modern studies of village anthropology (Gupta and Ferguson, 1997).

13. The role and value of ethnographic study more generally in the discipline of religious studies is discussed by Bowman (1992), and Jackson (1997).

14. See Park (1994) for examples.

15. As we have stressed elsewhere (Knott, 1998; Knott and Willmer, forthcoming), locality studies also have immense value for theologians. Their purposes, approaches and methods often differ to those of the Religious Studies scholar, but are complementary, and a valuable contribution to building up a body of data on religions in an area.

16. At Leeds, in the Community Religions Project, we have encouraged post-graduate students to do their own studies of this kind, e.g. Kalsi (1992), on Sikhs in Leeds and Bradford, and Lewis (1994) on Pakistani Muslims in Bradford.

17. Park refers to this as "decline and recycling" (1994: 211).

18. Neighbouring communities have included the Jewish population of Leeds, moving up and out of the area , Central and Eastern European settlers, and African Caribbeans, all with their shops, social and cultural centres, and places of worship. The hall adjoining the Sikh temple has been let in recent decades as a Church of God of Prophecy and a Hindu temple.

19. These were just some of the questions considered at an international conference on religion and locality held at the University of Leeds in 1998 and in the associated forthcoming papers.

20. In his article on the scholar as a cultural critic (1998), Jensen challenges McCutcheon's criticism (1997) of scholars who confine themselves to insider's representations of religion. I would support Jensen's view of the value of such representations as "a first step", particularly in terms of their public educational value.

21. Such notions may themselves be the effect of other types of scholarly research and publication on religion, e.g. on the nature of "world religions".

References

Anderson, Benedict, 1983, *Imagined Communities: Reflections on the Origin and Spread of Nationalism*, Verso, London.

Binfield, Clive, 1994, "The history of Button Hill: an essay in Leeds non-conformity", in A. Mason, ed., *Religion in Leeds*, pp. 79-107.

Bowman, Marion, 1992, "Phenomenology, fieldwork and religion", *Occasional Paper*, 6, British Association for the Study of Religions.

Burlet, Stacey & Reid, Helen, 1998, *Faith in the Future: People of Faith, Social Action, and the City of Leeds*, Department of Theology and Religious Studies, University of Leeds.

Byatt, A. S. 1993, *Angels and Insects*, Vintage, London.

Cady, Linell E., 1998, "The public intellectual and effective critique", *The Council of Societies for the Study of Religion Bulletin*, 27:2, 36-8.

Casey, Edward S., 1996, "How to get from space to place in a fairly short stretch of time: Phenomenological prolegomena", in S. Feld and K. H. Basso, eds, *Senses of Place*, School of American Research Press, Santa Fe, pp. 13-52.

Christie, Agatha, 1930, *The Murder at the Vicarage*, Collins, London.

Community Religions Project Research Papers, New Series, 1984-, Department of Theology and Religious Studies, University of Leeds, Leeds.

Earle, John R., Knudsen, Dean D., Shriver, Donald W., 1976, *Spindles and Spires: A Re-Study of Religion and Social Change in Gastonia*, John Knox Press, Atlanta.

Eriksen, Thomas Hylland, 1995, *Small Places, Large Issues: An Introduction to Social and Cultural Anthropology*, Pluto Press, London.

Feld, Steven & Basso, Keith H., eds, 1996, *Senses of Place*, School of American Research Press, Santa Fe, New Mexico.

Geertz, Clifford, 1983, *Local Knowledge: Further Essays in Interpretive Anthropology*, Basic Books, New York.

Gupta, Akhil & Ferguson, James, eds, 1997, *Anthropological Locations: Boundaries and Grounds of a Field Science*, University of California Press, Berkeley.

Hastings, Adrian, 1987-1988, "Fifty years of theology at Leeds", *The University of Leeds Review*, 30, 73-94.

Hinnells, John, ed., 1998, *A New Handbook of Living Religions*, Penguin, London.

Jackson, Robert, 1997, *Religious Education: An Interpretive Approach*, Hodder and Stoughton, London.

Jensen, Tim, 1998, "The scholar of religion as a cultural critic: Perspectives from Denmark", *The Council of Societies for the Study of Religion Bulletin*, 27:2, 40-3.

Johnson, Walter, ed., 1982, *Journals of Gilbert White*, Futura, London. [First published 1928.]

Kalsi, Sewa Singh, 1992, *The Evolution of a Sikh Community in Britain*, Community Religions Project, University of Leeds, Leeds.

Knott, Kim, 1984, "Community religions at the University of Leeds", *Community Religions Project Research Papers (NS) 1*, University of Leeds, Leeds.

104

– 1986, *Hinduism in Leeds*, Community Religions Project, University of Leeds, Leeds.
– 1995, "Women researching, women researched: Gender as an issue in the empirical study of religion", in U. King, ed., *Religion and Gender*, Blackwells, Oxford, pp. 199-218.
– 1998, "Issues in the study of religions and locality", *Method and Theory in the Study of Religions*, 10:3, 279-90.
Knott, Kim & Kalsi, Sewa Singh, 1994, "The advent of Asian religions", in A. Mason, ed., *Religion in Leeds*, pp. 161-79.
Knott, Kim & Willmer, Haddon, forthcoming, "Religion and locality: An agenda for research and teaching", in K. Knott, H. Willmer, A. Mason and K. Ward, eds, *Religion and Locality*, Community Religions Project, University of Leeds, Leeds.
Lewis, Philip, 1994, *Islamic Britain: Religion, Politics and Identity among British Muslims*, I. B. Tauris, London.
Mason, Alistair, ed., 1994, *Religion in Leeds*, Alan Sutton, Stroud.
Mayer, Adrian, 1960, *Caste and Kinship in Central India*, Routledge and Kegan Paul, London.
McCutcheon, Russell, 1997, "A default of critical intelligence? The scholar of religion as public intellectual", *Journal of the American Academy of Religion*, 65:2, 443-68.
Metcalf, Barbara Daly, ed., 1996, *Making Muslim Space in North America and Europe*, University of California Press, Berkeley.
Park, Chris C., 1994, *Sacred Worlds: An Introduction to Geography and Religion*, Routledge, London.
Pope, Liston, 1942, *Millhands and Preachers: A Study of Gastonia*, Yale University Press, New Haven and London.
Pye, Michael, 1977, "A paper presented at the Senior Seminar, 16 March 1977", *Community Religions Project Working Paper 3*, University of Leeds, Leeds.
Religious Research Papers, 1981-4, Department of Sociology, University of Leeds, Leeds.
Sahgal, Gita, and Yuval Davis, Nira, eds., 1992, *Refusing Holy Orders: Women and Fundamentalism in Britain*, Virago, London.
Smart, Ninian, 1989, *The World's Religions*, Cambridge University Press, Cambridge.
Toon, Richard, 1977, "A study of the Sikhs in Leeds", *Community Religions Project Research Paper 3*, University of Leeds, Leeds.
Werbner, Pnina, 1996, "Stamping the earth with the name of Allah: *Zikr* and the sacralizing of space among British Muslims", in B. Daly Metcalf, ed., *Making Muslim Space*, University of California Press, Berkeley, pp. 167-185.
Willmer, Haddon, 1996, "Religion and locality", working notes.

Follow the Genes:
Religion as a Survival Strategy

Gary Lease

Professor & Chair, History of Consciousness Department
University of California, Santa Cruz, USA

The Problem

David Noel Freedman, one of the grand old men in the study of Jewish scriptures, is coordinating a project that will end in a so-called World Parliament of Religions. *The Rivers of Paradise* will attempt to focus on the "great personality religions of the world," as he calls them: Judaism (Moses), Islam (Mohammed), Buddhism (Buddha), Confucianism (Confucius), and Christianity (Jesus); Hinduism is left out, by the way, because it is a "case of classic polytheism." The final goal is to promote peace among these five major religions, and education, through this new book, through the university, and through the proposed Parliament, is the way to achieve it (Reisberg 1998: A9). This undertaking represents nothing more than the attempted redemption of contemporary public society, while the academic study of religion is the tool to gain that elusive end. This is very serious work, of that one may not doubt; but it also represents at the very least a misunderstanding of the university and the academic study of religion. How is it that we have reached such a state of confusion?

In a recent article Ivan Strenski has reiterated his notion that our "beliefs about studying religion" are equated with "our thinking about religion" (Strenski 1998). An obvious consequence of this position would be a fundamental shift in understanding the task of the modern university, and above all the academic study of religion as part of higher education. Knowledge, its hard-won presence, its constant need of revision, its demand for never-ending critique: that is what the university is about. Both university and the study of religion therefore have as both vehicle and goal the achievement of knowledge and its clarification, not the realization of the object of study itself. While one must admit that the confusion between the study of various areas of human endeavor and world phenomena on the one hand, and the actual reality of the object studied on the other, is found all too often in contemporary universities, that is in no way sufficient justification to continue such practices: on the contrary, such misuse of the academic pursuit should be all the more forcefully contradicted in both practice and word. Where social scientists use their study of public constructions such as politics and its many mechanics, societal relations, and the forces binding them together to forge persuasions among their students regarding the proper or necessary political activity, they have confused their study with its object; and where scholars of religions seek to heal society, to gain interior (and sometimes exterior) liberation for individuals, or to empower their students for particular struggles, they go well beyond what the university is called upon to do: they transform the call to "know" about religions into a call to "do" religion (Lease 1998b). As a trenchant critic of such confusion has recently and bitingly described the situation, "a study of religion directed toward spiritual liberation of the individual or of the human race as a whole, toward the moral welfare of the human race, or toward any ulterior end than that of knowledge itself, should not find a home in the university ..." (Wiebe 1998: xiii).

If "doing" religion, however, is not the goal of its study, then how may one best pursue knowledge of this enormously variegated human experience? In my judgment three directions offer contemporary scholarship the most fruitful sources for the study of religion: the notion of religion as a "natural" concept; the interaction between religion and that other great human construct, the law; and finally, the anchoring of a theory of religion in the biological sphere.

"Natural" Histories of Religions

Religions, like all other human constructions, make claims about experienced reality. Evidences are mined from "natural" histories of these experiences and hardened into facts. The "natural" character of such undertakings lies, of course, in the constantly changing identity of reality, be it of the individual organism or its creations, be it of society or its institutions. A so-called natural history seeks to trace emergence, or primal identity;

development, or mature identity; and dissolution, or death of identity. There, obviously, is the rub: a natural history takes not only origin and development seriously, but above all the death or disappearance of the phenomenon or organism under study. This is true for physical reality, including humans, their planet and indeed the entire universe, and it is true for religion.

Concretely, this means for the study of religion that such natural histories of religions seek, first of all, to trace the origins or sources of observed religious experiences and their resulting claims. Since no reality in which we live, including religions, lies outside of change, the 'pedigree' of reality is vital to understanding it at any given stage. Identifying and locating the origin of a religion allows one to avoid the trap of uniqueness that leads to the non-rational legitimation of claims as reality.

Such histories also attempt to trace the development or patterns of change in a particular religion over time. Only in this way does a religion become intelligible: one sees that the particular phenomenon under study does not have to be the way it, in fact, is. Its history, in other words, tells us how, and with what connections, it arrived to confront us. Reality is contingent, and so is our understanding of it, and history is the medium by which we master that fundamental fact. Without a coherent account of the process of change that lies between the narrated emergence and the present point of observation, establishing the identity of a religion becomes difficult if not impossible. And without an identity, there is not intelligibility.

Finally, natural histories of religion seek to track the death or demise of a religion. All evidence that can be shared points to the utter impermanency of reality. It is in death that origins and history reach their union and intelligibility becomes possible. It is finally the acknowledgment of identity's impermanence that completes a natural history. The death of a religion is not the wages of sin, but rather the consequence of having existed at all.

Constructing "natural" histories of religions would mean that one never comes to closure on what constitutes the 'object' of such a history. The target, or particular religion in view, would always be shifting, would always be contingent, would never be final, just as with all our other rational objects of knowledge. Indeed, the evidences that one might adduce for such a history would also always be in movement. The ethical, moral, ritual, and intellectual choices that adherents of a specific religion consider to be demanded by their beliefs, or demanded by 'religion' in general, would constantly be changing, would never be absolute.

A "natural" history of a religion would never posit the 'reality' or better, the validity of any religion's claims or persuasions (beliefs) as the object of study and intelligibility, but rather the origins, the history, and the death of such claims and their resulting functions. In other words, desire and need are not identical: a genuine science of religion would acknowledge that a choice of reality does not constitute hegemony over all of reality or over others. Study of religion is not the giving or bearing of testimony to the "truth" of a particular religion, or religion in the abstract: it is not an act of belief (Lease 1998a: 140-143).

The plain fact of the matter is that the history of religions is like any other history: it suffers from the same weaknesses and limitations. "Don't speak to me about writing for future generations," protested the Prussian Field Marshal, Carl Friedrich von dem Knesebeck shortly before his death in 1848: "it isn't worth the effort." Why not? one might ask. Knesebeck had the answer at hand: "That collection of old gossip that you call 'history' is, when all is said and done, nothing but fable and poetry, at best a witness for the prosecution." (Fontane 1998: I,37). The creation of history cannot, try as we may, recreate the reality from which it wishes to speak. When Faust, in Goethe's version, makes his bet with Mephistopheles, he is waiting for the moment in which he can say: "Wait! Stay! You are so beautiful!" The emphasis is usually seen in the character of the beautiful. But the real problem lies in the desire that the beautiful remain with him. No matter how hard one presses the human memory, the reality that is sought is lost forever. Every memory is also a source of powerful pain. Histories of religions paint pictures of the past in the attempt to recover a lost reality, an attempt that is doomed to failure from the very beginning. The mythologizing of past, present and future is religion's chief tool in the attempt to stabilize a world that is constantly disappearing. Using myth religions seek frantically to achieve a direct connection to a facticity that is always changing, always dying. The attempt to retain as direct experience what has already occurred will always fail because past reality cannot come again. The result is constant pain: the pain of having lost reality. "Truth or illusion, George: you can't tell the difference, can you? But we have to act as if we could." (Albee 1962). As a wounded animal lies in its sick bed, so is the human memory of the past; and when it is driven out of its bed the pain is great, strength gives out, the original life is no longer present. The reality one sought to capture cannot be retained; only the pain remains (Lease 1999: 53).

Religion and the Law, or What gets to count as religion?

The question of what place religion occupies in our larger social life is an almost classic case of the intimate relationship between religion and the law. A colleague of mine observed some years ago that the parallel to the Jewish Teacher, Jesus of Nazareth, and his saying that the "meek shall inherit the earth," was Leo Durocher, well-known baseball manager of the 1950s, who once observed that "nice guys finish last." A more plastic manner of expressing the tension inherent in the role of religion in public life can scarcely be imagined. These are real tensions, not illusionary ones, and they have real consequences.

In our own time we have seen National Socialist Germany co-opt the major Christian churches in its spasm of totalitarian control and self-destruction, using particularly Roman Catholicism to organize public ritual and the celebration of fascist political domination (Lease 1995: 135-187). In Yugoslavia, or more specifically Croatia, we have seen the church co-opted by a national movement hardly distinguishable from its German masters, celebrated in Archbishop Stepinac's welcome of, and submission to the Croatian fascist leader Pavelitch; as a result he was received nearly with rapture in convents, monasteries, seminaries, and the Catholic press throughout the land. Yet only last year did the present Catholic pope, John Paul II, beatify the archbishop of Zagreb, calling him a martyr to "the atrocities of the Communist system" (Butler 1996). In contemporary Germany there are still echoes from the Federal Constitutional Court's ruling of four years ago forbidding the Bavarian State from ordering a Christian crucifix to hang in every public school room (Der Spiegel 1995). And in the United States there continues sharp controversy over whether the Congress and the states should amend the Constitution to permit prayer in school classrooms; the struggle is, of course, over the questions of which prayer and whose composition? Or take the recent "Religious Persecution Act," passed by the United States Congress, that seeks to regulate what constitutes religious persecution throughout the world.

A major part of the problem lies, naturally enough, in the question of

111

definition: just what gets to count as religion and what does not in any given moment and any given society? Surely it is not obvious that courts, and the legal world, are the "natural" places for such a definition to be determined; yet that is what is happening as I write. Nor, I would argue, is the issue of definition simply a matter of counting votes. In a world beset with ever more dizzying diversity in culture, beliefs and political allegiances, a theory of religion is needed that can accommodate multiple definitions of religion rather than imposing one definition upon all others. For the role religion can play in public life is highly impacted by the definition of religion with which the society begins. Where, then, does the work on such an act of definition take place? In many instances today it is lawyers, judges and legislative bodies who are making these decisions. Let me offer but one pregnant example.

A South African colleague, Martin Prozesky, and I submitted a critical suggestion to the South African Constitutional Assembly in 1995, arguing that certain language, in particular the preamble words "May God Protect Our People," was discriminatory of non-theists. In many cases our suggestions were followed, but the preamble phrase cited above was allowed to stand. As a consequence, Prozesky appealed in 1996 to the South African Constitutional Court. Last year its decision was handed down: the word "god" was to be left in the Constitution's preamble, not as an example of discrimination, but because there is no discrimination. Our arguments had demonstrated to the court that the word "god" in our contemporary and extremely diverse society had no substantive meaning at all. "God," in other words, is an empty cipher: it has, according to the Court's decision, "no particular constitutional significance ...", but rather is a "time-honoured means of adding solemnity used in many cultures and in a variety of contexts;" as such, this word ("god") has "no operative constitutional effect ..." and thus has "no effect on the rights of believers or non-believers" (Constitutional Court of South Africa 1997: par. 28).

Without doubt the area of religion and law is one of the most thorny, but also most fruitful sources for the study of religion today. As we can see in the examples just given, far-reaching determinations and definitions of what may represent religion are being decided in court rooms around the world. The student and scholar of religions should be able to understand this process, and in some cases even offer aid in sorting out precedents, connections, and above all consequences of such rulings.

Religion and Biology

In a recent remarkable study on the American pronghorn, a wildlife biologist concludes that this unique animal species has survived from another world, namely the late Pleistocene extinctions of North America; with luck, he suggests, "they will always be there, to remind us of just how fast a North American cheetah could run." In other words, though the predator has long ago disappeared, the surviving prey species still manifests those adaptations that allowed it to survive its predators. It is, in the author's wonderful phrase, chased by "the ghosts of predators past" (Byers 1997: 244).

Weston La Barre, the well-known anthropologist, has characterized belief in god, and indeed the production of religion, as a "biopsychological relationship peculiar to human biology" (La Barre 1970: 20). But recently Jeffrey Masson has reminded us how naked we come to the world when dealing with religion. Studying the case of a "natural" youth, a boy kept imprisoned from early childhood until his teens without either human contact or experience of the natural world, he notes how the first observers of this human were struck by the absence of any and all categories that might be termed religion (Masson 1996: 90; 149). Is it possible that evolutionary hangovers rather than specific genes lie at the heart of the human creation we call "religion"?

Using Byers' example of the American pronghorn, what if we were to view religion as a set of artifices, artifacts, and strategies by which the human species moved from being a prey species to a predator species? In other words, what if we took as our point of departure the definition of religion as a complex strategy designed as a system of values, reinforced by ritual, to locate our origin and our fate outside of ourselves, with the goal of this strategy being the effort to cope with an initial prey experience and an eventual shift to outright predation, ultimately ending in preying on ourselves? What if the human species is chased by the ghosts of predators past, and still displays its strategic adaptations for surviving those predators?

Byers' central thesis is that "predation has a pervasive, far-reaching effect on the evolution of social adaptations in ungulates such as pronghorn ... and ... the behavior of pronghorn, like the anatomy and running ability, often reflects past rather than current adaptation" (Byers 1997: xvi). Why this adaptive process should not apply to the evolution of the human species, which began originally as an herbivore, is not obvious. In other words, as Byers argues, why should "historical interpretation in behavioral ecology" not be raised to "equality with explanations that are based upon current utility"? (Byers 1997:13). Certainly the prey experience of early humans must have called forth adaptive strategies, however the memories of those moments have faded. How were decisions made regarding who would sleep at the edge of the fire or the mouth of the cave, i.e. who would be the first prey taken that night? Even more to the point, how were those decisions, however arrived at, accepted by those whom they impacted? After all, they were ultimately life and death selections! Certainly some of the basic strategies that would have enabled both leaders to make decisions about who would be the next most likely prey, and those candidates to accept willingly such decisions, can be found in the many persuasions featured in religions regarding the overcoming of death, life after death, the good of the whole, sacrifice for a greater good, and so on. Such belief structures could indeed be understood as the result of strategies developed for prey situations, and which have remained anchored in the human tool kit for survival, not, of course, in La Barre's Freudian sense, but in an evolutionary and functional sense.

If such a theory were to hold, then both the origins and the beginnings of religion would be located in a bizarre set of human practices and thought as an evolutionary response to a millennia-long prey/predator relationship, and as such has remained with humans as an evolutionary hangover. Some of our primate neighbors, particularly the ones that are more pedal (baboons, orangutans, chimps) are still heavily preyed upon, especially by the cats (leopards, lions). But with our own elimination of such predators (except in a few isolated locations), the problem has been reduced for the human species: we are now the most efficient predators prowling the globe. We left the trees, went to the savanna, and became predators ourselves. Which means, in effect, that we became competitors for the same food sources, which, in turn, made us by definition a prey species for the predators who were bigger and better at it than we were.

The result, as we know, is that the human species became a better predator, in the overall picture, for a wide variety of reasons. But what lingers are the evolutionary traces of prey behavior, developed in response to heavy predation. The physical traces of this development are few and not always clear; but the human psyche and its behavior do betray these traces more clearly. When things go bump in the night, it's not the boogeyman we expect, but that saber-toothed cat or giant cave bear that could run as fast as a horse. No wonder our hair stands up, or what is left of it (our backs "run cold" when the muscles that used to control the hair that used to be there contract). It was very dangerous business to be human, as we can still see in various places in the world today. India is a classic example. In several heavily tiger-populated forests, humans are a natural prey species for the big cats, not just the focus of so-called "man-eaters" who are injured or otherwise driven to hunt humans. And our experience with grizzly bears on the North American continent, and contemporary experience with polar bears are further such moments. Who can forget the story of John Patterson and the lions of Tsavo? Young male lions, uninjured, found a useful menu among railroad workers on a bridge project in late 1890s Africa. It took Patterson and his companions some seven months to eliminate them (Patterson 1996). The eery movie "The Ghost and the Darkness" makes very clear what it is to be a prey species as a human (1996). And so, of course, does war (Ehrenreich 1997).

Concluding Thoughts

If scholars were to pursue natural histories of religions instead of campaigns for the truth of a particular religion disguised as history, then we might well see religions take their proper and rightful place among the many human artifacts designed to tell our species' stories. If scholars were to probe more carefully the legislative and legal attempts to define, and thus impose, definitions of religion on societies, then we might well see religions function less as imposed orders of discipline and more as chosen interpretations of a kaleidoscopic reality. If scholars were to look more penetratingly at the links between religions and human biological development, as for example in the prey/predator theory sketched here, and if such a theory were to be demonstrated and widely accepted in a society, then we might well see a marked change in the role that religion would be allowed to play in a human community. No longer the legitimator of predatory political regimes, no longer the imposer of dogmatic and exclusionary definitions upon those who might think differently; religion would function less in public, shared life than in diverse, private life. Is such a thing possible?

References

Albee, Edward, *Who's afraid of Virginia Woolf?*, Atheneum, New York, 1962.

Butler, Hubert, *Independent Spirit*, Farrar, Strauss, New York, 1996.

Byers, John, *American Pronghorn: Social Adaptations and the Ghosts Predators Past*, University of Chicago Press, Chicago, 1997.

Constitutional Court of South Africa, *Case CCT 6/97*, 1997.

Ehrenreich, Barbara, *Blood Rites: Origins and History of the Passions of War*, Metropolitan Books, New York, 1997.

Fontane, Theodor, *Wanderungen durch die Mark Brandenburg*, "Die Grafschaft Ruppin", Büchergilde Gutenberg, Frankfurt am Main, 1998.

Lease, Gary *"Odd Fellows" in the Politics of Religion*, Mouton de Gruyter, Berlin, 1995.

Lease, Gary, "Rationality and Evidence: the Study of Religion as a Taxonomy of Human Natural History," in: *Rationality and the Study of Religion,* edited by J. Jensen and L. Martin, Aarhus University Press, Aarhus, 1998a: 136-144.

Lease, Gary, "Public Redemption: Strenski's Mission for Religious Studies," in: *Journal of the American Academy of Religion* 66/2 (1998b): 377-380.

Lease, Gary, "What are the Humanities and why do they matter?", in: *Bulletin of the Council of Societies for the Study of Religion* 27/4 (1998c): 91-95.

Lease, Gary "Religion gleich Weltbild? Zur Problematik einer Begriffsbestimmung," in: *Religion im Wandel der Kosmologien,* edited by Dieter Zeller, Peter Lang, Frankfurt, 1999: 47-54.

Patterson, John, *The Man-Eaters of Tsavo,* Pocket Books, New York, 1996 (1907).

Reisberg, Leo, "A Sage of Biblical Studies," in: *Chronicle of Higher Education*, 14 May 1998: A9.

– "Das Kreuz mit dem Kruzifix," in: *Der Spiegel* 33/14 14 August 1995: 22-34.

Strenski, Ivan, "Religion, Power, and Final Foucault," in: *Journal of the American Academy of Religion* 66/2 (1998): 345-367.

Wiebe, Donald, *The Politics of Religious Studies*, St. Martin's Press, New York, 1995.

Reflections on 'Theses on Method'[1]

Bruce Lincoln

Professor, Department of History of Religions
University of Chicago, Chicago, USA

I have always shied away from writing about questions of method, for I have generally found others' attempts unsatisfying: at best, too abstract and bloodless; at worst, hollow and pretentious. As I see it, know-how comes not from reading or writing about methodology, but from practical engagement with concrete data and the honest reflection on the inadequacies of one's prior understanding that grows out of such engagement. I wouldn't short-circuit this process if I could, but more to the point, I don't think it can be done.

The only times I've overcome my aversion to explicitly methodological essays were when good friends and valued colleagues prevailed upon me to do so. The first such occasion came in 1984, when Cristiano Grottanelli, then a visiting professor at the University of Minnesota, suggested we sketch out an overview of research in history of religions, past, present, and future. His proposal led to some fascinating conversations and a jointly authored paper that we presented to Minnesota's Center for Humanistic Studies. Shortly after publishing our paper, the Center died – presumably as a result – and virtually no one outside Minnesota ever saw the paper. It has recently been reprinted, however, much to my trepidation.[2]

Given such an inauspicious beginning, I was able to avoid like endeavors for more than a decade until Brian Smith asked me to participate in a panel at the American Academy of Religions in 1995. The panel was to discuss Brian's splendid book, which demonstrates how the system of homologies (*bandhu-*) developed by the priestly authors of the *Brāhmanas* serves to naturalize the social hierarchy and to legitimate their own privileged position within the caste order.[3] I anticipated with pleasure the opportunity to celebrate a fine work of critical spirit, marked by clarity of vision and painstaking research. Subsequent discussions disabused me of this notion, for I soon learned that the other members of the panel, which had been organized by a leading Jesuit Indologist, intended to focus attention on what they regarded as unseemly "Brahmin-bashing". My "Theses on Method" were written to defend Brian's book against their attacks and more broadly, to articulate a rationale for the embattled fragment of our discipline that remains committed to critical research.

Somewhat to my surprise, the session was well-attended and my remarks seemed to strike a nerve. Some people were outraged and others delighted, which is just as I would have it. Upon return to Chicago, I whimsically decided that my theses should be nailed – actually, thumbtacked – to a door, and my office was the obvious candidate. There they stayed for a few weeks, disappearing now and then for surreptitious photocopying. Ultimately, the theses became notorious enough that people began writing to me and asking for copies, at which point I decided to have them published.[4] I feel honored that Messrs. Rothstein & Jensen think them worth reprinting in this splendid collection, but I can't help feeling that the editors' otherwise astute judgment must have failed them in this instance.

*

1. The conjunction "of" that joins the two nouns in the disciplinary ethnonym "History of Religions" is not neutral filler. Rather, it announces a proprietary claim and a relation of encompassment: history is the method and religion the object of study.

2. The relation between the two nouns is also tense, as becomes clear if one takes the trouble to specify their meaning. Religion, I submit, is that discourse whose defining characteristic is its desire to speak of things eternal and transcendent with an authority equally transcendent and eternal. History, in the sharpest possible contrast, is that discourse which speaks of things temporal and terrestrial in a human and fallible voice, while staking its claim to authority on rigorous critical practice.

3. History of religions is thus a discourse that resists and reverses the orientation of that discourse with which it concerns itself. To practice history of religions in a fashion consistens with the discipline's claim of title is to insist on discussing the temporal, contextual, situated, inter-

ested, human, and material dimensions of those discourses, practices, and institutions that characteristically represent themselves as eternal, transcendent, spiritual, and divine.

4. The same destabilizing and irreverent questions one might ask of any speech act ought be posed of religious discourse. The first of these is "Who speaks here?", i.e., what person, group, or institution is responsible for a text, whatever its putative or apparent author. Beyond that, "To what audience? In what immediate and broader context? Through what system of mediations? With what interests?" And further, "Of what would the speaker(s) persuade the audience? What are the consequences if this project of persuasion should happen to succeed? Who wins what, and how much? Who, conversely, loses?"

5. Reverence is a religious, and not a scholarly virtue. When good manners and good conscience cannot be reconciled, the demands of the latter ought to prevail.

6. Many who would not think of insulating their own or their parents' religion against critical inquiry still afford such protection to other people's faiths, via a stance of cultural relativism. One can appreciate their good intentions, while recognizing a certain displaced defensiveness, as well as the guilty conscience of western imperialism.

7. Beyond the question of motives and intentions, cultural relativism is predicated on the dubious – not to say, fetishistic – construction of "cultures" as if they were stable and discrete groups of people defined by the stable and discrete values, symbols, and practices they share. Insofar as this model stresses the continuity and integration of timeless groups, whose internal tensions and conflicts, turbulence and incoherence, permeability and malleability are largely erased, it risks becoming a religious and not a historic narrative: the story of a transcendent ideal theatened by debasing forces of change.

8. Those who sustain this idealized image of culture do so, *inter alia*, by mistaking the dominant fraction (sex, age group, class, and/or caste) of a given group for the group or "culture" itself. At the same time, they

119

mistake the ideological positions favoured and propagated by the dominant fraction for those of the group as a whole (e.g. when texts authored by Brahmins define "Hinduism", or when the statements of male elders constitute "Nuer religion"). Scholarly misrecognitions of this sort replicate the misrecognitions and misrepresentatiosn of those the scholars privilege as their informants.

9. Critical inquiry need assume neither cynicism nor dissimulation to justify probing beneath the surface, and ought probe scholarly discourse and practice as much as any other.

10. Understanding the system of ideology that operates in one's own society is made difficult by two factors: (i) one's consciousness is itself a product of that system, and (ii) the system's very success renders its operations invisible, since one is so consistently immersed in and bombarded by its products that one comes to mistake them (and the apparatus through which they are produced and disseminated) for nothing other than "nature".

11. The ideological products and operations of other societies afford invaluable opportunities to the would-be student of ideology. Being initially unfamiliar, they do not need to be denaturalized before they can be examined. Rather, they invite and reward critical study, yielding lessons one can put to good use at home.

12. Although critical inquiry has beome commonplace in other disciplines, it still offends many students of religion, who denounce it as "reductionism". This charge is meant to silence critique. The failure to treat religion "as religion" – that is, the refusal to ratify its claim of transcendent nature and sacrosanct status – may be regarded as heresy and sacrilege by those who construct themselves as religious, but it is the starting point for those who construct themselves as historians.

13. When one permits those whom one studies to define the terms in which they will be understood, suspends one's interest in the temporal and contingent, or fails to distinguish between "truths", "truth-

claims", and "regimes of truth", one has ceased to function as historian or scholar. In that moment, a variety of roles are available: some perfectly respectable (amanuensis, collector, friend and advocate), and some less appealing (cheerleader, voyeur, retailer of import goods). None, however, should be confused with scholarship.

Notes

1. The thirteen points listed here were originally published in *Method and Theory in the Study of Religion* 8 (1996): 225-227. They are reprinted here with permission of the editors and publisher, E. J. Brill.
2. Cristiano Grottanelli and Bruce Lincoln, "A Brief Note on (Future) Research in the History of Religions" *University of Minnesota Center for Humanisic Studies, Occasional Papers*, No. 4 (1985). Reprint in *Method and Theory in the Study of Religions* 10/3 (1998): 311-25.
3. Brian K. Smith, *Classifying the Universe: The Ancient Indian Varna System and the Origins of Caste* (New York: Oxford University Press, 1994). While Smith's book is the definitive treatment of the topic, I am pleased to have anticipated some of his analysis in my article on "The Tyranny of Taxonomy," which was the inaugural lecture of Minnesota's ill-starred Humanities Center. They also published it as a pamphlet in 1985 and a revised version appeared in *Discourse and the Construction of Society* (New York: Oxford University Press, 1989), pp. 131-41.
4. They first appeared in *Method and Theory in the Study of Religions* 8 (1996): 225-227.

A Radically Social Theory of Religon

Burton L. Mack

Professor, Claremont School of Theology, Claremont, USA

Religion is the term critical scholars use to register an assumption about a certain set of social practices. The set includes such things as performing *rituals*, producing *myths*, cultivating *symbols*, defining social roles (for the *shaman* or *priest*), and constructing institutions for the care and reproduction of the set. Like *religion*, these terms are abstract generalizations, much in need of detailed definition and description. The assumption, however, is that, taken together, they form a coherent conceptual system, and that this conceptual system is derived from observations of human activities, and thus refers to a sphere of creativity and performance integral to the human enterprise of social formation. To borrow some language from Althusser, religion thus conceived is a "semiautonomous instance" among other instances (practices) within the political, the economic, and the ideological structures of a society. It should therefore be possible to describe these religious practices as they occur in the context of a given society or cultural history, note changes in different social situations, compare phenomena cross-culturally, test the assumption of a semiautonomous social system, and work toward the construction of theories to explain religion as a collective social construction.

This conception of religion is obviously not the way in which religion is understood in popular parlance and by scholars within various theological, philosophical, historical and hermeneutical traditions that occasionally turn their attention to the study of religion. The dominant view has been that religion is not a human social *construct*, but a *sui generis* phenomenon, the human *response* to manifestations of "the sacred," an order or entity of the divine that transcends the realm of social reality. The current form of this dominant view, especially in circles influenced by American thought, is that religion is mainly a matter of personal desire for contact with the divine and for transformations that elevate the individual into a transcendent realm of "spiritual" reality. This focus upon personal

123

religious experience appears to be the result of (1) a cultural shift in popular fascination with psycho-religious experimentation, in combination with a kind of legitimation it has received from (2) the phenomenology and history of religions.

The earlier historians of religion were not so sure about the ontological reality of a spiritual realm, but this did not lead them to pursue a radically social theory of religion. That is because they were fully immersed in the heady atmosphere of the Enlightenment with its discovery of "reason" and its concept of the individual, rational man. The myths and rituals of other peoples and cultures, by contrast, were seen as strange persuasions, much more difficult to understand than the Christian (Protestant) beliefs with which these scholars were familiar, and which in any case they thought of as a penultimate phase in the history of enlightenment. Thus the questions that came to mind focused on the "beliefs" of "primitive" peoples imagined as precursors to Christianity and regarded as examples of pre-Enlightenment thinking. How could they (the primitives) possibly have come to believe such?, was the question that set the agenda.

It is no wonder theories of origin were proposed that, though set in "aboriginal" times and thus viewed as "primitive" stages of human development, imagined in contrast to both the Christian and the Enlightenment "stages" of Western history, were nevertheless reminiscent of Christian myth, ritual, and belief in vague and vulgar ways. The familiar concepts of the confused mental-psychological state of the unconverted, the disease of language characteristic for the barbarian, the notion of the "human condition" as one of alienation, the tragic event of revelation, the miraculous transformation, the mystery of the cosmos, and the forms of sacred epiphany have all been recast in first-time scenes, a theater of the grotesque imagined as the preconscious history of the modern, enlightened, rational man. The history of the study of religion and culture is dotted with these originary scenes from Rousseau to Girard (with striking descriptions of the "primitives" that border on originary scenes from W. Robertson Smith, the pan-Babylonians, the myth and ritual school, Edward Burnett Tylor, Levy-Bruhl, Freud, Adolf E. Jensen, and Walter Burkert). The standard critique has been to point out the logical fallacy by which the result of a process held to account for some novel manifestation is actually presupposed in the make-up of the prior situation. Think of trying to imagine the very first time a hominoid experienced a religious impulse, aha, feeling of guilt, sorrow, or awe. Think of doing that in order to catch a glimpse of the human as we understand it, while at the same time trying to account for it in terms of events held to be "primitive," "savage," or pre-human. Although these scenarios had to be invented by the scholarly imagination, and although no two agree on how it was that "civilization" and "religion" began (from Rousseau's depiction of the "noble savage" to Girard's collective murder), the concepts of origin and development, and the underlying notion of the rational and psychological debility of the "natural man," have had a profound effect on the way in which religion continues to be defined and conceptualized. Theories of origin have underscored the notion that religion is primarily a matter of rational and psychological adolescence, and this has regularly frustrated efforts to account for the obviously public, collective, non-sensationalist, intellectual and cultural features of religion wherever human societies have been observed.

It is true, the emergence of ethnography, sociology, and cultural anthropology as disciplines eventually had its effect on the study of religion. But even then the taint of mystification, and the modernist fascination with individualism as the lens through which all social effects are viewed and evaluated, have worked to foil the quest for a social theory of religion. Examples are rife in functionalist theories that, though they situate religion within complex social structures, fail to account for it in social terms, preferring instead to mark the ways in which religion functions to answer human "needs," often left unexplained and unelaborated under the rubric of society's "need" for cohesion, but frequently imagined still as an individual's "need" for identity, orientation, and anxiety reduction (à la Blumenberg), as if the "sacred" necessarily belonged in the picture for such to be achieved. Thus the study of religion has not been pursued in the interest of explaining religion as a human, social construction.

There is a feature article on "The Study of Religion" in the Harper-Collins *Dictionary of Religion* (pp. 909-917). The point is made that the academic study of religion should be understood as a "quest for new theories of religion." It then goes on to discuss the four major types of theory that the study of religion has produced. They are (1) "Origin Theories of Religion," including rationalist, sociological and psychological approaches; (2) "Functionalist Theories of Religion;" (3) the theory implicit to the "Phenomenology and History of Religion;" and (4) "Structuralist Theories of Religion." Except for the sociological approach associated with the work of Émile Durkheim, none of these theories dares to imagine religion radically as a human construction integral to the process of social formation. For the phenomenologists, religion is *sui generis*, a sphere of preoccupation apart from social existence. For the rationalists and the psychologists, religion has been viewed as an understandable mistake in the effort to account for personal visionary experiences (such as dreams, ghosts, the hidden "memories" of childhood traumas, desires, and awe in the presence of cosmic and astrological phenomena). Functionalist theories do understand religion as integral to complex, holistic social models. But the emphasis has been on particular societies as closed, organic structures, and the "functions" noted have not raised the question of why it is that religion (and not some other set of social factors) is thought to be the appropriate provider. Structuralist theories, on the other hand, are recommended in this article, with the proviso that "Diachronic, historical, or evolutionary stages are irrelevant to structural (synchronic) explanations of religion," and that the structural approach is "yet to be fully applied to the study of religion." Thus ends the feature article.

Taking this article as an apt description of the current state of the discipline, three observations may be made about the quest for a social theory of religion. The first is that, from among the "origin theories of religion," only Durkheim's theory of the social origins of religion "is fundamental to contemporary studies of religion." That is correct. The Durkheim tradition does not ontologize "the Sacred" or posit "religious experience" as a point of departure. One tracing of this tradition through additional contributions to theory by Dumézil, Lévi-Strauss, Dumont, Wheatley, and Jonathan Z. Smith, has been thoughtfully discussed in Smith's important book, *To Take Place*. Unfortunately, this stream of intellectual labor is not yet at the center of discussion or debate in the academies of religious studies. It should be.

The second observation is that, from among the various social theories that do have some currency in religious studies, only the structuralists have been firm in their rejection of both individualism and psychological explanations. This is clearly an advance. Unfortunately, even in the application of structuralist theory to religion, where critical analysis seeks to uncover the internal logic of religious systems, questions of the social origin, maintenance, and effectivity of religion are routinely avoided or even discounted as illegitimate for synchronic analysis. An adequate social theory of religion cannot afford to do so.

126

The third observation is that a vigorous tradition of quest for a comprehensive social theory has been left completely out of account. I refer to post-Marxist thought in debate with postmodernist critique, especially in circles influenced by the work of Louis Althusser. It is here that one can find a form of structuralist thinking that makes room for social process, practice, production, ideology, and history. This quest has great potential for overcoming the current impasse that stymies debate between structualist and functionalist scholars. Unfortunately, post-Marxist thinkers have not paid much attention to religion as a social practice or, as Althusser would call it, a "semiautonomous instance" within a social formation conceived as a "structure of structures." And of course, not many scholars in religious studies have been attracted to Marxist theories of social and cultural production. So the promise is waiting for those who may dare.

If the scientific study of anything requires the theoretical discussion and definition of its object, and if academic study in the human sciences requires a social theory of the human practice or production in view, scholars interested in the study of religion have much work to do. My own view is that bits and pieces of a radically social theory of religion are close to the surface in several academic disciplines, and that putting them together would be a fairly straightforward and very interesting cross-disciplinary effort, except for several bugaboos that appear to be the reasons for not forging ahead. They are of two kinds. The first has to do with the problem of semantics that came along with the fragmentation of disciplines in the humanities and human sciences, the acceptance of multiple perspectives on a social or cultural phenomenon, the sophistication we have achieved about the cultural determination of the "languages" we use to describe a given phenomenon, and the critique of Enlightenment thinking with its desire for objective description and rational explanation. This situation, often referred to as postmodernism, has frustrated efforts to pursue social theory or relate theories of language, thought, the arts and religion to more comprehensive descriptions and theories of social formation.

The resulting semantic morass has had the effect of calling into question much of the language that has traditionally been used in many academic disciplines in the human sciences. Serious contradictions, partialities, and conceptual problems have been disclosed in many of our intellectual pursuits, and these problems register cautionary limits on subsequent studies. But it is also the case that the fallacies discovered in a logic of argumentation have often been reduced to clichés that cut off further thought. In the case of religious studies, for instance, the onus has been placed on the off-handed use of a number of erstwhile respectable terms, including "referential," "reflective," "collective," "experimental," "arbitrary," "necessary," "essential," "genealogical," "causative," "effective," and "functional." ("Cognitive," "structural," and even "generative" are still acceptable, while "history" and "change," though denoting features of the social that cannot be denied, are no longer explanatory, being in need themselves of explication.) This terminological mine-field, easily expanded to include most of the technical terms in the study of religion, is both a blessing and a curse. Awareness of the conceptual issues it registers is absolutely necessary, of course, and that awareness has the potential of raising the level of conceptual precision as one procedes. But because of the onus on many of these terms, they now frequently function as red flags that thwart the engagement of extremely important considerations for the full description of the social production and function of religion that I imagine as the object for investigation. A radically social theory of religion will have to reinstate many of these terms, though with other, and perhaps more prescribed connotations than they have had in earlier academic treatments. Note that the red flags have often had the effect of closing off even the search for better, alternative terms to designate the function or relationship in need of conceptualization. If we can't find acceptable terminology capable of referring to the observable, public practices we start with as data, and we find ourselves fully engaged with the critique of each other's referential language, what *are* we talking about?

The other kind of bugaboo is much more insidious. Ghosts from the comfortable notions of religion as a traffic-with-transcendence are still haunting even the sociologists of religion. Spooking along the ill-defined borders of our knowledges, these ghosts ask to be left alone, that even though the study of religion must of course take a turn toward sociology, a place should be reserved for "meaningful religious experience." The appeal of this familiar spirit seems innocent, suggesting that it is only fair to grant personal religious experience a place in the larger scheme of things. But it actually serves as a cover for the thought that *maybe* there *is* a spiritual realm of the divine "out there," in addition to the worlds of empirical reality, social construction, and human thought and imagination which oth-

128

erwise have to describe the horizons for scientific and academic discourse. To hesitate on the question of whether religion is a human, social construct or a traffic-with-transcendence scuttles the project of a radically social theory of religion. It does so, not because the *philosophical* issue of what we can or cannot know about "ultimate reality" has to be left open (the space that excites *theologians*), but because of the *anthropology* at stake. Religion thought of as traffic-with-the-divine implicitly works with an anthropology of the autonomous individual, not with a social anthropology. Thus the challenge of working out a theory of religion as a social construct is easily frustrated at every turn by fascination with the individual, the anthropology called individualism that now dominates the study of religion. There is no need to deny the significance of religion for an individual, or to overlook the many ways in which individuals within a society experience, interpret, and manipulate a religion, because a radically social theory of religion can account for them as products of a social formation. But personal religious experience is not a firm support for any theory of religion, much less a social theory. And so, noting that the features of a religion available to us as data are all social, collective, shared, public, debated, negotiated, and cultivated agreements and practices, a social theory is required, and the ghosts should be asked to stop flitting about and get on with their own task of inhabiting a memorial to the notion of epiphany. What an elegant theory it *was*. What a grand monument it deserves.

What then? Why then it would be possible to take charge of the academic investigation of religion in concert with other disciplines in quest of social theory. And the age-old questions that ran into dead ends when asked about religion as a response to "the sacred" could now be asked again, this time with a new set of contextual features and factors in view. Think of what it would mean, for instance, to reactivate the question of motivation, now asked of social constructs instead of personal "needs" and "desires." Why religion? Why does a group in the process of social formation produce the practices we call religion? Why? Suddenly the question of "motivation" could make very good sense again. It certainly gets to the heart of a matter that could not be discussed as long as the gods were still in the picture, either as ghosts or as primary agents. And it immediately generates a fresh set of equations begging to be solved. Just think of romping again through the considerable learning achieved in the disciplines of ethnography, cultural anthropology, and the histories of cultures and religions with the question of Why religion? in mind. Relieved of the embarrassment of inappropriately using the languages of personal psychology when talking about matters of social experimentation and the reaching of collective agreements, it would be okay to ask the Why? question, this time as a quest for language appropriate to a social anthropology. We have learned much about the social reasons for the creation of other social systems, how they are produced, reproduced, work and are worked in practices integral to social formations. Languages, kinship systems, systems of classification, technologies of production, modes of distribution, social structures, role assignments, modes of calculation and the keeping of accounts, and more, have been thoroughly studied and explained in relation to the human enterprise of social formation. Why not include religion?

To include the study of religion in the larger-scoped academic quest for a comprehensive social theory may be difficult. That is because wrenching rearrangements in the current structures of academic disciplines and programs would be called for. And as for the shifts in conceptuality required of those specializing in religious studies, as well as the need for methods and interdisciplinary connections appropriate to a quest for social theory, I suspect that a new mode of collegial conversation would have to be devised to replace the current strategies for protecting theological sentiments. I have no prediction to offer. But I do have two suggestions in regard to what an appropriate method might look like, one teaser about the difference such a shift would make for the kinds of questions we might ask, and one speculation on the shape of a radically social theory of religion and society.

On method, I would first like to highlight the importance of Jonathan Z. Smith's program of research which I understand as a rigorously controlled, comparative exercise in the description and classification of religious practices. I have discussed his program elsewhere, both as a four point process appropriate for historical studies (Mack 1996), and as a rationalized method of description which aims at theoretical constructions (Mack 1987, 1992). Briefly, the four operations are (1) *description*, (2) *comparison*, (3) *redescription* and (4) the *rectification* of descriptive categories. It is important to mention that the rectified categories would then enjoy a level of generalization and abstraction capable of theoretical testing. The point I want to make about Smith's program is that it is fully appropriate for a quest for a social theory of religion. It is unabashedly empirical with regard to data, historical with regard to description, and rational with regard to the sense of a given religious practice.

The second suggestion I have to offer on method stems from my attempts to apply Smith's program to the study of Christian origins. I have found it helpful to position a given myth, ritual, text, rhetoric, or social practice at its own intersection of what I have called *social formation* and *mythmaking* (Mack 1995, 11-15). This adds the dimension of process or production to a Smithian agenda of redescription, and it sets the stage for asking some serious questions about the relationship of a myth to the process of social formation. As one might suspect, my studies have high-lighted the ideological strategies for legitimizing social experiments. It may be too early to say that anything of value has been learned for social theory, but at least it has been possible to illustrate and discuss the social and intellectual production of a religion *as* a human construction *within* a social history instead of having recourse either to mythic origins, or to an abstract system of logic, philosophy, or theology ontologized and removed from social history.

Now for the teaser. Since I think it important to raise the question of motivation as part of the quest for a social theory of religion (the Why religion? question referred to above), and since I know full well that all talk of motivations and/or functions is currently taboo in cognitive and structural approaches to religious systems, I'll have to sneak up on my colleagues in the hope of catching them off-guard. I'd like to illustrate just how differ-ently older questions might look if we took seriously the quest for a radi-cally social theory of religion. What, then, might we propose as the human interests that converge in the processes that produce myths, rituals, sym-bols, shamans, etc.? Well, what about starting with that term, *interests*? I have been thinking about this term as a way to include religious studies in a post-Marxist, postmodern quest for social theory. I first took note of it in the way Jonathan Z. Smith used the term, always a very helpful point of departure for me, a notation which I registered at a precise point in my introduction to *Violent Origins* (Mack 1987, 69), the protocol of a con-ference on ritual at Stanford in 1983. I like the term because it works so well as a collector of connotations that can advance a social theory project: (1) The term is currently being used by social theorists to capture the sense we have that a social system both limits and directs the use of power, persuasion or force in just certain directions, thus giving us the impression of purpose, objective, and motivation. (2) The term does not have any distinctively religious connotations, but can be used in regard to any system of signs, practices, or social structures, including religion, when such a practice is interrogated as to its *raison d'etre* and/or function within the larger whole. (3) It can easily bear the connotation of inquisitiveness, thus making it possible to include intellectual activity and cognitive functions within the cluster of activities that produce a social system. (4) And yes, it definitely carries the connotation of reward due an investment, a nicely phrased motivational nuance for the intellectual labor required to produce a religion. (5) It is also thoroughly constructive, or can be, as a general term for collective motivation. That means that one would be free to start the investigation of Why religion? without having to first parry the usual litanies of "the human condition" (always problematic) or "the human potential" (usually for divine enlightenment/transformation)" in the prolegomenon. A fresh start!

But can anything be said about the "interests" that might make some social sense of religion? Well, they would not have to be much different in kind than the interests that produce other social systems. And what are *they*? Are they not interests in the human enterprise itself? Why not recognize the range of human interests that come into play in the process of social formation? Why not start with the observation that the human enterprise of social formation is an excessive overreaction if thought of in terms of "meeting" necessary, natural survival "needs"? Why not bewonder the complex systems of signs and practices that make social formation possible. Why not entertain the possibility that the processes of constructing, maintaining, and reproducing such systems are evidence for the investments humans make and the interest humans take in living together? The interests invested in the process of social formation cannot be thought of on the model of an individual's psychological profile. Interests of all kinds are always products of relations with others. Social theory will have to give an account of the interests that collect in the myths, symbols, codes, and systems of signs and practices that structure a social formation. Why not include religion among the systems that belong to the complex structures of a society? Why not work toward a theory of religion as a contribution to the quest for a comprehensive social theory of social formation based on collective human interests? What might that particular contribution be?

It is not possible to anticipate exactly what such a quest might stumble upon as a replacement for the gods. But we do already know very much about the social circumstances, situations, and effects of religious practices. All we need to do is take these practices seriously as important for the human enterprise of social formation. My speculation is that, given the complex task of the human enterprise that social formation is, religion may be found to fill a niche or provide a particular function just as important and integral as any of the other systems of social structuration and practice. We know that myths are a way of shaping the collective imagination of a people's past, ancestors, and events thought to have established their world within its horizons. We know that rituals focus upon practices that are important for both social and material production, that rituals call attention to these practices as worthy of close observation, and that rituals set these practices in marked-off times and places for controlled, precise performance, public observance, and social occasion. We also know that every people has a set of stories that tell why the codes and conventions of their culture are the right way to manage life together. What if we thought of these displacements in space, time, and imagination as a registry of the ways in which a group has settled upon such things as shared "memories" of the past, attitudes toward generational continuities, precedent social agreements, and invitations to consider the right ways to do things? What if we thought of them as fleshing out what Bourdieu has called a *habitus*, noticing that many of the figures projected into the *habitus* by religious practices represent interests, relationships, and attitudes that could not easily be pointed out by observation of the average daily round? What if myths and rituals are important ways of reproducing *habitus*, and *habitus* is a pedagogy for meditations on and instruction in conventions fundamental for the maintenance of the society? Of course there is a gap between the *habitus* and the way the social order actually works. The *habitus* is never a mirror image of a society as it actually exists and works. That does introduce the possibility of thinking about, elaborating, and manipulating the arrangements of the *habitus* itself as if it were an "other world." Interest focused solely upon the internal logic and configuration of an imaginary world might certainly frustrate attention to issues of social and material production, supposing a culture took that direction. But the gap

133

between the imaginary world and the world of the everyday also creates the space and the imagery for the perceptive cogitation, reflection, play, experimentation, winking, appreciation, and calculation that constitute social existence. And the facts of the case are that the symbols of the mythic world take on political and cultural representations about which ideological battles often rage. If so, religious studies might have quite a contribution to make to a comprehensive social theory. Social formation may well be a more complex process than a combination of political, economic, and ideological practices as they are now being discussed among us by social theorists. The social anthropology implied by the interests that may be discovered in the quest for such a comprehensive theory might well be mind-boggling.

Eventually, the evidence for practices that do not readily support such an anthropology of human interests in social formation would also have to be taken into account. I am thinking of such practices as predation, abuse of power, greed, and violence, all of which are currently calling for explanation. The lines of inquiry most compatable with my suspicion of a constructive theory of interests would not look for impediments in the "nature" of the human as is now the tendency. Instead, we would want to investigate the circumstancial factors in social configurations where such practices tend to occur on the one hand, and find some way to ask about the effective social and cultural difference that myths make on the other. Comparative studies of social situations, as well as of societies, cultures, and religions would seem to be the next logical step. We ought eventually to be able to say which combinations of human interests would be more helpful than others, supposing, for instance, that we settled on the construction of social democracies as our best bet for the forseeable future (McGowan).

If so, what might be the social role of the scholar in religious studies? Well, the social role depends on the theory of religion dominant in the academy and current in the society. If a people were able to come to terms with the concept of religion as a collective, human construct integral to the structures of society, and if they found it possible to admit in public forum that religion makes a difference in the way a society works, and if a people were willing to consider the effective differences various religions make in the ways people socialize and think about themselves in our multicultural world, a very interesting public role for the scholar could be imagined. Who else would there be to generate and lead public forum on the social and cultural consequences of a religion? If religion *is* of social and cultural consequence, why not ask the scholar of religion to join the ranks of cultural critics, those in our societies charged with helping us understand the interests that surface in literature, the arts, the media, the market, and what we now call popular culture? The role would be that of a public pedagogue, I should think. Unfortunately, at present in America, that dimension of a scholar's intellectual labor is hardly thinkable. So we not only have more theoretical work to do, we may also have a new role to play, supposing the object of our study turns out to be a practice of social significance.

References

Althusser, Louis (See Resch)

Blumenberg, Hans, *Arbeit am Mythos*. Frankfurt: Suhrkamp, 1979. English translation: *Work on Myth*. Translated by Robert M. Wallace. Cambridge, MA: The MIT Press, 1985.

Bourdieu, Pierre, *Outline of a Theory of Practice*. Translated by Richard Nice. Cambridge: Cambridge University Press, 1982. (The French edition is not available to me.)

Burkert, Walter, *Homo Necans: Interpretationen altgriechischer Opferriten und Mythen*. Religionsgeschichtliche Versuche und Vorarbeiten 32. Berlin and New York: Walter de Gruyter, 1972. English translation: *Homo Necans: The Anthropology of Ancient Greek Sacrificial Ritual and Myth*. Translated by Peter Bing. Berkeley: University of California Press, 1983.

Freud, Sigmund, *Totem und Tabu: Einige Übereinstimmungen im Seelenleben der Wilden und der Neurotiker*. Vienna, 1913; Frankurt: Fischer, 1940. English translation: *Totem and Taboo*. London, 1950.

Girard, René, *La violence et le sacré*. Paris: Grasset, 1972. English translation: *Violence and the Sacred*. Baltimore: Johns Hopkins University Press, 1977.

HarperCollins *Dictionary of Religion* (See Jonathan Z. Smith).

Jensen, Adolf, *Mythos und Kult bei Naturvölkern*. Wiesbaden: Steiner, 1951. English translation: *Myth and Cult among Primitive People*. Chicago: The Chicago University Press, 1963.

Levy-Bruhl, Lucien, *Les fonctions mentales dans les societes inferieures*. Paris: F. Alcan, 1910. English translation: *How Natives Think*. London: Allen & Unwin, 1926.

Mack, Burton L., "After *Drudgery Divine*," *Numen* 39/2. 1992: 225-233.

Mack, Burton L., "Introduction: Religion and Ritual," *Violent Origins: Walter Burkert, Rene Girard, and Jonathan Z. Smith on Ritual Killing and Cultural Formation*. Edited by Robert G. Hamerton-Kelly. (Stanford, CA: Stanford University Press, 1987) 1-70.

Mack, Burton L., "On Redescribing Christian Origins," *Method and Theory in the Study of Religion* 8-3. 1996: 247-269.

Mack, Burton L., *Who Wrote the New Testament: The Making of the Christian Myth*. HarperSan Francisco, 1995.

McGowan, John, *Postmodernism and its Critics*. Ithaca, NY: Cornell University Press, 1991.

Resch, Robert Paul, *Althusser and the Renewal of Marxist Social Theory*. Berkeley: Universityof California Press, 1992.

Rousseau, Jean-Jacque, *Discourse sur l'origine et les fondaments de l'inegalite parmi les hommes*. Paris: Editions Sociale, 1954.

Schluchter, Wofgang, *Rationalism, Religion, and Domination: A Weberian Perspective*. Berkeley: University of California Press, 1988.

Smith, Jonathan Z., editor, *Dictionary of Religion*. HarperSanFrancisco, 1995.

Smith, Jonathan Z., *Drudgery Divine: On the Comparison of Early Christianities and the Religions of Late Antiquity*. London: School of Oriental and African Studies; Chicago: The Chicago University Press, 1990.

Smith, Jonathan Z., *To Take Place: Toward Theory in Ritual*. Chicago: The University of Chicago Press, 1987.

Smith, W. Robertson, *Lectures on the Religion of the Semites*. London: A. & C. Black, 1907

Tylor, Edward Burnett, *Religion in Primitive Culture*. Volume 2 of *Primitive Culture*. New York: Harper, 1958.

Tylor, Edward Burnett, *Researches into the Development of Mythology, Philosophy, Religion, Art, and Culture*.2 Vols. London: John Murray, 1871. (See, especially, chapters 5 and 6, "Emotional and Imitative Language.")

Tylor, Edward Burnett, *Researches into the Early History of Mankind and the Development of Civilization*. London: Holt, 1865.

Weber, Max (See Schluchter)

Secular Theory and the Academic Study of Religion

Luther H. Martin

Professor & Former Chair, Department of Religion
The University of Vermont, Vermont, USA

> And you thought you'd give me some more material?
> Alas, I've got too much already ... I don't need any more data.
> What I need is a theory to explain it all.
> – Morris Zapp (Lodge 1984: 28)

I

The academic study of religion, as the rubric itself suggests, should conform in principle to the same protocol as does the academic study of *anything*. Earlier views of "religion" as *sui generis*, together with consequent arguments for some special method that is itself "religious" or that "brackets" what is considered to be "religious" from academic inquiry, deny this fundamental premise. The academic study of religion should, in other words, be in no way privileged – unless, of course, the counterintuitive claims and assumptions characteristic of religious expression be accepted as somehow true (in the ordinary sense of this judgement). Otherwise, something other is at stake in the ubiquity and perseverance of religion than its manifest appeal. To discover this significance requires that the study of religion be *theoretically* based.

Theory is but a kind of generalization; both attempt to explain the greatest amount of data in terms of the fewest number of principles. The former is distinguished from the latter, however, in that theoretically based generalizations should be reflexively established, they should somehow be testable and, if deemed valid, they should provide explanations. In the study of religion, generalizations are based on data concerning certain kinds of human practices, whether discursive or non-discursive, which are generated by comparative (anthropological) and historical research, each of which have their own theoretical problematic (Martin 1997c and Martin 2000).

Traditional examples of theories that offer explanations for religion include intellectualist theories which hold as their primary assumption the view that human beings have a fundamental interest in rationally understanding their environment. This view, consequently, approaches religions primarily in terms of their discourse, i.e., their myths, understanding them as early examples of intellectual activity. In reaction to this rationalist view, born of the Enlightenment, some nineteenth-century Romantic theorists argued that religious practices were expressive of some other feature of human life, e.g., the psychological or the social, and they defined religion, consequently, as a symbolic phenomenon. Arising also from Romanticism was an explanation of religion in terms of its nonrational features. These emotivist theorists explained religion primarily in affective terms and focused on extraordinary personal experiences of some transcendent or universal "other". (On these three classical theories of religion, see Marett: 1932: 1 and J. Z. Smith 1995: 1068-1069.)

Clearly the human sciences cannot test theories of religion in ways appropriate to the natural sciences. Unlike the invariable laws of nature sought by the natural sciences, the human sciences, including the study of religion, can attempt, however, to differentiate between valid and invalid generalizations – stereotypes, for example, or ideologically produced fictions. Writing of historiographical generalization, Louis Gottschalk has proposed that validation should:

> at least conform to all the known facts so that if it does not present definitive truth it should at any rate constitute the least inconvenient form of tentative error. That means that it must be subject to certain general standards and tests – of human behavior, of logical antecedents and consequences, of statistical or mass trends (Gottschalk 1963: vi).

A brief consideration of emotive or affective theories of religion can provide an example of such probative endeavors.

I have argued that the widely held theory about religion as personal experience in response to some transcendent "other" is invalid since it represents a generalization about religion based upon the data of a particular religious tradition, namely, the Protestant Reformation principle that "salvation is by [individual] faith alone as confirmed by an *experience* of grace".[1] In its American cultural context, this theological view of religion was given its first *theoretical* formulation by Jonathan Edwards in his "Treatise Concerning Religious Affections" (Edwards [1746] 1959), a work which has been judged to be "the most profound exploration of the religious psychology in all American literature" (Miller 1949: 177). Written in defense of the "Great Awakening", that first instance of large-scale revivalism that began in the 1720s and spread throughout the American colonies, Edwards held that "true religion consists so much in the affections, that there can be no true religion without them" (Edwards 1959: 120). The primary "objective ground" for these experiences is, he argued, "the transcendentally excellent and amiable nature of divine things, as they are in themselves" (Edwards 1959: 240). For Edwards, in other words, religion was based on an unmediated, personal experience in response to and confirmed by the sacred. This emphasis on individual experience relegates other religious practices such as discursive or ritual practices to outward and secondary expressions of that inward grace so cherished by Protestants.

A "Second Great Awakening" swept the United States at the beginning of the nineteenth century, associated interestingly with Edward's grandson, Timothy Dwight. This revival was reinforced by the influence of a popularized form of German Romanticism (Gabriel 1950), which had produced its own experiential view of religion that may be traced from Friederich Schleiermacher's speeches *On Religion*, first published in 1799, to its most influential theoretical articulation in Rudolf Otto's *The Idea of the Holy* (1917). Independently of Edwards, Schleiermacher had written similarly that "the sum total of religion is to feel that, in its highest unity, all that moves us in feeling is one" (Schleiermacher 1958: 49-50); "the true nature of religion is...[this] immediate consciousness of the Deity" (Schleiermacher 1958: 101). And like Edwards, Schleiermacher concluded that religious knowledge and organizations are but a secondary manifestation of this experience of unity with the Infinite (Schleiermacher 1959: 60-61, 101, 155-156).

At the beginning of the twentieth century, the American philosopher, William James, proposed essentially the same view of religion that had first been argued by Edwards — no longer in the discourse of Reformation or Romantic theology, however, but now in that of the newly defined field of psychology that James was so instrumental in popularizing. In his classic Gifford Lectures on *The Varieties of Religious Experience* (1902), James wrote that religion consists of "the feelings ... and experiences of individual men in their solitude, so far as they apprehend themselves to stand in relation to whatever they may consider the divine" (James 1929: 31-32), a definition of religion employed also by the philosopher, A. N. Whitehead (Whitehead 1926: 16, though without reference to James). For James, as for the Protestants that preceded him, "personal religion will prove itself more fundamental than either theology or ecclesiaticism. Churches, when once established," he asserted, "live at second-hand upon tradition; but the founders of every church owed their power originally to the fact of their direct personal communion with the divine" (James 1929: 31). Consequently, in the conclusion of James, "personal religious experience has its roots and centre in mystical states of consciousness" (James 1929: 370).

According to the *Encyclopedia of Religion* from 1987 little theoretical advance on the subject has been made since James. The author of the article on "Mysticism", after expanding on the characteristics of mysticism offered by James sixty years earlier, concludes that:

> all religions, regardless of their origin, retain their vitality only as long as their members continue to believe in a transcendent reality with which they can in some way communicate by direct experience (Dupré 1987: 246).

The condition requisite to the validation of generalizations about religion being based upon personal experience is preeminently that of an individualistic anthropology, a condition which did not exist in the cultures of Western antiquity, for example (Martin 1994), where the denigration of feeling in the face of reason by classical Greek culture would, in any case, argue in favor of intellectualist theories. Nor does this valuation of the individual over the collective characterize most of the modern, non-Western world (which is quite different than valuing the *raison d'être* of the social entity as the care of the individual, e.g., Pl. *Lg.* 9.875). Rather this individualistic anthropology arose with the Renaissance differentiation of the "humanities" from the "divinities" as a legitimate field of intellectual inquiry (*vide* "humanity. 4" *OED* 1971: 1346), and a concurrent emergence of an individualistic ideology, including individualistic psychology, the assumptions of which are so compatible with Reformation principles (*vide* "psychology: Note", *OED* 1971: 2347). While questions concerning individual religious experience may and certainly have been posed of such religions as Hinduism or Confucianism, they would seem to impose rather than reveal much of salience concerning such ritually and socially structured systems. Emotivist theories of religion are, in other words, culturally specific and, consequently, do not offer valid generalizations for the historical or comparative study of religion.

In contrast to individualistic psychologies, cognitive psychology offers a promising theoretical alternative in that it is concerned with those mental processes that are common to all humans. Since environmental (perceptual, cultural) input is attributed significance only as it is processed by human minds, the workings of the mind becomes central for understanding the production of any cultural formation, including the religious. This is not to suggest that attempts to map the workings of the mind will finally establish some sort of innate human "need" for religion; such mappings seek rather to identify a common mental architecture which has constrained the construction of a virtually infinite variety of human systems of meanings. In this regard also, cognitive psychology offers a promising alternative in that it seeks empirical, i.e., intersubjective validity for its conclusions. (For sustained attempts to connect cognition and culture specifically with reference to religion, see Lawson & McCauley 1990 and Boyer 1992, 1994.)

The alternative examples of psychological theories of religion, individualistic and collective, draw our attention to a second feature of theoretical generalization. Since such generalizations must be tested against the same comparative and historical data upon which the generalizations were based in the first place, it is *theory* and not data that finally determines our view of religion. Since theoretical formulations, as the example of emotivist theory suggests, are themselves subject to the historical influences of religious, political, economic, etc. interests, they must in turn be themselves rigorously subjected to their historical situation and to critical reflection.

II

The theory of religion with which I work (currently, at least) is that religion is (a) a social system (b) legitimated by claims to the authority of some superhuman power. This theoretical formulation offers a provisional or hypothetical sociological definition to be tested against the empirical research of cognitive psychology, on the one hand, and against comparative and historical research, on the other. Does this theory explain the greatest amount of data in terms of these two features? Do significant exceptions remain? or does the theory so over-determine the data to be selected that exceptions are *a priori* ruled out? Does the theory differentiate that which it explains from functionally similar systems?

Human beings, social scientists and philosophers seem to agree, are social animals, as the universal existence of human language, i.e., the means of intersubjective communication, argues. This sociability is apparently an innate characteristic of the species, whether the structures of this trait be explained as cultural elaborations of biology (Boyer, 1990, Burkert, 1996) or as the consequence of a domain-specific competence of the human mind (Hirschfeld, 1994). We can, in any case, conclude that such cultural products as religion are, at least, social facts.

Human beings organize their social productions systemically, which, to take our clue again from language, may be viewed as the establishment of closed sets of relationships in which the value of interdependent elements results solely from the simultaneous presence of the others (Saussure 1966: 114). Following the work of W. Robertson Smith, anthropologists identify but two types of social systems: "kinship" and "kingship" (W. R. Smith [1889] 1972: ch. 2). Smith defined "kinship societies" as those in which "[e]very human being, without choice on his own part, but simply in virtue of his birth and upbringing, becomes a member of" (W. R. Smith 1972: 29) – a notion of "natural societies" that may be traced from Aristotle (*Pol.* I. 1.4-6). By contrast, Smith defines "kingship" as a transformation of kinship groups into "an aristocracy of the more powerful kins" with a consequent unequal distribution of wealth (W. R. Smith 1972: 73). The difference between these two types might be summarized as a difference in the social distribution of power. Whereas power in kinship societies is disseminated more or less equally throughout the society (W. R. Smith 1972: 73), kingships are characterized by consolidations of power (see Sagan 1985: 236, 240; Martin 1997a and 1997b). These two types of societies are, of course, "ideal"; historical societies represent sundry incremental variations between these two types.

Social distributions of power may be differentiated further into specialized systems such as the political – concerned with the structures of power, the economic – concerned with rules of exchange, the ethical – concerned with principles of right relationship, the aesthetic – concerned with criteria of pleasure, etc. The special function of religious systems is to identify and maintain the markers of collective identity for the social entity – its history, for example, is often narrated in terms of origins from such superhuman powers as heroes or deities, its boundaries defined in such terms as ritual purity/impurity – and to establish the legitimacy of these markers by appeal to the authority of superhuman power. Such claims to legitimacy are claims to privilege deemed unavailable to "others", unless they too become subject to those claims and, consequently, to that group claiming legitimation on the basis of those claims. Such claims to legitimacy may escalate religious claims to the proposition that the religious system, especially though not necessarily when it operates in consort with the political system (Dumont 1980), is the system of systems, whether for a particular social entity or for an idealized and universalized utopia.

Whether and how religious systems are differentiated from their sibling systems is the consequence of their particular histories. In Judeo-Christian-Islamic cultures, for example, religions systems are identified with the moral, whereas in ancient Greece, morality was not deemed the purview of religion but of the intellectual system (philosophy). In the United States, the religious and the political systems are constitutionally separate but in ancient Greece and Rome, the former is embedded in the latter while in some contemporary Islamic cultures they are juridically identified.

Although systems common to a particular social group may be differentiated according to some specialized function, they replicate one another formally, not only as constructs constrained by common cognitive processes (Sperber 1996: 101) but also as structures produced by a common social history. Confederations of kinship societies, for example, tend towards confederations of kin deities, or towards polytheism, whereas condensations of power in kingship societies tend to be characterized by some form of heno- or monotheism. In this perspective, religion is a social system that is formally identical to any other system in a given society. Whether or not they are identified with their sibling systems, embedded within or deemed to be independent of them, the analytical *differentia* for religious systems remains their claims to the authority of superhuman power.

Superhuman power may be imagined anthropomorphically or theriomorphically as in the case of theistic systems, or dendromorphically, petromorphically, etc. as in the case of "animistic" systems, or abstractly, as exemplified by the Chinese notion of "Tao" – which in the context of that culture is itself further imaginable aesthetically ("Taoism"), ethically, socially, politically ("Confusicanism"), theistically (in "traditional" local practices), etc. Further, superhuman power may be imagined as supernatural. The Olympian deities of ancient Greece, for example, were understood as superhuman but not supernatural: whereas they were possessed of greater power than humans, they were nevertheless still subject to the same laws of nature (i.e., fate). The creator deity of Christianity, however, is imagined (anthropologically) as a supernatural power, standing above the nature he created and capable of altering its very laws (e.g., miracle). In other words, all supernatural images are superhuman but not all superhuman images are supernatural.

By analytically differentiating religion from other social systems in terms of claims to superhuman power, we are able to avoid the functionalist tendency of analyzing virtually anything and everything as "religion". This definition precludes, for example, the popular cold-war-era analysis of Marxism as a "religion" (if a demonic one!), for whatever one might conclude of Marxism, its appeal to legitimacy is not to superhuman power but to a materialistic historical dialectic. Similarly, Freud's appeal to the inevitable and ubiquitous conflict between nature (id) and the environment (civilization, internalized as superego) as the explanation for the dynamics of the psyche precludes, by the definition under consideration, the analysis of Freudianism as a religion – although Jungianism, it would seem, well conforms to the criteria of religion here suggested (Noll 1997).

The generalization about religion as a social system legitimated by claims to the authority of superhuman power is, admittedly, a minimalist theory of religion. Although it does account for a large amount of religious data, more so, I would argue, than the two theories mentioned earlier and the one briefly essayed, and it does so while still distinguishing religious from non-religious systems, it does so in a wholly formal way. Like any social system, however, religion is a *human* affair. It remains for specialized scholars of the various religious systems and of their traditions to amplify such formal analyses of religious systems with those historically produced and transmitted social practices, both discursive and non-discursive, which establish each and every religion system as a unique system of meaning for its participants and practitioners.

III

If the academic study of religion should conform to the same protocol as the academic study of *anything*, then the role of the scholar of religion should conform to that which is appropriate to academic study generally. This academic study, nowhere defined more clearly and forthrightly than by Max Weber, should be "in the service of self-clarification [what I have meant by theory] and knowledge of interrelated facts [what I have meant by systems]." The academic study of religion, Weber continues, should "not [be conceived as] the gift of grace of seers and prophets dispensing sacred values and revelations, nor does it partake of the contemplation of sages and philosophers about the meaning of the universe" (Weber 1919: 152). This is religious *practice*. "In the lecture rooms of the university," Weber concluded, "no other virtue holds but plain intellectual integrity" (Weber 1919: 156). "Integrity" is a value often invoked, within the academy and without, as a noble virtue devoid, however, of much specificity. I invoke it here, in the spirit of Weber, to indicate commitment to the academic ideal of theoretically based inquiry leading to explanatory principles supported by intersubjective conclusions.

Unlike some earlier attempts to limit the study of religion to an empathetic understanding of others, such intellectual integrity in the academy requires this study be a *critical* discipline as well. As such, the role of the scholar of religion must finally include a responsibility to venture judgements about religions. Such critique might be of religious claims which are based upon common sense, on the one hand, or of those born of propaganda, on the other. Vico defined common sense, a consequence of the social nature of human beings, as "judgement without reflection, shared by an entire class, an entire people, an entire nation, or the entire human race" (Vico 1970: 21), an example of which are the views of religion as experiential discussed above. Propaganda, on the other hand, is the ideological challenge to social consensus by special interest groups (Merton 1968: 160, 563), whether those groups might be exemplified by some new religious movement interested in propagating its own view of religion or the study of such groups from a particular ideological perspective even if in the context of the academy itself. Neither common sense nor propaganda are necessarily false; neither, however, do common assumptions nor fervent advocacy establish validity. Born of comparative as of specialized research, the critical assessment of religious claims as well as of explanatory generalizations about religions constitute finally the public task of the scholar of religion.

Note

1. The following example is taken from Martin 1993: 76-77, and used here by permission; see also Martin 1994: n. 53.

References

Boyer, Pascal, *Tradition as Truth and Communication: A Cognitive Description of Traditional Discourse*, Cambridge University Press, Cambridge, 1990.

– "Explaining religious ideas: Elements of a cognitive approach, *Numen* 39, 1992: 27-57.

Burkert, Walter, *Creation of the Sacred: Tracks of Biology in Early Religions*, Harvard University Press, Cambridge, MA, 1996.

Dumont, Louis, *Homo Hierarchicus: The Case System and Its Implications*, rev. ed., University of Chicago Press, Chicago, 1980.

Dupré, Louis, "Mysticism", in Eliade, Mircea (Gen. Ed.), *Encyclopedia of Religion*, Macmillan, New York, 1987, 10: 245-261.

Edwards, Jonathan, *Religious Affections*, Smith, John E. (Ed.), in Miller, Perry (Gen. Ed.), *The Works of Jonathan Edwards*, vol. 2, Yale University Press, New Haven, 1959.

Gabriel, Ralph H., "Evangelical religion and popular romanticism in early nineteenth-century America", *Church History* 19, 1950: 34-47.

Gottschalk, Louis, "Forward", in Gottschalk, Louis (Ed.), *Generalization in the Writing of History*, The University of Chicago Press, Chicago, 1963: v-xii.

Hirschfeld, Lawrence A., "Is the acquisition of social categories based on domain-specific competence or on knowledge transfer?", in Hirschfeld, L. A. and Gelman, S. A. (Eds.), *Mapping the Mind: Domain Specificity in Cognition and Culture*, Cambridge University Press, Cambridge, 1994: 201-233.

James, William, *The Varieties of Religious Experience*, The Modern Library, New York, 1902.

Lodge, David, *Small World*, Warner Books, New York, 1984.

Lawson, E. Thomas and Robert N. McCauley, *Rethinking Religion:*
Connecting Cognition and Culture, Cambridge University Press, Cambridge, 1990.

Martin, Luther H., "The academic study of religion in the United States", *Religio, Revue pro Religionistiku* 1, 1993: 73-80

- "The Anti-individualistic ideology of Hellenistic culture", *Numen* 41, 1994: 117-140.
- "Akin to the gods or simply one to another? Comparison with respect to religions in antiquity", in *Vergleichen und Verstehen in der Religionswissenschaft*, in Klimkeit, Hans-Joachim (Ed.), Harrassowitz, Wiesbaden, 1997a.
- "Biology, sociology and the study of religion: Two lectures", *Religio, Revue pro Religionistiku* 5, 1997b: 21-35.
- "Rationality and relativity in history of religions research", in *Rationality and the Study of Religion*, Jensen, Jeppe Sinding and Martin, Luther H. (Eds.), Aarhus University Press, Aarhus, 1997c.
- "Comparison", in Braun, Willi and McCutcheon, Russell T. (Eds.), *Guide to the Study of Religion*, Cassell Academic, London 2000.

Merton, R. K., *Social Theory and Social Structure*, Free Press, New York, 1968.

Miller, Perry, *Jonathan Edwards*, W. Sloane Associates, New York, 1949.

Noll, Richard, *The Aryan Christ: The Secret Life of Carl Jung*, Random House, New York, 1997.

OED, *Oxford English Dictionary, The Compact Edition*, Oxford University Press, New York, 1971.

Otto, Rudolf, *The Idea of the Holy*, Harvey, J. W. (Trans.), Oxford University Press, New York, 1958.

Sagan, Eli, *At the Dawn of Tyranny: The Origins of Individualism. Political Oppression and the State*, Alfred A. Knopf, New York, 1985.

Saussure, Ferdinand de, *Course in General Linguistics*, Bally, C., Sechehaye, A., Riedlinger, A. (Eds.), Baskin, W. (Trans.), McGraw-Hill, New York, 1966.

Schleiermacher, Friedrich, *On Religion: Speeches to Its Cultured Despisers*, Oman, J. (Trans.), Harper and Brothers, New York, 1958.

Smith, Jonathan Z. (Ed.), "Theory", in *The HarperCollins Dictionary of Religion*, HarperCollins, San Francisco, 1995: 1068-1070.

Smith, W. Robertson, *The Religion of the Semites: The Fundamental Institutions* [1889], Schocken, New York, 1972.

Sperber, Dan, *Explaining Culture: A Naturalistic Approach*, Blackwell, Oxford, 1996.

Weber, Max, "Science as a vocation" [1919] in: *From Max Weber: Essays in Sociology*, Gerth, H. H. and Mills, C. Wright (Trans. and Eds.), Oxford University Press, New York, 1946.

Whitehead, Alfred North, *Religion in the Making*, Cambridge University Press, Cambridge, 1926.

Suggested Readings

Jensen, Jeppe Sinding and Martin, Luther H. (Eds.), *Rationality and the Study of Religion*, Aarhus University Press, Aarhus, 1997.

Martin, Luther H. (Ed.), *History, Historiography and the History of Religions*, special issue of *Historical Reflections/Réflexions Historiques* 20, 1994.

McCutcheon, Russell T., *Manufacturing Religion: The Discourse on sui generis Religion and the Politics of Nostalgra*, New York/Oxford: Oxford University Press, 1997.
Wiebe, Donald, *The Politics of Religious Studies: The Continuing Conflict with Theology in the Academy*, St. Martin's Press, New York, 1999.

From Theology to World Religions:

Ernst Troeltsch and the Making of *Religionsgeschichte*

Tomoko Masuzawa

Associate Professor at the Program in Comparative Literature
University of Michigan, Ann Arbor, MI, USA

Few people today seem to question the truism that *religion* is everywhere; that there have been diverse *religions* throughout the world and through-out history. Indeed, it is generally assumed that the world can be mapped, and world history charted – though not very neatly – in terms of so many religions swarming the earth. Accordingly, the scholarly field of "religious studies" – and by implication the individual scholar as well – is mapped onto this virtual terrain. In view of the overwhelming truth-effect of the world-religions discourse, it seems all the more incumbent on us students of religion not to start our business having already bought into this imag-ined or imaginary topography. We should rather be prepared to position our scholarly practice at an oblique, critical angle to this plane of map-ping.[1]

To assess the exigencies of our present positioning, we might recall the situation of an earlier generation of scholars, who resolved to regard theo-logical apologetics as at once a fact (that is, as a certain mass of data to be taken into account) *and* a problem (something to be dealt with and kept at bay). In an analogous way, we are confronted by the powerful yet innocuous-sounding discourse of world religions as at once an incontro-vertible fact and an enormous problem. One might add, extrapolating from this analogy, that just as it was not God but rather the overbearing institution of theological discourse that needed to be dodged and objecti-fied then, it is not religions as such (whatever they are) but rather the growing and monopolizing enterprise of world-religions discourse that needs to be at once kept at arm's length and actively analyzed now.

I am not sure if an attempt at resisting, disengaging, or obliquely engag-ing this growth industry of a discourse necessarily guarantees one's posi-tion as properly critical, scholarly, and/or secular. I wonder, for that matter, whether the condition of being secular is in the last analysis a useful category in describing or legitimating one's scholarly practice today. Being secular, in the sense relevant to academics, appears to imply a particular intellectual and moral attitude of vigilance and abstinence. This attitude has been historically (and overwhelmingly) determined by the complicated, highly ambivalent relation many a *Religionswissenschaftler* hitherto has had to certain strands of (mostly Christian, mostly Protestant) theology. As such, the pertinence of the religious-secular dichotomy itself seems rather provincial. It has a way of distracting our attention from where it is due: the more imperious discursive practice and ideology in which we have been entrenched for a century.

My starting point, then, is this basic recognition: if by scholars of religion we mean those of us who are making a living in the domain of the lately dominant world-religions discourse while capitalizing on its impressive market value, we cannot simply assume that our line of work is intellectually responsible just because it is economically viable. As a way of driving a small critical wedge into the seamlessly prevalent, thoroughly naturalized ideology of world religions, this essay will focus on a particular moment in the history of that discursive formation, a moment when an eminent theologian, Ernst Troeltsch, subtly reconfigured his vocation in view of a new reality around him, in two of his essays written twenty-five years apart.

The career of Ernst Troeltsch (1865-1923) roughly spanned the period of transformation in the meaning of the terms "world religions," from the frankly evaluative sense (*qua* "universal religions," which meant certainly Christianity, probably Buddhism, and possibly Islam) to the avowedly neutral and inclusive sense (*qua* "living religions of the world").[2] As someone positioned to be a pivot in this historic turn, Troeltsch's situation could be described in multiple ways: while he was thoroughly schooled in the idealist and historicist traditions of the German academy, he increasingly gained an audience in the English speaking world; while he was a systematic theologian, he is also counted among the earliest sociologists of religion; in effect, he was a leading Christian spokesperson by profession, and at the same time a pioneering "historian of religion" of a particular sort.

It is to be remembered that, in the course of the nineteenth century, "history" was becoming an academic vocation, as it was being gradually dissociated from merely antiquarian or moral interests and emerging instead as an essential scientific discipline foundational to all areas of human sciences, or *Geisteswissenschaften.* It is generally understood, moreover, that Germany, and German universities in particular, were the fountainhead of this intellectual current running across Europe and beyond. Concurrently, detailed and systematic studies of the textual sources of various ancient civilizations were gathering force. One of the most prominent emblems of this surge in serious scholarship, which helped enhance, consolidate, and organize the knowledge of the great religious systems, was the compilation of the fifty-volume compendium, *The Sacred Books of the East,* a massive international collaborative effort carried out under the general editorship of F. Max Müller, the reputed founder of the *Religionswissenschaft*. It was also during this time that terms like "comparative religion" and "history of religion(s)" were becoming familiar designations for new types of scientific discourse and for those endeavors motivated principally by philological, archaeological, and anthropological – rather than confessional and missionary – interests.

As a chief exponent of the history-of-religions school (*Religionsgeschichteschule*), Troeltsch was arguably the first and the foremost among the systematic theologians who took the reality of other religions to heart. As his 1897 essay, "Christianity and the History of Religion," announces in no uncertain terms, his highly cultivated historical consciousness – which he credits to his German education – drove him to concede that "the rise of a comparative history of religion has shaken the Christian more deeply than anything else" (Troeltsch 1991, pub. 1897: 77).

This sentiment – that the reality and actuality of other religions and other cultures somehow had a profoundly unsettling effect on the presumptions and self-confidence of Christian orthodoxy and its institutions – has been pervasive and persistent to this day, so much so that probably few would deem it necessary to transport one's thought back to that time and ask why such a momentous crisis of confidence should have taken place just then. Viewed historically, this turn of events, if true, could not have been a result of some educated Europeans beginning to have higher opinions of some long-standing Oriental societies. For, if most inhabitants of the nineteenth century seemed to have had little respect for Orientals, they had simply "forgotten" what their eighteenth-century predecessors "knew." That is to say, many of the pre-nineteenth-century European literati – whose outlook was by no means hidebound but rather progressive and frankly revolutionary – were in the habit of harboring highly positive, in fact unrealistically elevated images of venerable Oriental societies, particularly when it came to the ancient Egyptian dynasties and the Chinese Empire. These regimes were typically fantasized and touted – especially by the Freemasons and other exponents of the Radical Enlightenment – as the epitome of an admirably stable civilization governed by the universal principle of Reason (cf. Marshall and Williams 1982; Reichwein, 1925; Bernal 1987: 161-188). All the same, this Oriento-mania of eighteenth-century Europeans apparently proved no detriment to their self-esteem or to their own universalist ideals. Much to the annoyance of these Enlightenment intellectuals, the old, unenlightened regime of European Christendom and its functionaries, far from faltering in the face of the increasing reports on other religions, remained recalcitrantly stable, defiantly unshaken.

Admittedly, what appears to have been unsettling was not the mere knowledge of the non-European and non-Christian societies but rather the discovery of historicity itself, the realization, in other words, that no one, no body of knowledge, and no vantage point escapes the pall of historicity, that is, the particular and contingent determinations of its own moment. The new historical sensibility not only brought to the forefront the incontrovertible actuality of non-Christian peoples; a decidedly more devastating consequence for "us," the European Christians, in Troeltsch's view, was that it brought home "the mutability of Christianity ... it destroyed the Catholic fiction that the church simply represented the continuation of original Christianity, as well as the Protestant fiction that the Reformation represented its restoration" (Troeltsch 1991: 77). Historical consciousness, or historicism of the nineteenth century, had, or was felt to have had, a profound leveling effect on all truth-claims and values, including those of religion. It seemingly had an effect of cutting Christianity down to size, relegating it to the status of just one of many religions around.[3] As Troeltsch puts it: "Christianity lost its exclusive-supernatural foundation. It was now perceived as only one of the great world religions, along with Islam and Buddhism, and like these, as constituting the culmination of complicated historical developments" (p. 78).

This relativizing tendency of thought had been summarily denounced as "the most prevalent form of unbelief" only half a century earlier by Frederick Denison Maurice, the first prominent author of so-called comparative theology. But now it appears that even the systematic theologians, the apparent spokespersons for the confessional community, could not summarily dismiss it. Equipped as he was with ever greater knowledge of the past and a heightened sense of historicity nurtured by Germanic scientific training, Troeltsch could no longer respond to the challenges of history by simply reiterating and amplifying the universalist-supremacist claim of Christianity as Maurice, Bishop Wordsworth, and James Freeman Clarke and others had done (Maurice 1846; Clarke 1871; Wordsworth 1893). Inevitably, then, the theologian came to confront the perturbing questions: "What would become now of Christianity's exclusive truth or even of its decisive superiority? Above all, what would become of the belief in an exclusive revelation?" (Troeltsch 1991: 78).

Troeltsch does not issue an answer to these ominous questions. What is remarkable is that he, without missing a beat, changes the subject and converts what is clearly a problem of threats specifically directed to the authority of Christianity (i.e., threats to its exclusive validity over against all other religions) into a problem of threats to *religion in general.* Thus he continues without pause: "But the consequences go even further. Not only the truth and validity of Christianity but also those of *religion itself, as a unique sphere of life,* disappear in this maelstrom of historical diversity" (78; emphasis added). This conversion is immediate and without explanation or apology, so much so that the reader is afforded no time to take stock of its significance. Troeltsch himself is obviously aware of this transitive moment, if only to the extent that he feels the need to assure his reader that this shift is but a matter of "going further."

But this is surely more than a question of going further. At this textual juncture, not only does Troeltsch shift the attention away from the immediate difficulty facing the confessional Christian community, but by so doing he also conjures up, out of thin air, something like "religion itself, as a unique sphere of life." To be sure, it is difficult for us today not to be taken in by this rhetorical move that glosses over an evasion and non-sequitur, saturated as we are by the world-religions discourse; for this discourse unequivocally takes for granted this very notion of "religion" as a "unique sphere of life" and presumes this sphere to be prevalent throughout the world and throughout history. Neither was Troeltsch lacking, for that matter, in a sympathetic audience among the comparative historians of religion of his own time. Max Müller and Rudolf Otto, for example, like Troeltsch himself, had a personal commitment to Christian faith as well as a sentimental attachment to the notion that all human beings without exception were endowed with some distinct and irreducible capability or sensibility specific to the Infinite, the Holy, the Absolute. On the basis of this conviction, they probably took some comfort privately in the thought that this made all human beings potential Christians, even if they are not in actuality. Liberal Christians like Troeltsch and Otto were by then generally prepared to accept the fact of religious diversity and respect the viability of "other religions" – and to do so has been more or less a matter of good public policy ever since – provided that they could remain entitled to their private thoughts as a matter of "faith."

Notwithstanding the compelling power of these opinions, notwithstanding, moreover, our well-schooled habit of believing rather moralistically that somehow this segregation of the private from the public, as well as the non-aggression pact that this arrangement makes possible, is for the good of humanity, let us take a moment and insist: Whatever happened to the question of the "decisive superiority" of Christianity? What about its "belief in an exclusive revelation"? Why does Troeltsch evade this issue and, if the answer seems rather obvious, we might as well ask: whence comes this conjuring of a new problem instead?

In the paragraphs immediately following the passage quoted above, "religion itself" – which has suddenly made its appearance out of the blue – comes to be endowed with a sense of reality of majestic proportions, not through demonstration but by the sheer force of elocution. Here, it is "history" that turns around and comes to the aid of the theologian at the crossroads. As Troeltsch goes on to suggest, if historical-scientific knowledge was what brought about the crisis of faith, it is also a historical science (*qua* history of religion) that could bring new knowledge to bear on the reality of the "unique sphere" that is religion.[4] But in order for that to happen,

> We simply must learn to view religion more sympathetically; to free ourselves
> from doctrinaire, rationalistic, and systematizing presuppositions; and to focus

more intently on the characteristic, distinctively religious phenomena and personages rather than on average people. *Then the deepest core of the religious history of humanity reveals itself as an experience that cannot be further analyzed, an ultimate and original phenomenon that constitutes,* like moral judgment and aesthetic perception and yet with characteristic differences, *a simple fact of psychic life. Everywhere the basic reality of religion is the same: an underivable, purely positive, again and again experienced contact with the Deity* [emphases added]. This unity has its ground in a common dynamism of the human spirit which advances in different ways as a result of the mysterious movement of the divine Spirit in the unconscious depth of the human spirit, which is everywhere the same. Unable to attain its goal in the short span of individual life, this movement is effected through the co-operative efforts of countless generations as they are grasped and led by the divine activity, surrendering to it and experiencing its true import in ever greater fullness and profoundness. (Troeltsch 1991: 79)

And a little later, he reiterates this concerning the matter of affinity – if not to say identity – of religions, expressed above in theological terms, in a manner more directly resonant with the ecumenical language of world-religions comparativists:

If we go beyond the accidents of time and space, personality and tradition, we find everywhere a very similar truth. We note a great sense of awe before the mystery of a supersensible world that speaks its word within the course of everyday life: whether it comforts people or frightens them, it always disrupts the slumber of a purely innerworldly existence. We also note the manifestation of divine forces in nature, and the authorization of moral and legal norms on the part of the Deity. Above all we note the higher goods of eternal blessedness and the rise of the belief in redemption. All these phenomena are properly viewed as belonging together, as requiring a unified, comprehensive treatment. (p. 81)

The frankness of these assertions is useful. Even if this undisguised universalism expressed by sheer force of dogmatic declaration is unnerving to the contemporary scholar of religion, the idea itself seems to be consistent with those of the key twentieth-century exponents of history and phenomenology of religion, including Otto, G. van der Leeuw, Eliade, and others; as such, it is an idea ingrained in the discourse of world religions and, by implication or by association, in the enterprise of religious studies. Even if some of us would rather contest than accept this presumption of the unity of "religious experience" as the basis of our discipline, there is little doubt that this is how the academy of religion scholars is perceived from without, and by some from within as well.

To cite a recent incident illustrating this point, in the spring of 1996 a postcard was sent to the members of the American Academy of Religion in the name of Bill Moyers, announcing the forthcoming broadcast of his interviews with Huston Smith entitled "The Wisdom of the Faith." On this note Moyers describes the Academy as an organization "dedicated to exploring, affirming, and educating the public about the religious dimension of human existence," and his guest, also a member of the Academy, as one who "has immersed himself in the world's great religions, seeking to discover the distilled wisdom of the human race." This odd missive to the Academy from somewhere within should come as no surprise to anyone who has lately sampled books on world religions. For, from the elementary logic and the rhetoric of these texts, one gets a definite impression that the business of religious studies is indeed, as Moyers puts it, "to let the best in each faith shine through [our] understanding" after a due immersion in the world's great religions. It is as though, by virtue of being members of this professional guild, we were subscribers by default to some versions of Troeltschean thesis, or to the idea of the essential unity, *au fond,* of the divergent religions, with a heavy emphasis on the inviolably authentic depth of experience.

The idea of the complementary contrast between the surface differences and the depth affinity of all religions, of course, may be called a rather old idea put to a new use – the idea at least as old as English Deists, many of whom opined that "religion" as a genus is one, whereas its "sects" and "denominations" as species are many (cf. Lash 1996; Pailin 1984). Whereas the Deists often got into trouble with authorities for their views in their days, we on the contrary would be hard pressed now to find a religion writer who dares to contradict the notion of the fundamental commonality or unity of religions. The disciplinary establishment of religious studies today seems to hold fast to this bottom line: Religion is found everywhere; it is an essential and irreducible aspect of human life; it should be studied.

And if we take into consideration the constitution of the Academy as a whole, it seems to imply also: it should be studied concertedly, comparatively.

Meanwhile, it should be remembered that, to his credit, the lessons of history that Troeltsch drew in due course were considerably more nuanced and thoughtful than those earlier quotations would suggest. As he was to conclude in an essay written a quarter of a century later, what history was apt to exhibit, in his view, was not unity and universality at all but, on the contrary, individuality:

> History cannot be regarded as a process in which a universal and everywhere similar principle is confined and obscured. Nor is it a continual mixing and remixing of elemental psychical powers, which indicate a general trend of things towards a rational end or goal of evolution. *It is rather an immeasurable, incomparable profusion of always-new, unique, and hence individual tendencies, welling up from undiscovered depths*, and coming to light in each case in unsuspected places and under different circumstances. [...] Thus the universal law of history consists precisely in this, that the Divine Reason, or the Divine Life, within history, constantly manifests itself in always-new and always-peculiar individualizations – and hence its tendency is not towards unity or universality at all ... It is this law which, beyond all else, makes it quite impossible to characterize Christianity as the reconciliation and goal of all the forces of history, or indeed to regard it as anything else than a historical individuality. (Troeltsch 1957, pub. 1923: 44-45)

Here, with a single stroke empowered both by the authority of German systematic theology and by the equally formidable authority of German historical science, Troeltsch definitively severs the question of the absolute validity – or absoluteness, as he puts it – of Christianity from the question of its universality in the empirical-objective sense. For what he says here is tantamount to a declaration that, for any foreseeable future, or perhaps for the entire duration of history that remains, the claim for the universality of Christianity – or of any religion – is destined to remain strictly a matter of conviction interior to a person or to a race, and that the source of such conviction is ultimately "the evidence of a profound inner experience"

(55) and nothing else. It is above all this interior of *experience* that he and many historians of religions after him have admonished us to view "more sympathetically"; accordingly, we have been advised, we must "free ourselves from doctrinaire, rationalistic, and systematizing presuppositions," so that we may discern "the deepest core of the religious history of humanity."

In sum, the question of the absoluteness and the universality of Christianity is finally brought to a standstill, as the problem comes to rest in a state of profound ambivalence. For, on the one hand, it is no longer tenable, if one is to remain consistent with the lessons of history, to count on the future hegemony and universality of Christianity in any overt, material, and historical sense. But on the other hand the dream of unity and universality is very much viable, it seems, in the dominion of "undiscovered depths" that are said to be revealed time and again in certain recondite recesses of human experience, the kind of experience "that cannot be further analyzed, an ultimate and original phenomenon that constitutes ... a simple fact of psychic life." This latter domain, for all its inaccessibility – or perhaps precisely because of it – constitutes a much more durable, difficult to refute, morally sacrosanct basis for a belief in unity and universality, whether such a belief is held as an article of faith or as a heuristic principle.

There is, however, a significant price to be paid for such a reconfiguration and re-authorization of theological absolutism. By *psychologizing* the question of absolute validity in this manner and by turning the meaning of the absoluteness of a theological claim into something strictly interior to a person or to a "race," Troeltsch implicitly accepts as given the individuality and plurality of believers and of "races." The elemental assumption here is that different persons and different peoples adhere to different ideas of foundational truth within their own personal or "racial" psychic life, and that each of these ideas carries with it its own absolute conviction and universalistic appeal, and, taken together, these separate psychic interiors are mutually inviolable, non-negotiable, and irreconcilable. What can, by contrast, be defended and advocated in the exterior realm, that is to say, in the non-theological or non-confessional public discourse, is therefore no longer Christianity or any other religion in particular, but "religion itself, as a unique sphere of life."

If this situation seems rather grim for theologians – indeed, disastrous for their prospect as public intellectuals – it was a great boon for the historians of religions then in ascendancy. This historical juncture may very well have been an unprecedented opportunity to reconfigure and re-fit a theologian into a new career as a historian of religion, as exemplified by Troeltsch himself.[5] At the same time, this moment also makes visible the origin, so to speak, of the suddenly powerful idea of "religion" as such, or in Troeltsch's own words, "religion itself, as a unique sphere of life." After all, this concept of religion as a general, trans-cultural phenomenon yet also a distinct sphere in its own right is a foundational premise essential to the enterprise of history of religions as the latter is envisioned by Troeltsch and others. But this concept is patently groundless; it came from nowhere, and there is no credible way of demonstrating it factually and empirically. Only when we are already compelled by the assumption – and we often seem to be – that religion is thus unique and universal, are we sure to find it confirmed everywhere, like a figure in the carpet. Furthermore, as we witness the emergence of the idea in this instance, it becomes evident that, from the beginning, this abstraction of an idea came fully endowed with all the weight and the moral charge – one might call it *cathexis (Besetzung)* – once in the domain of liberal Protestant theology, now that this theology has found itself up against the wall of its own undeniable historicity.

But this is not all. Troeltsch's intellectual passage eventually went beyond this familiar domain of classic world-religions discourse, where historians recover the unique genius of each "tradition," comparativists demonstrate diversity, plurality, and affinity among "traditions," theologians confess and confirm the absoluteness of their "tradition" when they are among their own kind and, when with others, speak the language of ecumenical empathy, and everyone claims to believe in the authenticity of experience and in the deep unity of all religions in their universal yearning for spirituality and peace.

As we recall, Troeltsch argued that the absoluteness of (each) religion is not only a matter of an individual personal conviction but also something intrinsic and interior collectively to a particular *race*. This, it appears, is a necessary implication of his understanding that all cultures and religions are historically determined and therefore particular. In his view, the dominion of a religion gradually comes to be shaped and circumscribed by a specific race in the course of history, irrespective, it seems, of the place of origination of that religion. What this means in the case of Christianity is as follows:

> It is historical facts that have welded Christianity into the closest connection with the civilizations of Greece, Rome and Northern Europe. All our thoughts and feelings are impregnated with Christian motives and Christian presuppositions; and, conversely, our whole Christianity is indissolubly bound up with elements of the ancient and modern civilizations of Europe. From being a Jewish sect Christianity has become the religion of all Europe. It stands or falls with European civilization; whilst, on its own part, it has entirely lost its Oriental character and has become hellenized and westernized. Our European conceptions of personality and its eternal, divine right, and of progress towards a kingdom of the spirit and of God, our enormous capacity for expansion and for the interconnection of spiritual and temporal, our whole social order, our science, our art – all these rest, whether we know it or not, whether we like it or not, upon the basis of this deorientalised Christianity. (Troeltsch 1957: 53-54)

This view is consistent with those of many nineteenth- and twentieth-century writers intent on appropriating Christianity fully and exclusively for the west while drawing a delicate line of separation between the European Christianity and its Semitic-Oriental origin. Once Christian religion is permanently – "indissolubly" – fused with the historical destiny of Europe and its recent triumphs, there resurfaces anew, in Troeltsch's writing, the question of the universality of Christianity and, concomitantly, the question of its *exclusive* validity. This resurgence, as might be expected, is not without some ominous implications.

Troeltsch himself however does not seem to harbor any misgivings – or irony, for that matter – when he finally proclaims that Christianity's "primary claim to validity is thus the fact that only through it have we become what we are ..." (p. 54). And when he suggests that without Christianity "we can lapse either into a self destructive titanic attitude, or into effeminate trifling, or into brutality" (p. 54), there is nothing particularly self-chastising about this assertion, as it becomes clearer presently. Scarcely a page later he goes on to proclaim, with sobering clarity, this:

160

> Christianity could not be the religion of such a highly developed racial group if it did not possess a mighty spiritual power and truth; in short, if it were not, in some degree, a manifestation of the Divine Life itself. (p. 55)

There is something nearly fatalistic – in fact, tragic, in the Romantic sense of the word – about this sense of European destiny, which is now for Troeltsch clearly a palimpsest for the religion of a self-sacrificing god. For, as he goes on to reflect – the year is 1923 – in the wake of the Great War and in the shadow of his own approaching death,

> our life is a consistent compromise as little unsatisfactory as we can manage between [Christianity's] lofty spirituality and our practical everyday needs ... This tension is characteristic of our form of human life and rouses us to many a heroic endeavor, though it may also lead us into the most terrible mendacity and crime. Thus we are, and thus we shall remain, as long as we survive. We cannot live without a religion, yet the only religion that we can endure is Christianity, for Christianity has grown up with us and has become a part of our very being. (pp. 54-56)

What is most remarkable here is not so much the melodramatic self-con-gratulatory appraisal of Christian Europe – after all, there is nothing new about that – but rather the forcefulness of the fusion between a religion and a historical cultural domain, and, as its corollary, the compelling notion that Christendom *qua* Europe constitutes a well-bounded totality. Some of the immediate consequences of these ideas are disturbing. For one, this would mean that only those Europeans who "have grown up" with Christianity – for generations, presumably, and not those oppor-tunistic or recent converts – would count as real Europeans. Conversely, those who are Christians but whose birthplace and/or ancestry is else-where would be only secondarily Christians, as it were. They are either fossil remnants of some stunted growth and illicit offshoots that failed to become part of the vital mainstream (i.e., heretics, renegades, para- and pseudo-Christians), or else recent converts, above all in the colonies, who are only vicariously or subordinately Christian. In either case, according to this view, the identity of such a non-European Christian must be pre-sumed to be essentially split, and one wonders how such a person or such a people with a constitutionally divided subjectivity is to be positioned

161

with respect to the absoluteness of Christianity. Furthermore, in this conceptual framework where a religion and a civilization are made coeval and considered a totality, it is difficult to conceive of any kind of border region without evoking the problematic notion of syncretism, any kind of dissent or displacement without the even more suspect notions of impurity and inauthenticity.

With regard to the question of the validity of religions other than Christianity, Troeltsch acknowledges the legitimacy of their truth claims in principle – and he assumes, like many others before and after him, that religions do make truth claims – and he suggests that they be measured by the same yardstick. Certainly, he would allow, all the successes and advantages that Christian Europe has enjoyed in recent centuries do not automatically "preclude the possibility that other racial groups, living under entirely different cultural conditions, may experience their contact with the Divine Life in quite a different way, and may themselves also possess a religion which has grown up with them, and from which they cannot sever themselves so long as they remain what they are. And they may quite sincerely regard this as absolutely valid for them ..." (Troeltsch 1957: 55-56).

It is however unnecessary and injudicious, in his view, to ascribe to every existing religion the possibility of its being absolutely valid. Most of the lesser religions, Troeltsch opines, do not even aspire to be absolute or universal. One can presumably discriminate such modestly finite religions from the grandly universalist ones, once again, by the same measure. That is to say, the rule of thumb amounts to this: a universal religion is distinct and unique in its character, its identity is consistent and constant, and above all, it flourishes and endures. Hence Troeltsch:

We shall, of course assume something of this kind only among nations which have reached a relatively high stage of civilization, and whose whole mental life has been intimately connected with their religion through a long period of discipline. We shall not assume it among the less developed races, where many religious cults are followed side by side, nor in the simple animism of heathen tribes, which is so monotonous in spite of its many variations. These territories are gradually conquered by the great world religions which possess a real sense of their own absolute validity. But among the great spiritual religions themselves the fundamental spiritual positions which destiny has assigned to them persists in their distinctness. If we wish to determine their relative value, it is not the religions alone that we must compare, but always only the civilizations of which the religion in each case constitutes a part incapable of severance from the rest. (p. 56)

In the end, then, we find Troeltsch speculating on and investing in the continuing prosperity of the European expansion project, with a promise and hope of possibly large future returns, perhaps in the end the return of the unencumbered Absoluteness and true Universality of Christianity itself.

Today, most historians of religions would likely protest that Troeltsch went too far, that it was unnecessary for him to take this last step beyond our tensely quiescent world of pluralist truce, where multiple, strictly historicized traditions of absolutes coexist, each enlivened by its own genius or, if one prefers, by "the mysterious movement of the divine Spirit in the unconscious depth of the human spirit." We might therefore regard with regret the fact that Troeltsch's imagination gratuitously reached out to the universe of such an all-out war of competition, where each of these individual absolutisms is made to don the full armor of a particular historical civilization with all its material accoutrements and to do battle with one another for survival and for the eventual mastery over all challengers. In other words, today's historians of religions might insist, despite Troeltsch's own excesses, that the pluralism of culture-specific absolutes presupposed in the world-religions discourse does not have to lead to the kind of global competition and the battle of the continents as envisioned by him, that his conclusion was in fact an illicit extension of this discourse, and that this transgression had the effect of plunging him right back to the domain of dogmatic theology. Certainly, it would seem, this final outcome of Troeltsch's deliberations counterbalances, if not to say contradicts outright, the presumably humbling effect of the discovery of radical historicity. History is said to have taught him and his fellow Christians the mutability and the irreducible particularity of their religion; the lessons of history were supposed to have compelled them to realize that theirs, too, was just another religion ardently claiming to be absolutely valid and uniquely universal. But was this realization, this hard-won new knowledge, all that humbling?

The idea that the "historical consciousness" somehow chastised "the West" continues to be as strong as it remains questionable. Whether or not one manages to abstain from taking the transgressive last step of Troeltsch's, the blanket belief in the morally curative or prophylactic power of historical consciousness – which, in some other contexts is often touted as a prize possession proper only to the West – is suspect. The notion seems to have given a cover, if not to say false consciousness, for certain historians of religions because it leads them to imagine that they are inoculated against theological dogmatism and racial bigotry solely by the virtue of their *being historical,* whatever is meant by this well-worn mantra. As the case of Troeltsch is but one indication, we have good reason to suspect that, as far as the greater Europe's stakes are concerned, there is no ideological disjuncture between the theological discourse and the world-religions discourse. Rather, the discourse of world religions came into being as a substitute and solution to the particular fix that confounded European Christianity – that is to say, the imperial Europe that claimed Christianity for itself – at the end of the nineteenth century.

This is as much as to suggest that the problem with the world-religions discourse probably is not its residual Christianity or crypto-theology. *Our* problem, in any case, is something far more powerfully and insidiously present in the hegemonic discourse about religion and religions, as this discourse constitutes reality not only for the self-claiming Christians or for the self-claiming Europeans but for us all, albeit in varying ways. In fact, when the contemporary scientists of religion denounce what they deem a remnant of Christian theology allegedly found amidst secular, non-denominational, scholarly discourse, this "theology" tag at times seems to be something of an effigy. Be that as it may, if we are to be serious about the critical intentions of "religious studies," an effective strategy is not an exorcism of the undead but something more tediously difficult: a rigorously historical discourse analysis.

Notes

1. This essay constitutes a segment of a monograph-length study which examines the formation of the world-religions discourse, entitled *The Invention of World-Religions.*
2. Elsewhere in the larger work mentioned in note 1, I examine this shift in the meaning of the word "world religion" (*Weltreligion* and *Wereldgodsdienst* in German and in Dutch, respec-

tively) from the narrower sense in contradistinction from "national religion" (*Landesreligion* and *Volksgodsdienst*) to the more and more inclusive sense now familiar to us. The phrase itself seems to derive from the earlier use by German and Dutch scholars active in the 1870's and 1880's, including Otto Pfleiderer, Abraham Kuenen, C. P. Tiele, L. W. E. Rauwenhoff, and P. D. Chantepie de la Saussaye.

3. In 1964, Mircea Eliade expressed this sentiment when he described what he termed "the grave crisis brought on by the discovery of the historicity of man": "This new dimension, the historicity, is susceptible of many interpretations. But it must be admitted that from a certain point of view the understanding of man as first and foremost a historical being implies a profound humiliation for the Western consciousness. Western man considered himself successively God's creature and the possessor of a unique Revelation, the master of the world, the author of the only universally valid culture, the creator of the only real and useful science, and so on. *Now he discovered himself on the same level with every other man, that is to say, conditioned by the unconscious as well as by history* [emphasis added] – no longer the unique creator of a high culture, no longer the master of the world, and culturally menaced by extinction." Mircea Eliade, "The 'Origins' of Religion," originally published in *History of Religions,* 4 (1964); revised and reprinted in Eliade: 1969: 51.

4. In this respect, too, Eliade echoed Troeltsch almost exactly, with further embellishment. See other essays included in *The Quest* (Eliade 1969), especially "A New Humanism"; "The History of Religions in Retrospect: 1912 and After"; "The Quest for the 'Origins' of Religion"; "Crisis and Renewal."

5. This, of course, is not to suggest that Troeltsch in any way ceased to be a theologian at some point. On the contrary, the fact that he does not abandon his identity as a theologian and confessional Christian by becoming a historian makes his example particularly instructive, as he makes visible the nature of the relation and the tension between the two.

References

Clarke, James Freeman, *Ten Great Religions: Essay in Comparative Theology,* Boston: Houton Mifflin, & Co., 1871.

Eliade, Mircea, *The Quest: History and Meaning in Religion*, Chicago: University of Chicago Press, 1969.

Lash, Nicholas, *The Beginning and the End of 'Religion'?* Cambridge, UK: Cambridge University Press, 1996

Marshall, P. J., and Glyndwr Williams, *The Great Map of Mankind: Perceptions of New Worlds in the Age of Enlightenment,* Cambridge, MA: Harvard University Press, 1982.

Maurice, John Frederick Denison, *The Religions of the World, and their relations to Christianity,* London: John W. Parker, 1846.

Pailin, David A., *Attitudes to Other Religions: Comparative religion in seventeenth- and eighteenth-century Britain,* Manchester, UK: Manchester University Press, 1984.

Reichwein, Adolf, *China and Europe: Intellectual and Artistic Contacts in the Eighteenth Century,* trans. by J. C. Powell, London: Kegan Paul, Trench, Trubner, 1925.

Troeltsch, Ernst, "The Place of Christianity among the World Religions" (originally published in 1923), in *Christian Thought: Its History and Application,* edited and with an introduction by Baron von Hügel, New York: Meridian, 1957: 34-63.

Troeltsch, Ernst, "Christianity and the History of Religion" (originally published in 1897), in *Religion in History,* translated by James Luther Adams and Walter F. Bense, Minneapolis: Fortress Press, 1991: 77-86.

Wordsworth, John, *The One Religion: Truth, Holiness and Peace desired by the Nations, and revealed by Jesus Christ,* London: Longmans, Green, 1893.

Critics not Caretakers:

The Scholar of Religion as Public Intellectual[1]

Russell T. McCutcheon

Associate Professor, Department of Religious Studies
Southwest Missouri State University, Springfield, MO, USA

The moment you publish essays in a society you have entered political life; so
if you want not to be political do not write essays or speak out.
– Edward Said (1996: 110)

The historian of religion cannot suspend his critical faculties, his capacity for
disbelief, simply because the materials are "primitive" or religious.
– Jonathan Z. Smith (1982: 60)

What is the role of the scholar of religion in public life? This question,
posed by the editors of this volume, is related to one currently being discussed in a number of books that have recently appeared in the United
States: What is the role of religion in public life? As might be expected,
virtually all of the answers to this second question involve an increased
role for "faith" and even theology in the intellectual, social, economic, and
political affairs of the modern state. Most often, the destabilizations of so-
called objectivity and science brought about by postmodern critiques are
the means by which writers attempt to return religious commitment to
public life. As one of the more notable contributors to these debates,
George Marsden, has put it, given that "many of the original reasons" for
excluding religious faith from the academy and matters of public concern
have, along with other Enlightenment notions, recently come under
severe critique, "is it now time to reconsider the rules that shape the most
respected academic communities?" (1994: 8-9).

 Because the question of religion's role in matters of public concern is
clearly of relevance to theologically inclined commentators on civil life –
we could go so far as to label this group of writers "public theologians" –

what, precisely, has all this got to do with the scholar of religion? My thesis is that debates on the resurgent role of religious commitment in public life ought to attract the interest of the scholar of religion precisely because they are evidence of our own failure as public intellectuals. Outside of a small number of readers and writers, few members of our own society – let alone our fellow members of the academy – know what we do or know who we are, let alone are influenced in their public decisions by our scholarship. When one examines the books written by public theologians (most often they turn out to be Protestant Christians), it is as if the academic study of religion – even its earlier incarnation as comparative religion – had never existed nor made any significant contribution to the human sciences.

A Problem of Our Own Making

What we should note from the outset is that the very phrasing of the question, "What is the role of religion in public life?" already presumes that the issue of what exactly religion is has already been settled. Virtually no one in this debate presumes that religion is the result of alienation caused by socio-economic relations (Marx and Engels), that religion is an illusory practice of wish fulfillment (Freud), that religious practices and stories symbolically deny the contingency and transience of life and human institutions (Bloch 1994), that religion is but one species of anthropomorphism (Guthrie 1993), or that religion is but an evolutionarily developed mechanism (Burkert 1996). If any of these alternative options were seriously entertained, then we would think twice about the role religion plays in a culturally, economically, and technologically diverse/complex state.

It should be apparent, then, that this unarticulated consensus concerning the self-evidently positive and enriching role that religious commitment plays in political affairs betrays the silence of scholars of religion. If the reading public was familiar with the work of those scholars mentioned above, then perhaps people would not gloss so easily over the messy parts of religious behavior and institutions. Therefore, the public theologians' question, "What is the role of religion in public life?" should instead be phrased, "What is the role of the scholar of religion in public life?", for it falls to us to pose potentially unflattering questions concerning a human institution our peers generally privilege and protect from critical examination.

To begin answering the editors' question, I would like to suggest that, as many currently understand their role, scholars of religion generally have little contribution to make to public issues. The methods most widely used in our field, phenomenology and hermeneutics, are directly implicated in the absence of critical and public intelligence in the field. In their insistence that religion is comprised of *sui generis*, non-falsifiable meaning derived from a private experience of mystery, awe, power, or the sacred that can only be described, intuited, felt, and understood by the outsider, scholars of religion have created sufficient conditions for their own political malignment and cultural silence in contemporary public debates. Clearly, our public role has something to do with the theory of religion that grounds our field.

One of the implications of this failure of critical nerve is that scholars of religion find themselves all but speechless when it comes to addressing issues of public concern. To be sure, we can describe assorted claims, translate back and forth between sides, try to interpret the sometimes obscure claims made by one or another side in any given debate or controversy, and provide historical and doctrinal context for this or that insider viewpoint. However, such is merely the job of a translator or color commentator, a role that some in the field think should occupy a greater amount of our time (e.g., see Judith Berling's [1993], Martin Marty's [1989], and Robert Wilken's [1989] Presidential Addresses to the American Academy of Religion). Conceived essentially as an exercise either in nuanced descriptions or reflexive autobiography, the study of religion has rarely amounted to more than a reporter repeating the insider's unsubstantiated claims, all the while invoking methodological agnosticism as their justification for doing so. Sadly, such scholars must inevitably remain silent when it comes to matters of explanation and critical analysis.

The Social Implications of Method and Theory

As already suggested, the very manner in which religion is conceived by many scholars of religion rules out our critical contributions to public debates. As already suggested, this is a matter of *theory*. From the outset, religion is presumed to be diametrically opposed to, and is in fact the victim of, so-called secular issues such as politics and economics. In other words, the sacred/profane dichotomy, which is itself one of the primary theoretical

169

tools used to maintain the autonomy and privilege of religious authority, is part of the problem. Take, for example, how religion is conceived by one prominent American contributor to these debates, Stephen Carter: it is self-evidently personalistic, moralistic, and experiential, and most definitely of the monotheistic variety (rarely do social systems outside of Judaism, Christianity, and Islam figure in these debates). "What does it mean," he asks, "to say that religious groups should be autonomous? It means, foremost, that they should not be beholden to the secular world, that they should exist neither by the forbearance of, nor to do the bidding of, the society outside of themselves" (1993: 34-35). Or, as Carter asserts a little later: "Religions are in effect independent centers of power"; religion is an "independent moral force" and, "at its heart, a way of denying the authority of the rest of the world; it is a way of saying to fellow human beings and to the state those fellow human beings have erected, 'No, I will *not* accede to your will'" (p. 35, 39, 41). It is on the basis of such a suspect understanding of religion that Carter argues for the legal, institutional, and social autonomy – and therefore public authority – of organized religion in America.

This very understanding of religion as socially autonomous grounds much of our field. Our almost exclusive reliance on the phenomenological and hermeneutical methods as the means for securing our intellectual and institutional turf has therefore ensured that scholars of religion have little or no voice in either the university or other public forums. This is the conclusion reached by the historians of religion, Cristiano Grottanelli and Bruce Lincoln, over a decade ago:

> There can be no shrinking away from the painful fact: the establishment of an autonomous field has, paradoxically, damaged the study of religion (and of religions) immensely ... The consequences of this situation may be summed up by stating that the discipline of "History of Religions" managed to marginalize itself in the name of autonomy. Its connections with history, anthropology, sociology, political science, and other relevant fields are scarce, while its ties with theology – however much they are denied – remain strong, if implicit, covert, and distorted. (1985: 8)

Based on the common religious/secular distinction (as if there exists a realm where issues of social power and privilege were not of relevance), a distinction that fuels the exceedingly misleading notion of the "separation

170

of church and state," "religion" is construed as an independent variable occupying the untainted realm of pure and private moral insight that is opposed to, and the salvation of, the messy public worlds of politics and economics. However, if this is the understanding that we carry with us, a dilemma faces scholars of religion. As the scholar of Christian origins, Burton Mack, phrases it:

> The usual approach to the definition of religious phenomena is ... limited to what moderns have imagined as the "sacred," or as reference to discrete "sub-cultural" systems of religion that take separate institutional forms. This way of defining religion leaves out of account the arenas of discourse, practice, and display where a society's values and attitudes are regularly cultivated in the "secular" realm. (1989: 30)

Much as an earlier generation of historians of religions argued that because religion is *sui generis*, sociologists and anthropologists cannot adequately study it, so too religiously committed writers such as Carter stake out an institutional and political turf through the deployment of strategies of containment and isolation.

However, such isolation, generated largely through issues of *theory* (religion is held to be *sui generis*) and *method* (scholarship is perceived to be a form of translation and commentary), excludes the scholar of religion from making a contribution to larger issues of public concern. If we follow the British literary critic Terry Eagleton and, at least in part, define the intellectual as "somebody who trades in ideas by transgressing discursive frontiers" (1992: 83), then such definitional and methodological autonomy – let alone the institutional autonomy scholars of religion require to survive in the university – effectively rule out all forms of transgressing, for the boundaries of just what is and what is not within the reach of the scholar of *sui generis* religion are quite clear (i.e., if there are no gods, no myths, no rituals, and no hierophanies, then it is hardly something about which the scholar of religion can have an informed opinion). As we all know, "the economics department is interested only in abstract models of a pure free enterprise economy; the political science department is concentrating on voting patterns and electoral statistics; the anthropologists are studying hill tribesmen in New Guinea; and the sociologists are studying crime in the ghetto" (Rai 1995: 138). And scholars of religion study

171

and comment on the free floating, *sui generis*, and sacred quality of private human experiences.

The effect of such a rigid compartmentalization, characteristic of the disciplinary, administrative, and funding structures of the modern university, is that certain transgressive questions, by definition, cannot be asked. This in turn prevents creative and oppositional scholarship; for moving across, between, and around disciplines means calling into question the rules by which we normally divide up, study, and understand "reality". Institutional as well as methodological containment and isolation make it all but impossible to assess the relations between these assorted pieces of the pie we call reality, let alone assess the very conditions (both intellectual *and* material) that are prerequisite for just these pie pieces and just this pie in the first place. This is surely one of the reasons why cross-disciplinary scholarship is met with suspicion in many sectors of the university – not least by scholars of *sui generis* religions. And this is precisely why the work of a scholar like Edward Said, whose book, *Orientalism*, transgressed so many traditional intellectual boundaries, can offer us one model for our role as transgressive public intellectuals.

"Religion is a Social Way of Thinking About Social Identity"

In the words of the sociologist Karl Mannheim, the scholar as translator is little more than one who "takes refuge in the past and attempts to find there an epoch or society in which an extinct form of reality-transcendence dominated the world, and through this romantic reconstruction [they] ... seek to spiritualize the present" (1985: 259). They are precisely the people involved in what Jeppe Sinding Jensen and Armin Geertz referred to as the "politics of nostalgia" (1991), an apt term first used by such mid-twentieth century U.S. historians as Richard Hofstadter and Arthur Slesinger Jr. to refer to a form of populist history writing (e.g., historical novels, fictionalized biographies, etc.) that stressed sentimental appreciation at the expense of critical analysis (Lears 1997: 60). If, instead, religion is conceived as but one aspect of human social practices and if, as the American scholar of religion, Jonathan Z. Smith, has suggested, the category "religion" itself is understood to be a second order category of description (where the first order constitutes the behavior or claims being observed and then described by scholars) and not a higher order category of redescription and analysis, then scholars of religion will have a significantly different role to play in both the reproduction of authority and in public debates where such authority is legitimized and contested. What I mean by this is that for scholars, the beliefs, behaviors, and social institutions usually grouped together and described as religion ought to be the subject of critical theorizing rather than mere description and appreciation. Whereas "religion," and claims about "world religions," might operate in the realm of description, when it comes to analysis (a higher order cognitive activity) both terms are replaced and reduced to talk of minds, economies, societies, classes, genders, etc.[2]

Our involvement in the public debate is, then, on the higher level of critical, comparative, redescriptive analysis and critique, all of which implies a critical theory of religion as an all too human institution. Whatever else religion may or may not be, then, it is at least a potent manner by which humans construct maps by which they negotiate not simply their way around the unpredictable natural world but also through which they defend and contest issues of social power and privilege in the here and now. To put it mildly, we can cite the scholar of Christian origins, Ron Cameron: "religion is a social way of thinking about social identity and social relationships" (Allen 1996: 30). Or, to make it somewhat more complex, we can draw on the work of such contemporary scholars as Jonathan Smith (1982), Bruce Lincoln (1994), Burton Mack (1996), and Gary Lease (1994), and say that religions are systems of social signification, encoded within narratives of the epic past and the anticipated future, coordinated within behavioral and institutional systems of cognitive and social control, all of which characterizes human responses to the various incongruities and disruptions that come with historical existence. Anthony Giddens, the British sociologist, comes close to this understanding when he writes that "myth both unites the group and provides an interpretive framework for coping with the exigencies of, and threats from, the natural world (Giddens 1984: 265); so-called religious systems, then, are perhaps the pre-eminent site for creating or contesting cognitive and social continuity and authority amidst the discontinuities of life.

For the scholar of religion as public intellectual, religious language, behaviors, and institutions are therefore efficient and often uncontested means for abstracting issues, claims, and institutions from the tug-and-pull of historical existence, ascribing a significance to them that affords

173

them a privilege that, by definition, extends to their participants and one particular view of how reality not only *is* but *ought* to be constructed. Unlike participants in these systems of signification, scholars of religion come upon the scene with sophisticated tools for comparing, analyzing, and critiquing the strategies by which communities decontextualize and marginalize, mythify and deify one side in what is more than likely a complex situation. In the very act of contextualizing and historicizing our data, we call into question the "aestheticization of the political" (Carroll 1995: 15), the "authority of detachment" (Merod 1987: xi), and the way ever changing instances are aligned with static essences. The scholar of religion as public intellectual is therefore involved in acts of resistance. Or, as the literary critic Fran Lentricchia wrote over a decade ago, "it is the function of the intellectual as critical rhetor to uncover, bring to light, and probe all such alignments. This is part of the work of ideological analysis" (1985: 149). As critical rhetor, the scholar of religion exposes the mechanisms whereby myths, truths, and norms are constructed and subsequently authorized, demonstrating the contingency of seemingly necessary conditions and the historical character of ahistorical claims.

Perhaps it is the realization of just this potential role for scholars of religion as public intellectuals that explains our absence from the citations of those public theologians who advocate an increased role for religious faith in the affairs of the state. For, after all, the scholar of religion as critical rhetor comes not to inform the world of how it *ought* to work, but explains how and why it *happens* to work as it does, making such critical scholarship a convenient resource to avoid when making pronouncements on the future of human meaning, the nation, or the world – claims that are either politically conservative *or* liberal, in support of dominant *or* oppositional regimes.

It is in their critical analysis of so-called religious institutions, traditions, myths, and rituals that scholars of religion can contribute most to uncloaking and laying bare the conditions and strategies by which their fellow citizens authorize the local as universal and the contingent as necessary. Such scholars find in seemingly insignificant gestures and rhetorical flourishes the makings of larger issues in the practice and reproduction of social power and authority. In our analysis of the manner in which humans represent the world and their place in it – let alone our analysis of the representations of our colleagues in the university! – we are equipped to scrutinize the ideological sleight of hand that leads to a seemingly perfect fit between the model constructed and sanctioned by the group in question, on the one hand, and reality, on the other. It is through the techniques of comparing and contextualizing competing representations that the public intellectual juxtaposes models of the world and attempts to determine why it is that such-and-such an institution or story accompanies this or that model.[3] Part of answering this "why" question will necessarily address the very real material and social interests that are at stake in authorizing this over than institution. If our colleagues fail to do this, we are justified to inquire into just what they are selling their readers and students when they uncritically reproduce authoritative accounts in merely descriptive scholarship.

The Status of "Religion" for Public Intellectuals

It seems sensible that religious devotees make claims regarding the autonomy and privilege of their experiences, behaviors, and institutions. After all, the label "religion" is a powerful and pervasive means by which a number of human communities authorize their claims of historic and practical import by, in Roland Barthes's words, dressing up their own creations in "decorative displays" to make them pass for "what-goes-without-saying" (1973: 11). Through their use of the tools of nuanced description, their effort to recover authentic meaning, and their disdain for transgressive questions, scholars of religion risk uncritically reproducing such claims of autonomy and authority. Where they could instead be involved in the active business of uncloaking the ahistoric rhetoric that makes its appearance in public debates, scholars of religion *qua* translators have instead opted for the highly conservative practice of entrenching ideologies and rhetorics – a point convincingly argued by Graeme MacQueen in his critical study of scholarship on myth. MacQueen argues that by creating of "myth" a seemingly uniform set of existentially meaningful narratives, largely concerned with ahistorical origins, scholars have ignored the relations between socio-political and gendered dominance and subordination in the societies they study. This "leaves students of myth in the dangerous position of lending unconscious support and legitimacy to structures of authority in societies that they study" (1988: 144).

What needs to be repeated is that for the scholar of religion as public intellectual, "religion" is a category that holds little analytical value. As both Pascal Boyer[4] and Jonathan Z. Smith,[5] have suggested, it is a second order category, and part of the problem to be studied, not a higher order category that is part of the analysis of human behavior: it is part of the data to be explained because, as they are commonly defined, religious discourses remove something (a claim, an institution, a practice) from history, thereby privileging it over all other historically-embedded claims and knowledges. Although such rhetoric is presumed by many in the field to be beyond critical analysis and reproach, public intellectuals must inquire into just what other part of our public debate would sanction a position that is based upon such ahistorical certainty, such undefended and indefensible self-evidency?

Conclusion: The Scholar of Religion as Culture Critic

> When one permits those whom one studies to define the terms in which they will be understood, suspends one's interest in the temporal and contingent, or fails to distinguish between "truths," "truth-claims," and "regimes of truth," one has ceased to function as historian or scholar. In that moment, a variety of roles are available: some perfectly respectable (amanuensis, collector, friend and advocate), and some less appealing (cheerleader, voyeur, retailer of import goods). None, however, should be confused with scholarship. (Lincoln 1996: 227)

If we follow Bruce Lincoln's advice and not act as cheerleaders or voyeurs, friends or advocates, what role is left? Both Lincoln and Mack recommend that we become culture critics, for the only role possible for scholars who see religion as a powerful means whereby human communities construct and authorize their practices and institutions (i.e., their "regimes of truth") is that of the culture critic.

"Culture," as in "culture studies," is the larger category into which religious practices and beliefs fall when they are correctly understood as being no different in origin or implication from other social authorizing practices. "Since modern societies in the western tradition make such a fuss about keeping religion separate from society," Mack writes, "we need the term culture to cover the phenomenon of values and attitudes cultivated within a society apart from overtly religious inculcation" (1989: 30).[6]

176

Scholars of religion as culture critics presume that so-called religious discourses, religious practices, and religious institutions are in fact part of the descriptive, historical data that requires critical study. As a culture critic, then, I can now return to one of the questions posed at the outset of this essay: What is the role of religion in public life? It should now be clear that, from my theoretical perspective, so-called religious systems are perhaps the pre-eminent site for creating social continuity amidst the discontinuities of historical existence. If this was our understanding of religion, we would see all the more clearly just what is at stake when our colleagues obscure matters by uncritically teaching and writing on insider claims concerning certain behaviors and institutions being socially and politically autonomous systems of faith or salvation.

Whether we like it or not, then, as teachers working in publicly funded institutions, we are public intellectuals already. Moreover, as writers who make public our private thoughts, we have, as Edward Said noted in one of this essay's epigraphs, already entered public, political life. The question is whether we will accept this role or, through our efforts to spiritualize and dehistoricize the people and practices we study, we will obscure both our data and our social role, thereby contributing to the very authorizing practices we could instead be studying and questioning. To me, the choice is rather straightforward: whether to reproduce or challenge the ideological mechanisms and alignments whereby description becomes prescription and the local is represented as universal. For, as I have argued elsewhere, "[t]o fail to make explicit the social and political motivations/benefits behind what the apparent majority of 'religionists' yet think to be the *sui generis* quality of religion, its texts, and its language ... is to fall considerably short of what the academic study of religion could be" (1991: 256).

I recommend that scholars of religion as public intellectuals should not simply describe religious claims; instead, they should accept the challenge of generating critical, scholarly theories *about* these normative discourses. As recently argued by the historian, Eric Hobsbawm, regarding the role of the professional historian, the scholar of religion likewise is involved in the "deconstruction of political or social myths dressed up as history" (1997: 273). As such, "a sceptical critique of historical anachronism is probably the chief way in which historians [and scholars of religion, we might add] can demonstrate their public responsibility" (Hobsbawm 1997: 273-274). Accordingly, we must presume that normative reflection is not inherently problematic – one could go so far as to argue that it may actually be inevitable that, to paraphrase Roland Barthes, contingent History is continually dressed up by communities as essential Nature; it just happens that the slippery nature of such rhetoric is precisely what we have tools to historicize and study. Finally, our scholarship is not constrained by whether or not devotees recognize its value for it is not intended to appreciate, celebrate, or enhance normative, dehistoricized discourses but, rather, to contextualize and redescribe them as human constructs.

Notes

1. A longer version of this essay first appeared in the *Journal of the American Academy of Religion* 65/2 (1997): 443-468; portions of that essay appear in this rewritten version with the kind permission of the journal's editor. The longer version of this essay also appears as a chapter in my forthcoming *Critics not Caretakers: Redescribing the public Study of Religion*, State University of New York Press, Albany, New York. My thanks goes to Burton Mack whose unpublished essay (1989) influenced me a great deal while writing this paper.
2. For a survey of some recent uses of the category "religion" see McCutcheon 1995.
3. Noam Chomsky's work in comparing U.S. media coverage of Cambodian (official enemy) and Indonesian (official friend) military atrocities in the 1970s is startlingly frank evidence of the way in which representations vary with socio-economic and geo-political interests. In *Manufacturing Religion* (1997; chapter 6) I have used a similar comparative method to examine the differing American scholarly and media representations of the so-called "self-immolations" of Vietnamese Buddhist monks in the early 1960s.
4. "The study of religion is an 'impure' subject [in the chemical rather than the moral sense], that is, a subject where the central or official topic is not a scientific object" (1996: 212).
5. "[T]he term 'religion' is not an empirical category. It is a second order abstraction" (1988: 233).
6. Needless to say, Mack immediately goes on to argue that such a change in datum would require us to reconceive and reorganize departments of religion which are still largely the product of a seminary model. An example of how the study of religion might be reorganized as the comparative study of culture is provided by Tim Fitzgerald (1995: 1997).

References

Allen, Charlotte, "Is Nothing Sacred? Casting Out the Gods from Religious Studies", *Lingua Franca* 6/7, 1996: 30-40.

Barthes, Roland, *Mythologies*, Annette Lavers (Trans.). Paladin, Hammersmith, London, 1973.

Berling, Judith, "Is Conversation About Religion Possible? (And What Can Religionists Do to Promote It?)", *Journal of the American Academy of Religion* 61/1, 1993: 1-22.

Bloch, Maurice, *Prey into Hunter: The Politics of Religious Experience*, New York: Cambridge University Press, 1994.

Boyer, Pascal, "Religion as an Impure Subject: A Note on Cognitive Order in Religious Representation in Response to Brian Malley", *Method & Theory in the Study of Religion* 8/2, 1996: 201-213.

Burkert, Walter, *Creation of the Sacred: The Tracks of Biology in Early Religions*, Harvard University Press, Cambridge, MA, 1996.

Carroll, David, *French Literary Fascism: Nationalism, Anti-Semitism, and the Ideology of Culture*, Princeton University Press, Princeton, NJ, 1995.

Carter, Stephen L., *The Culture of Disbelief: How American Law and Politics Trivialize Religious Devotion*, Doubleday, New York, 1993.

Eagleton, Terry, *The Significance of Theory*, Blackwell, Oxford, 1992.

Fitzgerald, Tim, "Religious Studies as Cultural Studies: A Philosophical and Anthropological Critique of the Concept of Religion", *Diskus* 3/1, 1995: 35-47.

– "A Critique of 'Religion' as a Cross-Cultural Category", *Method & Theory in the Study of Religion* 9/2, 1997: 91-110.

Giddens, Anthony, *The Constitution of Society: Outline of the Theory of Structuration*, University of California Press, Berkeley, 1984.

Grottanelli, Cristiano and Bruce Lincoln, "A Brief Note on (Future) Research in the History of Religion", Center for Occasional Studies' *Occasional Papers* 4, 1984-1985: 2-15. Reprinted in *Method & Theory in the Study of Religion*, 10/3 (1998): 311-325.

Guthrie, Stewart, *Faces in the Clouds: A New Theory of Religion*. Oxford University Press, New York, 1993.

Hobsbawm, Eric, "Identity History is Not Enough", *On History*. New Press, 1997.

Jensen, Jeppe Sinding and Armin W. Geertz, "Tradition and Renewal in the Histories of Religions: Some Observations and Reflections", in Jensen, Jeppe Sinding and Armin W. Geertz (Eds.), *Religion, Tradition, and Renewal*, Aarhus University Press, Aarhus, 1991: 11-27.

Lears, Jackson, "Looking Backward: In Defense of Nostalgia", *Lingua Franca* 7/10, 1997: 59-66.

Lease, Gary, "The History of 'Religious' Consciousness and the Diffusion of Culture: Strategies for Surviving Dissolution", *Historical Reflections/Reflexions Historiques* 20/3, 1994: 453-479.

Lentricchia, Frank, *Criticism and Social Change*, University of Chicago Press, Chicago, 1985.

Lincoln, Bruce, *Authority: Construction and Corrosion*, University of Chicago Press, Chicago, 1994.

– "Theses on Method", *Method & Theory in the Study of Religion* 8/3, 1996: 225-227.

Mack, Burton, "Caretakers and Critics: On the Social Role of Scholars Who Study Religion", unpublished paper presented to the Seminar on Religion in Society, Wesleyan University, September 14, 1989.

— *Who Wrote the New Testament? The Making of the Christian Myth*, HarperCollins, San Francisco, 1996.

MacQueen, Graeme, "*Whose* Sacred History? Reflections on Myth and Dominance", *Studies in Religion* 17/2, 1988: 143-157.

Mannheim, Karl, *Ideology & Utopia: An Introduction to the Sociology of Knowledge*, Harcourt Brace Jovanovich, New York, 1985.

Marsden, George, *The Soul of the American University: From Protestant Establishment to Established Nonbelief*, Oxford University Press, New York, 1994.

Marty, Martin E., "Committing the Study of Religion in Public", *Journal of the American Academy of Religion* 57/1, 1989: 1-22.

McCutcheon, Russell T., "Ideology and the Problem of Naming: A Reply," *Method & Theory in the Study of Religion* 3/2, 1991: 246-256.

— "The Category 'Religion' in Recent Publications: A Critical Survey", *Numen* 42/3, 1995: 284-309.

— *Manufacturing Religion: The Discourse on Sui Generis Religion and the Politics of Nostalgia*, Oxford University Press, New York, 1997.

Merod, Jim, *The Political Responsibility of the Critic*, Cornell University Press, Ithaca, NY, 1987.

Rai, Milan, *Chomsky's Politics*, Verso Books, London, 1995.

Said, Edward, *Representations of the Intellectual*, Vintage Books, New York, 1996.

Smith, Jonathan Z., *Imagining Religion: From Jonestown to Babylon*, University of Chicago Press, Chicago, 1982.

— "'Religion' and 'Religious Studies': No Difference at All", *Soundings* 71/2-3 (1988): 231-244.

Wilken, Robert L., "Who Will Speak for the Religious Traditions?", *Journal of the American Academy of Religion* 57/4 (1989): 699-717.

Suggested Readings

Roland Barthes, *Mythologies*, Annette Lavers (Trans.). Paladin, Hammersmith, London, 1973.

Terry Eagleton, *Ideology: An Introduction*, London, Verso, 1991.

Frank Lentricchia, *Criticism and Social Change*, University of Chicago Press, Chicago, 1985.

Bruce Lincoln, *Authority: Construction and Corrosion*, University of Chicago Press, Chicago, 1994.

Russell T. McCutcheon, *Manufacturing Religion: The Discourse on Sui Generis Religion and the Politics of Nostalgia*, Oxford University Press, New York, 1997.

— *Critics not Caretakers: Redescribing the public Study of Religion*, State University of New York Press, Albany, New York, forthcoming.

Critics not Caretakers: The Scholar of Religion as Public Intellectual

Jim Merod, *The Political Responsibility of the Critic*, Cornell University Press, Ithaca, NY, 1987.

Edward Said, *Representations of the Intellectual*, Vintage Books, New York, 1996.

Jonathan Z. Smith, *Imagining Religion: From Jonestown to Babylon*, Chicago: University of Chicago Press, 1982.

Speaking Different Languages: Religion and the Study of Religion

Tim Murphy

Mellon Postdoctoral Fellow, Department of Religion
Case Western Reserve University, Cleveland, Ohio, USA

To begin with a simple fact: two languages, by their very two-ness, are different languages. To explain in English how something is said in German, is to speak the German in English. The words, or signifiers, may be identical but they are not spoken in the same language. Here, it is English which speaks German.

The metaphor of languages may be extended: domains of discourse, including domains of systematic inquiry as well as looser cultural formations, may be conceived, as they have since Wittgenstein, as "language-games" (see Wittgenstein 1958: 2-172). To truncate a long theoretical history, to say that X is a language-game is to say that a term within it is used according to the rules of that particular language-game. To use the same term in a different language-game is either to change its meaning or to equivocate. The age-old "picture theory" of reference overlooked this point and so was not capable of discriminating between differing uses of terms, but insisted rather that they be tied to their extra-linguistic referent (Wittgenstein 1958: 2-21). However, subsequent linguistics has shown that the referent is *another term* within the system of a language. The relationship between the term and a referent object is absolutely arbitrary and so cannot be determined by it as the picture theory had for so long insisted. That relationship is, however, what Wittgenstein called "rule governed" and what Saussure called "structured" (Saussure 1959: 114-117) There can be no appeal outside the system of a given language to describe the meaning of its term. That is simply to speak the first language in terms of a second.

Domains of inquiry or of culture are analogous to language-games, then, in two senses. First, terms have meaning only in relation to the rules of their use. Second, their meaning is defined *within a system* of meanings. This is to say that there is no "meaning as such," only particular meanings stipulated by *definite* language-games. As Lyotard and others have shown, this is no less true of science than of other cultural language-games. Science is a specific rule-governed language-game which stipulates the conditions under which statements can be falsified (for the rules of the language-game of science, see Lyotard, 1979: 23-27).

Once domains of inquiry are understood on the model of language we may then ask a basic question: how are various languages related to one another? Languages, in their relations with one another, are not simply equivocal. At any time a given language "speaks" another, while the other is merely spoken. That is, any given language may be either a metalanguage or an object-language. A metalanguage is any language, including cultural codes, which speaks another language (see Barthes 1973: 89-94). Any language can be a metalanguage because it is a matter of positionality, not of substance. Most natural languages and cultural codes carry this possibility only as an accidental potentiality. However, some languages are *designed* to speak other languages (or, at least, significantly more extensive in their capacity to do so). This is true of both religion and science.

Religion is a metalanguage, and this in two senses. First, "religion" is itself a metalanguage. That is, the category "religion," as it is used by both scholars and practitioners, functions as a classification of various phenomena, but also thereby as a characterization of them. It does not stand alone by itself; is a term within a discursive system (or systems; believers' use may vary from that of scholars; one school of scholarship from another), and this system of discourse is used to speak, to signify other domains of signification.

Yet again, so-called "concrete" religions are metalanguages in that they are systems of signifieds which are mapped onto various domains of reality, often purporting to speak the entirety of reality – speak, that is, to organize it semiologically according to the order of its own signifieds. In other contexts this is called "interpretation," but the term is so overused one must further specify what it means. The act of interpretation is semiotic: it is to grasp a series of signifiers, taken from one domain, and to *rename their meaning* in the terms of another domain. This, I would argue, is the essential act of "religion" and of religions.

The insight that the relationship between signifier and signified is arbitrary shows us *how* it is that religions speak the world. The overdetermined nature, or plasticity, of a signified such as "act of God," in a religious system, combined with the non-fixed relation it has with any given signifier, allows for the infinite (or near infinite) application of a signifier to such a signified. The signifiers can easily be substituted while the signifieds, in theory at least, remain stable. As Saussure pointed out, "[l]anguage is radically powerless to defend itself against the forces which from one moment to the next are shifting the relationship between the signified and the signifier. This is one of the consequences of the arbitrary nature of the sign" (Saussure 1959: 75).

Consequently, the language itself, as well as its application to the "world" must be *interpreted*: "[w]here there is a canon [structure, or system of signifieds, concepts, or "doctrines"], it is possible to predict the necessary occurrence of a hermeneute, of an interpreter whose task it is continually to extend the domain of the closed canon over everything that is known or everything that exists without altering the canon in the process" (J. Z. Smith 1982: 48). Religious interpretation, then, is both fixed and, in principle, infinitely permutatable. The art of religious interpretation is to find the bridge, the link, between a given signifier presented by the world and mapping it onto the appropriate signified. Secular critics of religion, because they have traditionally concentrated so exclusively upon the problem of the truth of the signifieds, i.e., on the signified-world relationship, have often overlooked the subtlety, ingenuity, and intelligence with which this activity is carried out. A good televangelist, for instance, within his or her language domain, can produce ingenious mappings of world-to-signifieds.

Science, too, is a metalanguage. It takes signifiers from the world at large, "data," and renames them according to the order of its signifieds, "law," "statistical regularity," "anomaly," etc. Where science differs from religion is not in the fact that its constraints are "external" as opposed to internal, but that the nature of the internal constraints are different, not only in content but in kind. Unlike religion, science's axioms *demands* the critical investigation of those very axioms, along with each and every result produced by the axiomatic constraints. As far as I am aware, this is not the case with any historical phenomenon to which the label "religion" can be properly applied. To be a member of a religion, some elements of the inherited axioms simply cannot be questioned. This does not mean that

185

none can; I am not making the tired Enlightenment claim that religions are "dogmatic" while science is based upon "free inquiry." Science itself, in the form of linguistics, has shown that to be a gross oversimplification. Furthermore, it is clear that, within certain axiomatic constraints, religions are often remarkably self-critical, even ingenious in the pursuit of this. The radicalness of this questioning, however, is inevitably more circumscribed than that of science. The scientist must be willing to abandon *any* given belief at any time.

Science and religion, then, are different and incommensurable language-games. The regime of truth is different in each. They cannot be subsumed by one another, though they can be spoken by one another. Even when they use the same signifiers these are attached to different and differing signifieds. Even the term "religion" as used in the science of religion simply does not mean the same thing as it used by practitioners of specific religions. The plasticity of the operative gesture of a metalanguage misleads many to believe that religion and science, or any other set or pair of metalanguages, can finally converge. The site of this convergence is typically stipulated as "the Truth." But this "Truth" is itself the signified of *some language*, typically "religion," a religion, or a school of philosophy. Linguistically, "truth in-itself," i.e., apart from any system of signifieds, is literally meaningless. Therefore, the move to an alleged convergence merely replicates the operational gesture: now a third language attempts to name the meaning of the relationship between the first two.

It is in this light that we may understand the interaction between the metalanguages of science and religion. Contrary to what classical phenomenologists have claimed, the science of religion does not seek to speak the believers language. It seeks to understand that language in terms of its *own* language. What is spoken outside the language of science (or a science), is simply non-science. It is therefore logically impossible for the science of religion to re-present the religious believer in their own terms. Neither is it desirable, at least not for the science of religion.

As Tony Edwards has very clearly shown, the conflict between religionists and the science of religion arises when their respective descriptions conflict (see Edwards 1994: 169-182). This, however, must be examined more carefully. These descriptions conflict, not in an isolated, head-to-head way, but as they are apprehended in yet another discursive domain, usually the so-called "public sphere." The problem is not *simply* with the

186

divergence of the two descriptions, but with the place each domain occupies within that third discursive domain. That is to say, "religion" and "science" have a predetermined, fixed value in the system of public discourse. The comparison of their respective descriptions is weighted within that domain, and the conflict arises, not only because each has differing internal criteria, but because each is a competitor for pride of place within the domain of public discourse (see Cormack 1992: 22-23).

From the foregoing analysis it is clear that this competition is not a competition from *within* the languages of religion or science, at least not *in strictu sensu*. It is a subtle shift from internal constraints to how the results of these constraints position that language within a third sphere (here, the domain of public discourse). Each does speak the other, and each fears being subsumed by the other; this is an undeniable fact of both their operational extension and the history of their relations. But the more specific site of this fear of subsumption is the loss of the power to *persuade*, i.e., diminishment of their respective positionality within a third discourse. The joke on both, of course, is that the public domain's structure of discourse functions completely independently of either. Its principles and system of classification *predetermine* where any and all of the statements of either will "reside." That is, public discourse *translates* the contents of religion and the results of science into its own terms. When either says something that cannot be stated in the terms of public discourse, it simply does not get said. Both scientists and religionists have had the frustrating experiences of either having their words "twisted around," or, of completely failing to call attention to something they believe is of vital importance. This is, again, because public discourse has a built-in taxonomy which decides in advance what is or is not important.

This raises a final question: what is the relationship between the science of religion and the public sphere? Again, we are confronted by two distinct domains of discourse. And again, although they share many signifiers, the *system* of signifieds is different. The most striking difference between the two domains is that they exist in completely different temporal horizons. That is to say, for the philosopher Plato can be a real "contemporary." The mundane distantiation of the past does not apply in scholarship in at all the same way as it does in the public sphere. Likewise, the horizon of the future of science and scholarship is far greater than that of the public sphere. Science lives within a future horizon which stretches out indefinitely. We expect the future of science to yield results which cannot be foreseen in the present. Given what we know of the history of science, we can only imagine that the problems, methods, and questions with which we deal today will bear no relationship to what is done in the future. And we are forced, *a fortiori*, to will this, to affirm this as the good for science. Consequently, we are also forced to live with an indefinite suspension of "belief."

Because it takes as its basis, as its guiding principle, the dictates of practical reason, the temporal horizons of the public sphere are much narrower than are those of the sciences. Likewise, the suspension of belief in an indefinite deferment to the future is not possible given the dictates of practical reason. Practical questions demand practical answers, answers which may form the basis for concrete plans which can be realized within a foreseeable time frame. The public sphere is necessarily constituted by these demands, and cannot have the patience to "wait and see," a gesture of deferral which is essential to science.

The scientist, then, speaks two languages, each of which is incommensurable with the other. As *citizen*, the scientist speaks one language; as scientist, he or she speaks another.

There is, however, a way in which the two languages overlap and intersect. Both scholars and the public domain produce and circulate representations. As Paul Rabinow has noted, *all* representations are social facts including those produced by scientists (Rabinow 1986: 234-261). These representations can be of diverse kinds: images of gender, of "natives," of foreign peoples' or leaders, of the realm of nature, of human nature, and so forth. When a scholar writes a book or an article on, for instance, Hinduism, he or she creates a social product which then enters into the system of social meanings in which it circulates. As Russell McCutcheon has argued, "scholarship, once published, read, and quoted, becomes a public, political act" (McCutcheon 1997: 460).

In point of fact, however, most scholarly productions do not circulate widely enough to be considered "social representations" in a serious sense. There are however, two ways in which they do effect the larger sphere of social representations. For one, they may indirectly effect the production of social representations by being "popularized." We need only think of the use of Carl Jung by Joseph Campbell, the use of Campbell by Bill Moyers and the Public Broadcasting System in the United States to see

188

how an entire domain of popularized theory can be constructed. More importantly, however, the institution of the university, intentionally or not, lends credibility to social representations at large. It does this indirectly by the phenomenon of "they say," the anonymous circulation of authorized "facts." The institution of the university implicitly authorizes information products. That it contests or even condemns many specific information products gets lost in the larger network of its relations to cultural production in society – relations that the university is often loathe to criticize because of the overall advantage it accrues from its being so positioned within them. The university, because of its place within public discourse, and because of the place of science within the university, implicitly authorizes information products by the sheer *mode* of its authority. That which is endorsed by the university is taken to be endorsed by science, and, since the university virtually endorses the public sphere, within public discourse, all one need do is invoke this authority. Consequently, like the magician's apprentice, once a work gets out of the scholar's hand, he or she loses much of the control over that work's career. This does not mean that a scholarly work automatically becomes "political," only that it always potentially may.

The scholarly work rarely, if ever, becomes political (or politicized) in and of itself. It does so because in the public sphere individual representations often help tell a larger story which a segment of the public, or the larger structures of public discourse itself, are urging upon society as "truth" (see Lyotard 1979: 27-53). These stories, ideologies, *grand récits*, etc., are part of a larger social fabric which legitimates certain kinds of socio-economic-politic arrangements. Scholars often do not realize this because they lack the ideological training and skills necessary to decipher the ideological function of a specific narrative or representation. All to often, scholars simply repeat some aspect of the dominant ideology while simultaneously denying that this aspect of their work – or any aspect – is either politically implicated or motivated. This is because what they mean by "political" is the specific *intention* on their part to advance a particular social agenda. In so saying, however, they are availing themselves of a crucial category of Liberal ideology, namely, the agent. The concept of the agent/actor as the (at least relatively) autonomous author of his or her own actions is so widely circulated a concept that it is, for the most part, uncritically accepted. That does not change the fact that it is a thoroughly

ideological concept, as well as the object of considerable ideological contestation. Besides this, it is often the case, at least in the United States, that
most scholars tend to agree with the larger narratives of society. Most
scholars, again, at least in the U.S., are Liberals. The two factors combine
to make ideological contestation *invisible* in most discursive contexts.

It is here where the roles of scientist and citizen converge. The task of
the scientist is to critically assess the representations produced by, for, and
in the public domain – including their own. In challenging the status of
particular representations, or particular classes of representations, it *may be*
the case that the scientist *qua* scientist thereby challenges the larger narrative which these particular representations are being used to tell. To challenge the image of the "primitive" may entail challenging the narrative of
"modern, industrial, society," i.e., that counter-image which is sustained
by its other. Whether the scientist's challenge goes that far will depend
upon the particulars of a given case. Not all representations are e*qually*
part of society's *grand recits*, nor are all narratives told to the same ends (see
Cormack 1992: 9-16).

On the other hand, as McCutcheon has noted, failure to challenge the
legitimating implications or use of a particular representation has definite
political implications (see McCutcheon 1997: 444-446). It is to let stand
those politics which do, in fact, exist. When representations are taken up
into legitimating narratives or other ideological devices, the possibility for
neutrality disappears. One either consents by silence or one engages.
Absence, as Cormack (and many others have noted) has a positive ideological function: "It is not simply a matter of avoiding some issues, but
rather of enabling the ideological argument of the text [or of society as a
whole] to be worked out unproblematically" (Cormack 1992: 32). Failure
to challenge representations the scientist knows are false (according the
criteria of science) is to *enable* the ideological mechanisms of a society.

The central points of contention, then, are over which representations
are being ideologized, if any, how, and to what specific ends. I disagree
with McCutcheon when he claims that "[t]he scholar of religion as public
intellectual is, *by definition*, involved in the act of resistance" (McCutcheon 1997: 452, emphasis added). The scientist *qua* scientist need not *necessarily* contest the system of social representations. This is because the scientist *qua* scientist holds to no totalizing ideology which creates a *systematic opposition* to any narrative or ideology. In the domain of public dis-

course the scientist *qua* scientist operates *ad hoc*, addressing only particular cases and occasions. Science as an ideological instrument undoubtedly exists. However, this is science as spoken by and in the discourse of modern, western, industrial societies, or "Science," if you will. It is not the same thing as the rule-governed activity in which practitioners of science engage. The scientist *qua* scientist does not operate within any grand narrative – not even science's own. The scientist *qua* scientist must be willing to abandon or overturn *any* belief at any time. As such, the scientist is neither friend nor enemy to anyone.

References

Barthes, Roland, *Elements of Semiology*, New York, Hill and Wang, 1973.

Cormack, Mike, *Ideology*, Ann Arbor, University of Michigan Press, 1992.

Edwards, Tony, "Religion, Explanation, and the Askesis of Inquiry" in Idinopulos, Thomas A., and Yonan, Edward A. (Eds.), *Religion and Reductionism: Essays on Eliade, Segal, and the Challenge of the Social Sciences for the Study of Religion*, Leiden, E. J. Brill, 1994.

Lyotard, Jean-François, *The Postmodern Condition: A Report on Knowledge*, Minneapolis, University of Minnesota Press, 1979.

McCutcheon, Russell, "A Default of Critical Intelligence? The Scholar of Religion as Public Intellectual," in *Journal of the American Academy of Religion*, 65/2, 1997: 443-468.

de Saussure, Ferdinand, *Course in General Linguistics*, New York, McGraw-Hill, 1959.

Smith, Jonathan Z, *Imagining Religion, From Babylon to Jonestown*, Chicago, University of Chicago Press, 1982.

Wittgenstein, Lüdwig, *Philosophical Investigations*, Third edition, New York, Macmillan Publishing Company, 1958.

Suggested Readings: Annotated Bibliography

Barthes, Roland, *Elements of Semiology*, New York, Hill and Wang, 1973.

– "From Science to Literature" in *The Rustle of Language*, Berkeley, University of California Press, 1989.

   The first work gives one of the more lucid and comprehensive expositions of how Saussure's linguistics can for the basis for a general semiotics. His description of the meta-language/object-language relationship is invaluable. The second work makes a compelling argument for the reduction of science to writing, i.e., science as a specific form of discourse, not as a eidetic knowledge.

Clifford, James, "On Ethnographic Allegory" in Clifford, James and Marcus, George E. (Eds.), *Writing Culture: The Poetics and Politics of Ethnography*, Berkeley, University of California Press, 1986.
> This, along with Clifford's other work, brilliantly analyzes the structure and function of ethnographic discourse. He convincingly demonstrates how this structure *constitutes* the ethnographic object.

Culler, Jonathan, *In Pursuit of Signs: Semiotics, Literature, and Deconstruction*, Ithaca, Cornell University Press, 1981.
> An excellent overview of these methods of literary criticism.

Derrida, Jacques, *Of Grammatology*, Baltimore, Johns Hopkins University Press, 1974.
> A brilliant and "dislodging" work, the reading of which is itself an experience. He discusses the relationship between science and writing and writing and culture in ways which have shaped much contemporary theoretical discussion.

— "Signature Event Context" in *Margins of Philosophy*, Chicago, University of Chicago Press, 1982.
> An excellent critique of the metaphysicalization of the concept of "context" in literary criticism, social science, and historical method.

Foucault, Michel, *The Archaeology of Knowledge and The Discourse On Language*, New York, Pantheon Books, 1972.
> One of the best technical analyses of the nature of discourse and its relationship to literature and philosophy.

Lincoln, Bruce, *Discourse and the Construction of Society: Comparative Studies of Myth, Ritual, and Classification*, New York, Oxford University Press, 1989.
> A very thorough and clear application of discourse theory to the study of religion-virtually the only one of its kind.

Nietzsche, Friedrich, *Zur Genealogie der Moral: Eine Streitschrift*, Berlin, Walter de Gruyter and Company, 1967.
> For all its controversial aspects, this work contains many brilliant *methodological* insights. It is especially useful in showing how interpretative systems absorb one another, and how the scholar of religion can learn from a diachronic analysis of this activity.

Silverman, Kaja, *The Subject of Semiotics*, Oxford, Oxford University Press, 1983.
> An excellent introduction to semiotics generally and Lacanian semiotics in particular.

Todorov, Tzvetan, *Introduction to Poetics,* Minneapolis, University of Minnesota Press, 1981.
— *Genres in Discourse*, New York, Cambridge University Press, 1990.
> Perhaps the best introductions to discourse theory available.

White, Hayden, *Tropics of Discourse*, Baltimore, Johns Hopkins University Press, 1978.
> A very fine analysis of the specific linguistic entities, i.e., tropes, which constitute the structure of discourse itself.

Religion, World, Plurality

William E. Paden

Professor & Chair, Department of Religion
The University of Vermont, Vermont, USA

Religion is not an *object* for which one can have an explanation, but a *word* which points to a variegated domain of different but related phenomena, each of which may appropriately require explanation – or multiple explanations – of a different kind. "Religion" is then not a thing but a start-up category pointing to a general realm or zone of cultural behavior, and that realm may conventionally be described as something like, "behaviors (whether verbal or nonverbal) that refer to and engage culturally postulated superhuman powers deemed to be sacred." While this initially distinguishes religion from science, morality, art and politics as various zones of culture that one may want to look into, it does not essentialize or entify religion. As a region of behavior, types of religion may then be examined just as one might analyze types of military, gaming and courtship behaviors and symbolisms. We, the interpreters, are the ones who postulate these distinctions, for purposes of analysis, and create models or prototypes by which to define and explore them.[1]

In this approach, religion is a broad area that includes not one but innumerable kinds and contexts of relationships with superhuman objects. A topic like this is not an object or datum for explanation any more than "America" or "Asia" is an object for explanation. It is rather a large region with much dimensionality and internal contextuality, with many significations and functions to insiders and outsider-interpreters, with permeable and contested definitional boundaries, a site where one may begin to investigate complexity, form sub-mappings, make discoveries, and, indeed, create new maps and discard old ones.

If religion is understood in this way, it is pointless to contend so wearisomely over what "it" "essentially is." Yet if a singular explanation of religion makes no sense, and the same could be said of music or art, there can certainly be theories of controlled, contextualized aspects of religion. And

193

the aspect we choose to look at already prefigures the kind of explanation one may expect. The primary need today for the secular study of religion is to clarify the relationship of various theoretic frames by making clear the aspect of religion they describe, while also generating more adequate cross-cultural categories and perspective.

An Aspectival Approach to Religion

Religious behavior is simply not monolithic: engagement with superhuman objects takes place at every cognitive level of human consciousness and in every cognitive domain, in every form of social dynamic and causality, in every conceivable historical environment and cultural context, in every type of mythological discourse and meaning-attribution, in every imaginable form of ritual performance and sensory environment – in short, through every genre of human behavior. By the same generic definition stated above, it would be religious to be possessed by a god in a trance state but it would also be religious to maintain fidelity to divinely endowed moral precepts. It would be religious to exercise altruistic care for others in the name of the teachings of the faith and also religious to abandon social attachments to others in order to seek other-worldly communion. For those under threat of chaos, it may be religious to see the "superhuman" as absolute order and stability, but for those bound and suppressed by their social identities, it may appear in the form of liberation from a given, corrupt order. "Religion," then, may either bind or unbind, separate or bring together, invite ascetic constraint or ecstatic dance. It draws on many trajectories of basic behaviors – like territorial marking, submission to authority, bonding, offering and gift-giving, atoning for offenses, sacrificing, communal sharing, and acts of loyalty.[2] Even what seems like a specific categorial theme like sacrifice turns out to not be unitary but quickly break down into quite different modalities and collocations (Strenski 1996: 19-20). The reason we have dozens of fairly reasonable theories of religion, myth, ritual and gods, is because each addresses an important aspect of the subject.

There is no apparent way out of this embarrassingly simple commonsense circularity in which explanations of religion are driven by chosen prototypes. Where "religion" is understood as social belonging, or as ecstatic apparitions, or as ritual, theory must follow suit. The gender dimensions of religion invite gender-factor explanation, out-of-body experiences invite theories of sleep-paralysis and brain-states, and historical changes and syncretisms invite historical expertise and analysis. Thus, Gananath Obeyesekere examines the susceptibility of Sri Lankan women to enter into orgiastic possession trances and applies Freudian theory about repressive sexuality. C. G. Jung looked at mandalic symbols and found emblems of psychological wholeness and polarity. Emile Durkheim studied totemic objects and, behold, found his theory of the totemic principle. Likewise, scholars explain variations on church attendance through notions of suburban change, explain religious submission through evolutionary concepts of authority deference, explain ceremony as a form of display behavior, explain the persistence of tradition by theories of cognitive transmissibility and memory-filters, explain millennialist cults by theories of social marginality, explain prayer by theories of object-relations, explain the rise and fall of cult leaders by theories of ego-inflation and paranoia, explain altruism [unselfishness] and self-abnegation by sociobiological theories of group survival, and explain religious conversions by psychological theories about identity transformation.

When theory works well at one site, the tendency is to hegemonize it, [domination of one site] even though rightness and fit applied to one set of behavioral constraints and defined conditions may be misplaced or irrelevant elsewhere. As theory, after all, is itself a form of political behavior, a kind of struggle for control of the ideological center, we do well to remember its coercive nature. Nor is it unnatural in itself to totalize, to make one's particular theoretic worlds into "the" world, to reduce chaos and complexity by unifying and ultimately inhabiting a world filled with one's own semantic field, a world "good to perceive," (Burkert 1996:165) – in this case, one's invested theory.

The Sui Generis Issue and Beyond

Critics of the idea that religion is a privileged, *sui generis* datum have challenged the discourse of the phenomenology of religion tradition and have attempted to replace it with more scientific, analytical agendas (Segal 1989; Penner 1990; McCutcheon 1997). Their view is that religion and "the sacred" are not unique, autonomous or privileged categories, or something with a supernatural content that requires spiritual intuition on the part of the scholar to be understood. The tradition represented by

Rudolf Otto and Mircea Eliade, the argument runs, epitomizes this privileging and is thus unworthy of the secular academy.

But exposing the theological and political rhetoric of ontological and administrative autonomy should not be an excuse to cease paying attention to what is "different" about the subject matter. All forms of behavior have their own features, their "own kinds" of traits. Moreover, the meanings attributed to actions by their performers – for religion, read "believers" – are part of the data of difference that the outside interpreter must pay attention to.

William James saw both sides of this issue well. On the one hand, he showed that one does not need to posit a special, distinct religious feeling or behavior as a category in its own right, as there is rather a "common storehouse of emotions" – and presumably, actions – "upon which religious objects may draw, ..." (p. 28) On the other hand, "[A]s concrete states of mind, made up of a feeling *plus* a specific sort of object, religious emotions of course are psychic entities distinguishable from other concrete emotions; ..." (p. 28). Religious behavior does not have to be theologically privileged and essentialistically "separate" to be simply different.

Religious humility and praise, then, are homologous with other forms of humility and praise, and yet are "different" from nonreligious humility and praise by virtue of the role of the postulated superhuman object and its significatory context in the mind of the participant. Any behavior, like kneeling, running, shouting, or submissiveness can have a different meaning depending on the context, and religious models function as differential contexts or frames for behavior just like any nonreligious setting does, e.g. athletics, war, or love.

While the behaviors which religion draws upon are from the same fund of general conduct available in nonreligious contexts, conduct which may occur without any superhuman objects – e.g. deference, trance, gift giving, contemplation, and protocols of purification – the superhuman factor in the equation generally adds authority and consequentiality, thus enhancing the intensity and commitment of the human response. In Peter Berger's words, "To go against the order of society is always to risk plunging into anomy. To go against the order of society as religiously legitimated, however, is to make a compact with the primeval forces of darkness" (p. 39).

At the same time, religious activity is more than just structures and analytical features of object-relations and enhanced empowerments. It is typi-

196

cally a way of living and perceiving the world that is invested with values and networked, textured significances conveyed by the participant's mythic tradition and mindset – in short, a form of world habitation. Again, to point this out is not to elevate or idealize the subject matter per se, for the same could be said of the world of psychotic depression or the world of crime. Every domain of experience and culture has a life and logic of its own and constitutes a piece of theatre where roles are played out.

In that regard, the critics of the idea that religion is "its own kind," in lumping Otto and Eliade together as essentialists, have tended to obscure the very significant contributions Eliade made to the analysis of character-istically religious world formations and behaviors. While Otto clearly emphasized the non-natural character of the numinous and capacity to apprehend it, Eliade, while occasionally speaking broadly about the spiri-tual implications of studying the history of religions, for the most part saw sacrality as a category of religious life bearing on the construction of reli-gious universes and thus a structural element in behavior that needed descriptive attention. In this sense Eliade is closer to the Durkheimians, who developed a discourse about the "irreducible" role and character of sacred objects within collective systems, and did so within a decidedly sec-ular conceptual frame (Paden 1994a: 198-206).

Religious Worlds

These considerations lead to the important concept of "worlds" (Good-man 1978; Paden 1994b, 2000). The concept of world assumes that exis-tence or "the universe" is not a given, known, already agreed upon refer-ent, but always a concomitant of interpretation, a product of particular ways of representing and inhabiting it. World thus describes versions of life-space without reducing those versions to an independent norm. The idea of world acknowledges these multiple orderings of reality by not assuming a single, a priori system of knowledge in terms of which all human experience should be described. For example, rather than viewing religions in terms of a given standard, religious or nonreligious, of what "the" world is and then seeing how they, the religions, represent it, the assumption is rather that religions themselves create their own versions of world.

The concept of world is then non-metaphysical. It is isomorphic with system, environment, place of habitation, horizon. It has no structural or thematic content. It is a category that directs attention to context while placing no categorial imposition onto cultural data. Rather, it is an orientational, comparative tool for asking about and identifying the very different contexts that may bear on the import of any particular object or event.

A world is the operating environment of behavioral and linguistic options which persons presuppose, posit and inhabit at any given point in time and from which they choose courses of action. Culture, accordingly, is not a single horizon of linguistic and behavioral expectations, but the entire set of shifting horizons and world-versions available to its members. Humans may act out or encounter many such worlds, even in the course of a day.

Religions provide a conspicuous instance of worldmaking because of the ontological character of their language. It is the nature of religious language to name and script the ultimate powers that determine, ground and empower existence itself, and to fill world-experience with their meaning, agency, presence and authority. Religion is a primary cultural/linguistic instrument for defining and explaining identity, fate, time, space, cosmic order, suffering, danger and other meta-categories. While ontologies can also be shaped by secular and scientific concepts, religious world horizons continue to abound with a vigorous cosmizing and nomizing life, to use Peter Berger's terms (Berger 1967: 19-28).

Broadly speaking, one might say that world habitation rather than "manifestations of the Holy" becomes here the more appropriate conceptual referent for describing religion. The hermeneutical shift is from a version of political monarchy ("the Sacred" as God), within the context of religious edification, to a decentered, pluralistic set of coexisting universes – reflecting a turn from the theological interests of divinity schools to those of the secular academy. But note that as a concept, world has a particularly open-ended character. It can refer to any world-version, religious or nonreligious. It may include the data of postulated experiences of otherness and superhuman powers as it may also feature the data of physical life. It can have virtually any content. It calls attention to the many matrices of experience such as ethnicity, geography, gender and social class that contextualize religious life so diversely. World is both something represented and something practiced; it is imaginal objects and bodies-in-performance; it can be static or mobile. It allows these not only as data expressive of the insider's realities, but at the same time as data for the interpreter to analyze, compare and explain. In its acknowledgement of religious content combined with the endless contextual variables constituting any system, it here reconciles at least some of the traditional concerns of the so-called phenomenology of religion with a socio-anthropological program, and also creates a matrix both for reformulating the notion of sacrality in a non-theological, non-foundationalist sense, and for regrounding comparativism.[3]

Sacrality

The term "sacred" is typically used as a noun, amounting to a kind of generic label for the transcendent, divine, or "wholly other" object of religious experience. But apart from the problem that this tends to foundationalize the referent of religion, it also limits the concept to substantive use rather than allowing it to have adjectival and adverbial meanings which draw attention to *how* insiders behave in relation to religious objects. Sacredness and holiness are not just attributes of objects, but also forms of behavior in relation to objects. The organizing factor in the constitution of religious domains is the constraining relationship between sacred objects and appropriate human responses to them, and "sacrality" can serve as a polythetic, umbrella term for those relational behaviors.

There are any number of ways of identifying these kinds of relationship to such objects. One might say that the superhuman is a realm that humans *receive* through states of possession, awe, gratitude, divination and fate, but also *give to* through acts of offering and sacrifice, and *interact with* through acts of exchange, prayer and communion, and *defend* through acts of protection, adherence to moral and ritual laws, and exorcism of impurities. Any sacred object may elicit any of these actions. Thus, superhuman objects in different religious systems may evoke similar behaviors; objects in the same religious system may evoke different behaviors; and the same object in a single system may evoke different behaviors at different times. Sacrality here refers to the place and requirements of an object within interactive systems, not just to a vague "transcendence."

It also follows that the experience of otherness or numinousness is understood here as *one* modality of religious objects (or relationship to them) rather than as a foundationalist entity hegemonized or essentialized as the single, dominant mode and reified as a phenomenological epithet for God. The superhuman realm may appear as mana-laden and revelatory, as an active agency, but *also* as an object to be kept from violation or defilement – a particularly salient distinction I have elaborated on elsewhere (Paden 1996b). The concept of sacred, superhuman objects needs to be emancipated both from a restrictive revelational model, and from a model that reduces these objects simply to referents of basic, counterintuitive "belief."

It is certainly the case that we need a wider, more complex accounting of superhuman objects and relationships to them. These objects of course not only include deities, ancestors, spirits, buddhas, holy persons, and so forth, but also places, writings, signs, icons, words, principles and symbols that represent any of these. While anything can function as a superhuman object, religious objects are constituted as much by the behaviors they require as by any self-defining mythologizations about their superhuman nature per se. If the objects can do what humans cannot, they start to qualify as superhuman, but this is not enough since cartoon and popular figures like Superman or space aliens can do what humans cannot yet they are ordinarily not objects constraining sacred behaviors.

While the modes of sacrality are not culture-specific, because they draw on human capacities, the content of sacrality is entirely system-specific. The office of the papacy is sacred to Catholics but not to non-Catholics; the Ganges river is sacred to Hindus but not to Jews; the history of the Emperors of Japan is sacred to Shintoists but not to Swiss Protestants; the Jiba in Tenri, Japan, is not the center of the world to those outside the Tenri-Kyo faith. Religious systems crystallize around their own objects, their own linguistic, ritual, historical and geographic "places," reciting quite different histories of the world, observing alternative world calendars, and making unequivocal allegiance to disparate systems of authority and lineage.

Comparative Perspective

Understanding the realm of religion means being grounded in comparative perspective. Comparative concepts show common, human processes amidst otherwise diverse cultures, while also allowing us to perceive and explain differences relative to those common forms, so that the study of religion develops by identifying both what is generic and what is specific in the subject matter. Generalizations about religion therefore issue from, and are accountable to, the kind of conceptual analysis that issues from responsible, controlled comparative work. Today comparison is not limited to marshalling parallel religious motifs, much less comparing religions as wholes, but analyzes religious factors as they interact with *any* of the patterns and variables that comprise the human situation.

Comparativism builds a vocabulary not available in the limited language of the religious insiders – just as economics builds a language beyond the vocabulary of any particular system, or comparative literature builds analytical terms beyond the poetics of any one tradition. This is at once the great de-provincializing achievement of religious studies and one of its most serious, ongoing problems, given the issues of commensurability between different cultural contexts. Yet one cannot even begin to describe and explain human behavior at any historical or ethnographic level without conceptualizations, which are themselves comparative formations. The issue is not whether to compare, but what to compare and how to get the comparability factor right.

Cross-cultural study certainly shows common features of religious worldmaking activity. Nor does connecting these features with generic human activity disregard their religious form. Humans *do* religious worlds. They make them as naturally as birds build nests. While every spider has a distinctive pattern of web-making, they all build webs. All religious worlds make pasts by transmitting memories of sacred, founding events and mythic histories; they all cosmicize or absolutize their own sacred symbols and authorities; they protect these symbols from violation; and they always renew their sacred objects and categories through periodic observances.

The discovery of otherwise unnoticed commonality and the discovery of otherwise unnoticed difference are therefore both functions of comparison. If religious cultures commonly conduct periodic rites of world-renewal, linking their community with "the Great Time" of myth, each one does so by giving a different content to what it is that is being renewed, e.g. hierarchic family relationships, or the dependency of laity and monks, or economic exchange alliances between villages, or the prestige of the founder. Moreover, if classic phenomenologies tried to illus-

201

trate the ubiquity of versions of sacred space and time, contemporary historians of religion are more interested in the way myth and ritual reveal particular, cultural worlds of gender, class, power, sexuality and "local knowledge." At the same time, differences do go all the way down to the individuals in the culture, and we should beware of essentialist projections onto what cultures think or do as wholes (Doniger 1996: 114-115).

The significant common factor in comparison here is that it is in every case *human beings* that are engaging in religious actions. An era of emphasis on cultural differences has either obscured or trivialized this bedrock, bioanthropological referent.[4] Religions share certain features because it is humans who are the actors, just as in every culture there are common factors in the way humans eat, work, sleep, make love, bring up families, play, and make art. Likewise, humans recite myth, offer to gods, and perform rites of purity. Again, if previously comparative religion abstracted out and focused on the religious content of these, we are today equally interested in the nature of recitation (who recites, and why, and how, and in what context), the politics of exchange, and the sociology of purity.

We therefore need not limit comparative religion to juxtaposing only religious material per se, but also see religious behaviors in the context of the kind of human behavior they are drawn from, not isolating religious versions as being "outside of nature's order altogether" (James 1985: 24). Comparativism enlarges its notion of patterns by not limiting them to an inventory of religious genres (prayer, priesthood, deity), because religion as a subject matter is filled with all the same "patterns" as found in human culture generally, e.g. authority, order, freedom, economic status, class and gender interests, types of environment, ego development and types of personality. This generates more complex templates of comparison, differentiated typologies, and thus more variations and bases for showing difference. Comparativism builds and extends its vocabulary by using all these crisscrossing matrices of understanding and explanation, thus acknowledging and addressing religion's complexity (indeed, the world's complexity), showing the relationship between religious and nonreligious realms, checking our propensity for conceptually monolithic packagings and reductions, and providing a zone of integration that joins the interests of the history of religions and the social sciences.

Finally, in all this connectedness of "religion" with comparative themes, all comparativism should be conducted by controlled, delimitative aspectual focus. Fitz John Porter Poole states this well: "Comparison does not deal with phenomena *in toto* or in the round, but only with an aspectual characteristic of them. Analytical control over the framework of comparison involves theoretically focused selection of significant aspects of the phenomena ..." (p. 414). Two or more objects may then be comparable in one respect, but not in others; they may have some point of commonality, but be unlike in every other way. Comparison has the right to pick out single points of analogy for its own theoretic purposes. In this way, comparative method is itself a tool of the general approach to religion outlined above that shows the subject matter to be modal and domain oriented. These domains, thematizations or conceptual zones may be large ("world," "authority"), small (hand-washing rites in Moroccan Muslim villages), and complex or formulaic (correlations between urbanization, kinship solidarity and Passover observance in industrial North America).

Religion and Nature: The Broad View

Negotiation with postulated superhuman objects and the sacralization of life environments in relation to sacred objects apparently count among the natural dispositions of human behavior. It is natural to bond reciprocally with these ostensible ruling forces of the environment, to give to them in order to receive from them. It is natural to defend these objects from any violation and to sense guilt, impurity or the need for atonement if infraction of their order occurs. It is natural to see the whole of time and space in terms of one's own ancestries and ritual categories, just as it is natural to equate one's moral order with the ultimate order of the universe and it is natural to find "the absolute," centripetally, in one's own communal shrine. It is natural to form boundaries of kosher and nonkosher, and it is natural to draw contemporary meaning from the founders and other mythic exemplars of one's collective memory. Likewise, the "doing" of myth and theology can be understood not just as disembodied speculation, but as a natural activity, a behavior, namely the behavior of meaning-giving, orienting, reciting, and performing. In such ways, the study of religion is the study of the variety and relativity of human worldmaking and the variety of cognitive situations that transmit or undergird both religious and nonreligious behaviors (cf. Boyer 1994).

These sacred, superhuman objects will have multiple functions both for insiders and according to interpreters. Any one function may be more or less relevant or operable depending on context. Thus, sacred objects: a) give focus and explicitness to values and worlds that would otherwise remain unfocused and implicit, b) give status, dignity, objectivity and stability to what would otherwise only be taken as transient human invention, c) provide an expanded, surplus repertory of imagination for the psyche and thus its capacity to express many voices, d) provide an alter-ego, an "other," in relation to which participants can form behaviors and attitudes that would be unexpressed without such a compelling object-relation, e) call forth more authoritative forms of respect, accountability, dependability and disciplined performance than would obtain through nonreligious conceptions, f) give a name to the forces of the adherent's world that appear to bear upon healing, strength in adversity, liberation, destiny and fate, and g) ritualize and anchor, at a postulated transhuman level, practices of social solidarity, status, and difference. Likewise, in the name of the superhuman, religion gives enhanced value and exemplary standards to particular behavioral qualities that vary from system to system but include, for instance, devotion, respect, honor, sense of purity, humility, courage, fortitude, integrity, capacity for selflessness, self-criticism, and the many versions of holiness generally. Other cultural forms like nationalism, ideologies, educational systems, and philosophies do some of this "virtue-enhancing," and certainly maintain some of the functions listed above, but it could be said that religion in its more conspicuous forms virtually specializes in it.

Yet none of this means "religion" is necessarily good or desirable or that "the sacred" is by definition simply a benign force in culture that radiates transcendental truths. The same force which mythicizes positive qualities can foster negative ones. Religious world views manifest the same human problems as any world views, and thus can become systems of aggression and violence, discrimination and subordination, fear and ignorance, colonialism and racism, paranoidal inflation and banal trivialization. The gods may be masks for fickle political honor, and the fact that they are deities does not mean they cannot be tyrants. Religious authorities are themselves subject to destructive paranoias. In these senses, religion attracts all that human nature has to offer, functional or dysfunctional, showcasing the range of human conduct. It is not something that simply shows us a divine, cosmic transcendence (classically, "the sacred"), but a part of the world that blends sacrality with webs of social power and political legitimation.

In this last regard, religious objects and behaviors are not only reflections of nonreligious objects and behaviors, but also the other way around. That is, religion throws perspective on our ordinary nature because it amplifies or intensifies features of behavior that are already there and implicit in quasi-religious forms. Both Durkheim and Eliade saw this well – the way societies elevate and idolize their heroes and give them a "supernature," construct social and political mythologies, and indulge in secular initiatory schemas and rites. So it is not just that religious praise is "like" ordinary praise, but also that ordinary praise is "like" religious praise. The analogies go both ways. In this way, religion shows us dimensions of humanity.

Final Points

In its pluralistic stance, this essay implicates certain notions of reflexivity and constructivism. Some clarification is in order.

I am not advocating that every interpretation of religion is merely capricious. That there is no uninterpreted world does not mean there is nothing out there (or in here). Agreeing with Byron Good's statement that "perspectivism is rooted in reality itself" (p. 177), my view is not that everything is an invention of the interpreter or that the world is "only" or "merely" in the eye of the beholder, but rather that the world is a multidimensional immensity that the interpreter selects from and observes in some particular context, and that one should be aware of the way interpretation both gains and limits access to what is there, and thus become accountable for why we choose to look at what we do. The study of religion can become a vast lesson in such reciprocities and positionalities – which is to say, in methodological reflexivity.

Because I am impressed by the relational, reciprocal nature of meaning and the way objects and world take place and form through human positionings, I prefer neither the objectivist view that reality is there simply to be represented by subjects, nor the subjectivist view that human interpretation makes it all up, but rather a reciprocity model wherein the world gives itself through the receiving and configuring acts of the subject. The approach is addressed more fully in my *Interpreting the Sacred* (1992: 110-135).

Are religious worlds "just" constructs? We speak of worlds as constructions at one level of generalization in order to point to the plurality and cultural relativity of reality-versions and the strong role of human activity in the formation of environments. But worlds, including religious worlds, are also environments to which one attends and responds.[5] In that setting, "making" a world is only one aspect of the process. Humans, as Paul Ricoeur puts it, also "render" a world, like an artist (1981: 116-120). They also surrender to it, discover and receive it, and give it back. Even to the extent that worlds are our creations, our cultural artifacts, they nevertheless present themselves already externalized to individuals and thus as non-arbitrary, given objectivities (Berger 1967: 3-28). This externalization and objectivation is certainly the case with language, knowledges, and all the arts and categories of any civilization. From this angle, worlds come to individuals already weighted with a certain ontological authority.

It follows that I would not restrict the notion of world to metaphors of building. Worlds are not just constructions, but habitations; not just inventions, but expressions; not just projections, but performances and engagements; not just fabrications but ways of seeing, doing and behaving.

It is not, then, that religious systems are without reality, without foundation, without reference, but rather that they posit and mediate their own realities, foundations, and references. Such a view takes every world as its own performance, voices and renderings. Indeed, these expressions are what we are trying to learn about. They are "the data." What we do with them is the work of analysis, comparison, explanation and evaluation.

In all, the huge domain of the history of religion – that interesting space of human possibilities – is not only a lesson in the nature of worldmaking, the mutually constitutive nature of human subjects and their sacred objects, and the revealingly various regimens and contents of those objects, but also an occasion for coming to clarity about how our categories both occlude and reveal what is there.

For the scholar of comparative religion there is surely here a new public-facing responsibility. That role goes beyond the de-exoticizing, irenical occupations of describing "the religions of the world," just as it is unrelated to the popular, universalizing discourses about archetypal spiritual journeys. The comparativist's task is to reintegrate the comparative, thematic study of religion with the general study of culture and society, an employment not to be left to social scientists or sociobiologists who harbor only western, essentialized or otherwise popular notions of "religion." Moreover, if the field of religious studies continues to view cross-cultural work as a sideline activity rather than a matrix for the study of any and all religion (e.g. Christian traditions, biblical religion), public knowledges about religion can only remain in their current undeveloped state, subject to the stereotypical templates and interests of committed insiders, market-feeding media editors, or New Age prophets.

Once comparativists are able to reconstruct their subject matter in the post-Eliadean era, prospects of translating knowledge to the lay public should follow, including works that can potentially influence the evolution of public education curricula and media journalism. A new realism about "religion" here will neither be an anti-theological broadside nor an essentialist privileging of a monolithic, spiritual "thing," but will embody an evenhanded perspectivalism that at once contextualizes religious activity within the various modes of human behaviors while also showing the way religious forms – just like those of politics, sport, music, and other developed institutions and vocabularies of culture – create their own evolving modes of human expression and habitation.

Notes

A previous version of this article, with the same little, appeared in Thomas A. Idinopulos and Brian C. Wilson (eds.), *What is Religion? Origins Definitions, & Explanations* (studies in the History of Religions, LXXXI), E. J. Brill, Leiden, 1994: 91-106.

1. A useful introduction to prototype theory as applied to religion is Saler 1993: 197-226.
2. Walter Burkert's *Creation of the Sacred* (1996) does an admirable job of examining several of these modalities in relation to specific biological, evolutionary contexts.
3. On the issue of a "new comparativism" see the panel on that subject published in *Method and Theory in the Study of Religion*, 8-1, pp. 1-49, with contributions by Luther Martin, Marsha Hewitt, Donald Wiebe, E. Thomas Lawson and myself.
4. Donald Brown's *Human Universals* (1991) is a useful account of the history of the question of anthropological universals, and a compelling case for reconsidering the issue. It includes an extensive annotated bibliography on the subject.
5. I draw the distinction of "attending" to the world vs. "constructing" the world from Tim Ingold, in Tim Ingold, ed., *Key Debates in Anthropology* (London: Routledge, 1996), p. 115. A section of this volume (pp. 99-146) includes a useful debate among anthropologists on the concept of the cultural construction of human worlds.

References

Berger, Peter, *The Sacred Canopy: Elements of a Sociological Theory of Religion*, Doubleday, New York, 1967.

Boyer, Pascal, *The Naturalness of Religious Ideas: A Cognitive Theory of Religion*, University of California Press, Berkeley, 1994.

Brown, Donald E., *Human Universals*, Philadelphia, Temple University Press, 1991.

Burkert, Walter, *Creation of the Sacred: Tracks of Biology in Early Religions*, Harvard University Press, Cambridge, MA, 1996.

Doniger, Wendy, "Minimyths and Maximyths and Political Points of View," in Laurie Patton and Wendy Doniger (eds.), *Myth and Method*, University of Virginia Press, Charlottesville, 1996: 109-127.

Good, Byron, *Medicine, Rationality, and Experience: An Anthropological Perspective*, Cambridge University Press, New York, 1994.

Goodman, Nelson, *Ways of Worldmaking*, Hackett Publishing Co., Indianapolis, 1978.

Ingold, Tim, (ed.), *Key Debates in Anthropology*, Routledge, London, 1996.

James, William, *The Varieties of Religious Experience*, Penguin Books, New York, 1985.

McCutcheon, Russell T., *Manufacturing Religion: The Discourse on Sui Generis Religion and the Politics of Nostalgia*, Oxford University Press, New York, 1997.

Paden, William E., "World," in Willi Braun and Russell T. McCutcheon, eds., *Guide to the Study of Religion*, Cassell, London, 2000: 334-347.

— "Elements of a New Comparativism," in *Method and Theory in the Study of Religion*, 8/1, 1996a: 5-14.

— "Sacrality as Integrity: 'Sacred Order' as a Model for Describing Religious Worlds," in Thomas A. Idinopulos and Edward A. Yonan (eds.), *The Sacred and its Scholars: Comparative Methodologies for the Study of Primary Religious Data*, (Studies in the History of Religions, Vol. LXXIII), E.J. Brill, Leiden, 1996b: 3-18.

— "Before 'the Sacred' Became Theological: Durkheim and Reductionism," in Thomas A. Idinopulos and Edward A. Yonan (eds.), *Religion and Reductionism* (Studies in the History of Religions, LXII), E.J. Brill, Leiden, 1994a: 198-210.

— *Religious Worlds: The Comparative Study of Religion*, 2d ed., Beacon Press, Boston, 1994b.

— *Interpreting the Sacred: Ways of Viewing Religion*, Boston, Beacon Press, 1992.

Penner, Hans H., *Impasse and Resolution: A Critique of the Study of Religion*, New York: Peter Lang Press, 1990.

Poole, Fitz John Porter, "Metaphors and Maps: Towards Comparison in the Anthropology of Religion," *Journal of the American Academy of Religion* 54, no. 3, 1986: 411-457.

Ricoeur, Paul, review of Nelson Goodman's *Ways of Worldmaking*, in *Philosophy and Literature*, Spring, 1980: 107-120.

Saler, Benson, *Conceptualizing Religion: Immanent Anthropologists, Transcendent Natives, and Unbounded Categories*, E.J. Brill, Leiden, 1993.

Segal, Robert, *Religion and the Social Sciences: Essays on the Confrontation*, Atlanta: Scholars Press, 1989.

Strenski, Ivan, "Between Theory and Speciality: Sacrifice in the 90s," in *Religious Studies Review*, vol. 22/1, 1996: 10-20.

Westernism Unmasked

Michael Pye

Professor, Institut für Religionswissenschaft
Universität Marburg, Marburg, Germany

Preview of arguments

The position expressed in this article is that it is intellectually viable, worthwhile and interesting to work out theories of religion which are not themselves religious. Such theories relate to phenomena or systems which can be identified in the wider context of human history, culture and society, and can sensibly be designated as religion(s) for the purpose of investigation. This will be illustrated under the heading "adumbrating the field" immediately below. The adumbration of a field provides a starting point for the identification of sources which provide evidence for the phenomena in question, the selection of appropriate methods for their study and for the engendering of theories to elucidate and explain them. Though the relation between method and theory is close and subtle, methodology will only be touched on in passing, since the relevant points have been set out recently elsewhere (Pye 1999). Here we shall proceed rapidly to a consideration of theory in the study of religion(s). Theories of religion may be described as scientific in so far as they are rational, empirical, explanatory and testable. Though common to all science, these features will be commented on with particular reference to the field in question.

Naturally, theories of religion are themselves developed in particular intellectual and social contexts, and have their own history. While there is an increasing recognition of the importance of this among specialists, it is argued below that several dominant conditions affecting recent and present work are among those least clearly seen. Accordingly a number of currently significant, but widely ignored conditioning factors will be pointed out under the heading "historical locations". In particular, there is a widespread view that scientific theories of religion are a product of "the western world" and are somehow reduced intellectually by being limited to such a world. Arguments are adduced against this view in the interest of promoting a more stable, interculturally recognisable understanding of the study of religions. Towards the end of the article, various questions which should be regarded as extraneous to the development of scientific theories of religion are briefly adduced under the heading "questions to be set aside". Though interesting in themselves, these questions have to be set to one side when proceeding scientifically, and they are considered here in order to indicate where the necessary distinctions between different kinds of reflection are thought to lie.

Adumbrating the field

Contrary to much vague discussion, it is not at all difficult to provide a tentative, open-ended adumbration of the field adressed in the scientific study of religions. This will be demonstrated by the following definition which is intended to be understood in terms of the well-known idea of family resemblances. The term religion may be used to refer to patterns of (i) various inter-related behaviours including, for example, ritual practices and the design and use of special sites and buildings, (ii) more or less normative beliefs, symbols, images and other representations, (iii) a variety of social forms such as mass movements, local gatherings, churches, special interest groups and the specialised roles of individuals, and (iv) a subjective focusing in an awareness of power, otherness, holiness, depth, security, healing, release, and so on. The order in which these four aspects are delineated is immaterial, and no one of them determines the others exclusively. Moreover the relations between them (six simple relations, not to mention complex ones) are as significant as the aspects viewed severally. These patterns can be distinctively documented in various cultures and can be seen to have developed and declined, to have been transmitted, to have been politically espoused or suppressed, and so on. They display signs both of mutual influence and of other similarities apparently related to the recurrent features of human experience. It pertains to this adumbration of the field to provide examples, and the reader shall not be left without them. Prominent examples of religion are the great cosmo-political systems of the ancient world, many of which persist in some form today or have successor examples such as Islam or the religions of specific peoples such as traditional forms of Hinduism, Judaism or Shinto. Many others are systems of salvation, release and guidance such as Buddhism, Christianity and smaller religious groups with their own specific teaching. Innumerable further examples could be named without difficulty, although their names may not be equally well known in all quarters (e.g. Byakko Shinkokai, Cao Dai, Umbanda) Many derivative and marginal cases have fewer of the common characteristics of religions but are nonetheless relevant for systematic observation and analsysis. Also relevant to the field of investigation are less clearly organised religious spectra which have been designated as civil religion, invisible religion, implicit religion, common religiosity, etc.. Given that there is such a field including a wide range of such phenomena, though not exhaustively delimited above, and that the field can be investigated, the question of the development of appropriate theory or theories arises.

This delineation of the object of study is an alternative version of one advanced quite a long time ago (Pye 1982: 70), where it was termed a heuristic or operational definition. This terminology diverges from that of Robert Baird who, inadvisedly following the usage of logician Richard Robinson, uses "functional definition" in an analogous way (Baird 1971: 6ff). In the present connection "functional" is a very unsatisfactory term, for it commonly implies an explanation (as in "functionalism") which goes beyond the heuristic. It should therefore be avoided in the initial adumbration of the field of investigation. In seeking what he intended to be a heuristic definition, Baird landed on a spot very close to Paul Tillich's definition of religion as "ultimate concern". However, this too should be avoided, for while seeming to be generally formulated it in fact implies a normative, participant's view as to what should count as valid or significant religion. It was of course worth considering whether Tillich's definition *might* be taken over as an operational one for the general study of religions, and at that time it was widely current. However I distanced myself from it precisely in the interests of distinguishing an operational definition from a normative one (Pye 1972: 10-12). As I pointed out then, there is much religion which is not really about "ultimate concern". Rather, it is about proximate concerns. Many examples of this could be drawn from all over the world, and it is strikingly the case in the countries of East Asia and Latin America. Thus we have a clear example of an idea which had penetrative theological force for its author, Tillich, but for this very reason, i.e. because of its one-sided, normative-definitive interest, was not in fact appropriate as an operational definition for the study of religions. The one-pointedness of such definitions always betrays their real import, as can easily be seen in the precursor definitions advanced by Schleiermacher (absolute dependence) or Otto (sense of the numinous), both of which are theologically derived and motivated. Compared with all these, the open-endedness of a (non-theological) "family-resemblance" operational definition of religion(s) and its appropriateness for the study of religions should be very obvious by now.

Relating method and theory

When people point out that the study of religions does not have any one single method which is unique to itself, this is often thought to imply that there can be no such discipline as the study of religions at all. Studying religions is just a part of history, or a part of sociology. What is overlooked thereby is that the study of religions does require a particular *clustering* of methods in order to do justice to its subject matter. This clustering of methods arises in part because of the nature of the sources which are, variously, written, oral and material. The need for an integrative clustering of methods arises in connection with attention being paid to these various kinds of source with regard to their relevance for the delineated subject matter, namely religion(s). As a result, the study of religions cannot be locked one-sidedly into the "historico-philological" method, if indeed any such investigatory method can still be purely maintained. Nor can it be located restrictively in social-scientific methods, as if the vast quantity of historical sources, both textual and material, could be relegated to the cellars. The main general steps in the method required for the study of religions are elucidation (of data), characterisation, comparison, and explanation. The first two of these may further be defined as *recognitional* in that their primary purpose lies in taking cognisance of a particular unit of data. Comparison and explanation, being more complex, can only take place on the basis of prior recognitional study.[1]

There is a complex relationship between sources, method and theory in the study of religions, not least because the scientific study of religions is already in progress, so that new steps taken within the discipline make use of, and test, previous theoretical advances. On the one hand the development of particular theoretical constructs is itself part of the overall method required for studying religions. On the other hand particular aspects of method may be specified in accordance with the steps taken in research and theory development, as in the sequence: elucidation, characterisation, comparison, and explanation. At the same time there are other features of method which, though not in themselves theoretical, are necessary if elementary steps in the investigation of the subject matter. An example of this would be the act of comparison, which is not in iself a "theory", although some theory might arise out of an act of comparison. As noted already, the study of religion(s) does not have any methods unique to itself, but it does have a typical *clustering* of methods which is particularly appropriate to its subject. The specific clustering of methods is devised not only to take account of the appropriate sources but also to mediate between the relevant data and theory development. As to theory, the main forms are general theory, morphology, typology, thematic analyses, and explanatory theory. The purpose of this paper is not to develop such theories in detail, which would take up far too much space, but to attempt to situate such theory development correctly. Suffice it to say that the argument does not take place in a vacuum, but in the context of my own attempts to contribute to theory development especially in the areas of morphology, tradition, syncretism and religious innovation.

Rational, empirical, explanatory, testable

The elementary features of any theory of religion(s) which could be regarded as "scientific" in the manner intended here are that it should be rational, empirical, explanatory and testable. Each of these features is necessary for a theory of religion(s) but only taken together do they become sufficient. They are commonplace features of modern scientific enquiry which do not require any particular justification by specialists in the study of religion(s). A few additional comments on each one is necessary, however, in order to exclude some common misunderstandings and to make the general position clear.

While the relations between religion and reason and/or rationality have been the subject of debate in endless variations throughout western intellectual history, these debates have usually been concerned with the evaluation of religious truth claims. In other words, they have mirrored the question of the relations between revelation and reason or faith and reason, as reflected upon in all the western theistic traditions. Interestingly these debates have not been paralleled closely in other cultures, in spite of the intimate relations between Indian logic and both Buddhist and Hindu thought. In some cultural contexts it is even difficult to explain what the debates have been about. However that may be, such debates are not directly relevant to theories of religion(s). The extensive book series entitled *Religion and Reason* edited by Jacques Waardenburg lives partly on the borrowed capital of this chapter of intellectual history while some of its titles move away from it into the scientific study of religions. The same may be said of Ninian Smart's *Reasons and Faiths* which is partly about traditional questions in the western philosophy of religion concerning the correlation of reason with faith, and partly, and perhaps more importantly, lays a foundation for a substantial comparative theory of religions (Smart 1958). On the relation between science of religion as a rational enterprise and other questions pertaining to religion and rationality see further in the section entitled "Questions to set aside."

More recent times have also seen specialised debates about the relations between apparently conflicting systems of thought which claim to be rational, or appear to sophisticated observers to imply such a claim. Thus there is the question of the relation between "magic" as a ritual system which is rational in its own right, and "observer rationality"(Winch, Evans-Pritchard). Whatever the interest of these debates, it should be clearly recognised that it is not for specialists in the study of religions to mount their own particular view of "rationality." Nor is it possible to pretend that there are various optional "rationalities" which could all be operationalised in the scientific study of religions. Specialists in the study of religions as a scientific enterprise can do no other than presuppose, and maintain, the rationality of the enterprise itself. As human beings, they can of course, if they wish, simply give up studying religions and pursue whatever other interests they may have. That is another matter. During the scientific study of religions the internal coherence of any one of the systems under study should be respected, at least at the recognitional stages of elucidation and characterisation (c.f. previous remarks on method). The manner of its plausibility for those who religiously entertain it or practice it is one of the features to be studied.

The second most important feature of any theory of religion(s) which could be regarded as "scientific" in the sense indicated above is that its reference is empirical. That is, it relates to historically or socio-scientifically documentable phenomena. Specifically, it relates to those which fall within the adumbration of the field. In this regard it is easy to be misled by the idea that "religion" is somehow in the mind. All religious systems exist at least in part in the minds of the believers or participants. But these believers are socially observable. They behave in various ways, and leave traces of activity and thought which become sources for the study of religions. Even more pernicious is the one-sided assertion that the object of study is located in the mind of the observer. In some sense, this is of course true. However it is not only located there. The study of religions refers to a field which is, in the common phrase, "out there". By contrast, if it is held that religious systems are "only" in the mind of the observer, or in some such sense "only" subjectively accessible by an observer, the theories produced will be scientifically ungrounded. For this reason "post-modernist" accounts of religion are often worthless. To put it another way, it is hard to find a post-modernist account of religion which is in fact about the field. By contrast the view is taken here that there are in fact data in the field which can be documented on the basis of sources open to more than one investigator and consequently studied in a publicly accessible manner. In this sense the reference of the scientific study of religions is empirical.

The third feature of a theory of religion(s) is its explanatory character. This means that the theory perceives and reports something which was not previously obvious to the casual observer or to the participant or actor in the religious system or situation. "Explanation" can be provided in two stages. Initially there is the stage of internal explanation, that is to say, the explication or clarification of coherences or structures within the system under study, viewed under its four main aspects (c.f. remarks under "adumbrating the field" above). It pertains to the rationality of theory that such coherences or structures are likely to be discernible in a series of separate cases or situations. Second, there is the stage of explanation in terms of historical, social, cultural or psychological factors other than the religious system or situation itself. This may be called functional explanation. It means that the religious and non-religious factors are correlated with each other in a manner which explains their mutual functions. It is desirable for this mode of explanation to be preceded by the first, since it is then less likely to be mistaken. For example, mistaken applications of Weberian explanation to Japanese religions have been based on a misunderstanding of the internal structuring of certain forms of Buddhism with regard to "this-worldly" and "other-worldly". In fact, both Pure Land Buddhism and even more markedly Shin-Buddhism, though entertaining the notion of rebirth in a "pure land" after death, display a this-worldly orientation as a result of a response to experienced grace, as in Lutheranism and Calvinism.

The fourth feature is testability. Though test-tubes can hardly be used in this regard the principle of testability is important in all scientific theory, for otherwise it languishes in the realm of speculation. In so far as theories of religion(s) display the three features already delineated, they are also in principle testable by other investigators attending to the same field. This may be difficult, for the field is changing, and disappearing, all the time. Usually it will be too late for another observer to study exactly the same phenomena. However, it should be possible in some sense to follow through the process of investigation and reflective analysis, once again, to such an extent that assent, or dissent, can be given by others to the results previously presented. To use a convenient German term, research should in principle be *nachvollziehbar*. This may be done by follow-up research in a given field, taking note of intervening social changes, or it may be done by a reworking of the accumulated data, taking new information and theoretical adjustments into account. Corrections do not necessarily invalidate the previous research. They adjust it and develop it.

Historical locations of theories of religion(s)

These elementary features of modern non-religious theories of religion(s) do not in themselves amount to a specific theory or theories, of which there have been very many. It is important to understand however that a theory of religion(s) can hardly arise as a complete abstraction. On the contrary, it can only be developed in the context of other intellectual movements. A theory of religion(s) may be the clear product of a particular, wider intellectual movement, it may be indirectly dependent on particular developments, or it may resist the general tide in some way.

It is not yet clear, for example, whether "post-modernism" as an intellectual movement will itself (or itselves) produce new theories of religion, simply destroy some previously current ones, or eventually turn out to have been largely irrelevant. Specialists in religion must be watchful in this regard. It is not self-evident that any one, rather recent intellectual movement is more likely to produce theoretical advances in the study of religion than those of previous intellectual movements which are now scorned. How much does it really help to designate particular theories of religion(s) as premodern, modern or postmodern, colonial or postcolonial? Sometimes one gets the impression that a theory of religion should be, above all, post-everything, and then it would be all right. I recently received an e-mail message with the structure: "Is there still anybody out there who thinks...if so I would like to hear from them!" The word "still" may sound rather plaintive, but often it is used as a term of abuse.

Nevertheless it has been evident for a long time, and at least for most of the twentieth century, that theories of religion(s) are themselves historically located, as clearly argued by Ernst Troeltsch. Typical of the twentieth century are influential works on the history of the study of religion(s), or historical appraisals of theory of religion(s), by writers such as de Vries (1961/1967) Evans-Pritchard (1965), Sharpe 1975), Waardenburg (1973, via source extracts), Preus (1987), Strenski (1987) and, most recently, McCutcheon (1997). There has been a parallel literature in adjacent disciplines such as social anthropology (Kuper 1973) and of course in the wider discussion of "orientalism." There has also been increasing interest in the historical characteristics of western studies of East Asian religions (Pye 1978, Girardot 1999, Urban 1999) and in particular of Buddhism (Almond 1988, Amstutz 1997).

However there remain very considerable problems with the available presentations of the history of the study and theory of religion(s). In particular there is remarkably little agreement about the pivotal role, for the western world, of the European Enlightenment. Sharpe emphasised nineteenth century evolutionism as the matrix for the comparative study of religions, while recently Preus has quite rightly been looking back to the seventeenth century for the emergence of particular constituents of such study (Preus 1998). Relevant features of the European intellectual movements prior to the Enlightenment are usually identified very tentatively by reference to authors of classical antiquity (for example, Euhemeros or Cicero). But what happened in between? Moreover there is no balanced account even of the modern European development of the study of religion(s) which takes account of the various national traditions involved. A number of contributions have sought to redress the balance with regard to the francophone tradition (see especially Despland 1991). The matter can also be pursued in articles relating to Scandinavia, Poland, Spain, and elsewhere, as abstracted in the bibliographical journal *Science of Religion* under the heading "history of subject". But the resultant picture has not been drawn together. Much of it goes ignored in English-language writing.

Some of the above mentioned works are very up-to-date, and appear to have gained a vantage-point which is "post-" everything so far thought of. Yet it is not at all clear that all the components in the history of the study of religions have yet been identified, or that they have been well correlated with each other. Some of the important phases are very obvious by now, for example: the Enlightenment, Romanticism, colonialism, the missionary movement, evolutionism, historicism, and orientalism. However other important contextualisers are not recognised. Their importance remains underestimated. Four may be named: neo-colonialism, cold-war-ism, oil wealth, and intercultural exoticism. Attention has been drawn to these before (Pye 1997) but the precise correlation of these with movements in the study of religion(s) has not even begun to be considered in detail. Thus while colonialism can be seen with relative retrospective clarity, leading to the use of the term "post-colonial", neo-colonialism appears to go largely unnoticed. The same applies to cold-war-ism. The history of theories of religion during the cold war, which covered half a century, will eventually have to be written with an adequate correlation of both sides. "Half a century" is approximate, but the Cold War did not immediately come to an end on the western side simply with the opening of the political frontiers. In fact, by many, it is still being waged, as I have argued in a paper entitled: "Political correctness in the study of religions: Is the Cold War really over?"[2]. Similarly oil wealth has led to a special brisance between the economic haves and have-nots and their diverse relations to the United States and its allies. Consequently quite special, and often misleading perceptions of Islam have become dominant, even while Islam-related studies are funded in part by the oil-rich. As a result the word "fundamentalism" has passed into widespread media use and has largely lost its value for theoretical analyses of religion. Finally, intercultural exoticism, in religious terms "New Age," has been the starting point for many students of the subject in recent decades and has to be understood both in relation to the home culture and to those used as exotic reference points. In short, if the history of the study of religion(s) is now being reconsidered under many aspects, these factors too need to be taken into account seriously.

But just how are theories of religion(s) related to a historical context? While it is important to appraise theories of religion in their intellectual and social context, it is not adequate to think that theories of religion are no more than the products of other things which are going on in "history." A scientific theory can be better or worse than others, and while its features can themselves be explained in terms of intellectual history the question of its appropriateness or validity remains to be answered. Moreover the force of any theory as related to knowable data, that is, its scientific plausibility, is likely to have some influence on its durability.

Westernism unmasked

It is notable that most accounts of the history of theories of religion(s) are restricted to western intellectual history. This is because it is widely assumed that the study of religion is a western "product" or "project." For one way of putting it we may quote some published lectures by Samuel Preus: "It [religion] is a product of history, and so is its study, as we practice it here and now – a peculiar product of Western historical experience and reflection." (Preus 1998: 3). It is fair to say that the phrase "a product of history", which is found here, is in widespread use. But in what sense does "history" have "products"? More limitedly we might wish to say that something is a part of history, in which case little is being said, for nowadays we not only have histories of the world, but even of "time" itself. Naturally everything knowable which has an empirical reference is a part of history in such a sense. Or we might wish to say that the study of religion is the "product" of other factors *within* history. From the context it would seem that this is what Preus is suggesting. Now while there is no doubt that it is at least this, and that western intellectual traditions have a wide influence on the way religion is viewed by the intellectual classes of non-western countries today, it remains a partial truth only. It really is astonishing that Eurocentrism (also widely adopted by North Americans) continues to have such a strong hold on writers in this field. Preus states it uncompromisingly as far as the modern study of religion in the west is concerned when, reflecting on its origins, he writes that "westerners were intellectually equipped" with "a second system of knowledge – namely, philosophy – grounded in the Greek discovery of the Logos." (Preus 1998: 3) He goes on to argue that this "universal reason" provided a perspective from outside religious cultures by means of which it became possible to reflect upon them. Assuming widespread assent to the premise on the part of his audience, he began his above quoted lectures with the question, "Something in our culture that nobody has quite figured out is this: why is the modern study of religion an invention of the West; why is it not done anywhere else quite like the way it is done here? Why does it not even seem to make sense in other cultures?" (Preus 1998: 3)

This premise is however only partially correct. It is right to suggest that "nobody else" has done "it" in quite the same way. Everybody does it in a slightly different way, which makes the intercultural location of the study of religion(s) interesting and instructive. But where is "here"? Is "here" Western Michigan University, where the lectures were delivered? That fine institution has a splendid tradition in the study of religions, which is however considerably shorter than the overall history of the subject. So we are led back to "the West," with its capital letter. What is this "West"? It was pointed out above that there is as yet no satisfactory history of the subject which takes into account the linguistic and cultural diversity even of Europe. It is time that the notion of the "West" was unmasked for what it is, an extremely slippery construct, pressed into service for the most diverse of reasons, usually veiling complexities which would disturb a politically desired image. By analogy with "orientalism" we may call this construct "westernism."[3]

Taking up the matter positively, it is also time that the reality of studies of religion(s) in various regions of the world was brought more steadily into view. Let us take one more cue from Samuel Preus. In his opening section entitled "Our agenda" he concludes by pointing out, very correctly, that a key feature of modernity is the perception of pluralism. And at the end of the first lecture he states that he thinks of "the study of religion as essentially critical, comparative and historical." (1998: 11) With all of these features we may concur unreservedly. What is left out from his account however is that all of these features were also available in eighteenth century Japan. Now this state of affairs, which by now has been documented for quite some time, should lead to a significant rephrasing of the general questions (and answers) about the historical location of the emergence of theories about religion(s). In particular, they cannot be regarded as the product of "the Greek discovery of the Logos." Specific elements have to be identified, and to this process the detailed work of Samuel Preus is a fine contribution. However these elements are not culture bound. In particular they are not bound to the culture of "the West." The identification of these features which are necessary for the development of a theory of religion(s) has the interesting and valuable effect of showing that it need not be regarded as ineluctably eurocentric.[4]

What are the main intellectual features in East Asia which made early modern thought on religion(s), with incipient theory-building, possible? While introducing the translated writings of the Japanese "Enlightenment" figure Tominaga Nakamoto (1715-1743, Tominaga being the family name) I attempted to identify these. Several of them overlap with features in western thought, significantly, while it is also interesting to see that there is some divergence. Five features arise in the context of religion itself, and these are: (1) the very idea of a critique of natural human existence (provided by Buddhism and Jainism), (2) the diachronic extension of independent lines of religious tradition allowing for retrospective reflection upon them, (3) diversification and reforms within major traditions (Buddhism and Confucianism) ensuring the absence of any single religious authority, (4) the idea that a religious teaching has to be related to a present time, with the implication that times and places are relative and particular (5), awareness of inter-religious rivalries and the possibility of harmonious relations, in short, of the plurality of religious systems. Three futher features are of a more general intellectual kind: (6) the perception that there is significant culture beyond one's own geographical and political borders (Europeans and Americans please take note!), (7) increasing chronological sophistication and the emergence of history writing based on such ideas as "doubt, argument, independence, selection and judgment," and (8) the development of detailed bibliographical skills which amounted to a systematisation of knowledge and a basis for "the investigation of things." To these intellectual features should be added the social basis for independent reflection on religion in eighteenth century Japan, namely the rise of a major non-political urban centre in Osaka with a partially leisured bourgeoisie. Finally, in addition to all these features of which a movement in thought might be regarded as the product, a thinker with creative ability was necessary to respond to the available cultural situation and produce a new idea, in this case a theory of tradition.

Just as it is possible to look back more carefully into western intellectual history, the same can be done for that of East Asia. All the above mentioned features can be explored in more detail and in more historical depth. For example, we find that the perception of the plurality of religions (referred to as "ways" or as "teachings") has a long and fascinating history in China and Japan, and led to the objectification (or even "reification") of named systems.[5] Or again, we find through the examination of the origins of Chinese bibliography that far from producing a religious "canon" of sacred scriptures it laid the basis for the analyis of diverse fields of knowledge. In the writings of Tominaga himself we find that the diversity of cosmologies leads him to the conclusion: "Teachings about the cosmos are in actuality quite vague and do no more than tell us of the inner working of the mind. Hence I say that the cosmos arises on the pattern of people's minds." (Pye 1990: 93) So we have an explanation, which others might call projectionism. To give one last example, he also concluded on the basis of textual analyses that the foundational sutras of Mahayana Buddhism were by no means uttered by the Buddha himself, a historical statement which was very unpopular at the time but was later completely vindicated. (Japanese Buddhist scholars were forced to return to it following interaction with Max Müller and others.) Thus it came about that there was in eighteenth century Japan a study of religion(s) which was "critical, comparative, and historical," to borrow the phrasing quoted earlier. This in turn is relevant to the general discussion of theories of religion. Rational, empirical, explanatory, testable: all these features can be found in the writings of Tominaga Nakamoto, composed in eighteenth century Japan.

Questions to be set aside

It has now become a commonplace in the study of religions to recognise the separation between theories of religion and religious views of the world.[6] However, it is not essential for a theory of religion which is not itself religious to be described as "secular," for this term implies an opposition between "secular" and "religious" which might or might not be warranted. Indeed, a scientifically coherent theory of religions might conceivably be consistent with one or more religious orientations. On the other hand it might and probably must conflict with a number of religious orientations or with statements arising out of them. There is therefore a question regarding the consistency of a general theory of religions with the intellectual content of particular religions. As an appendix to the other matters discussed above it may be helpful to lay bare in utmost brevity my own understanding of this question.

Stated most generally, all possible and non-mistaken knowledge must be consistent because all known thought processes take place within the single universe within which we find ourselves. Even with respect to other conceivable universes we are only able to project the possibilities known to us in the known universe. This projection might include, in general, the possibility of difference, but it cannot include any specific denotation of difference. This view is consistent with modern cosmology and physics, and yet, interestingly, ancient Indian cosmologies also conceived of an indefinite number of universes which are essentially similar. Ancient Buddhist cosmology is a fine example of this. Thus the consistency of universes is presupposed, even though people differ about their precise description.

Non-mistaken knowledge could include some knowledge which we might for some reason wish to describe as religious. Many religious statements on the other hand are evidently false. Some are false because they can be demonstrated to be inconsistent with other knowledge. Others, even though they somehow claim to avoid the challenge of correlation with other knowledge, are mutually exclusive. In so far as religious statements are overtly not in agreement, they cannot all overtly be true. Thus the possibility of framing statements which are both incontrovertibly true and in some sense "religious" must be regarded as being, at best, minimal. In other words, the possibility of a holistic view of knowledge is kept open, but at the same time it is recognised, indeed asserted, that many if not most religious statements cannot be regarded, in the last analysis, as correct knowledge.

Yet this state of affairs is not at all surprising if we take into account that "inexpressibility" is itself a widepread reference point in religious consciousnesses. The implication of this is that statements which seek to convey "expressional truth" (Robinson 1967: 49) in relation to that which is deemed to be "inexpressibly" valuable or significant cannot be otherwise than "worldly" or "conventional", and hence in some respect self-avowedly false. This relationship has been articulated in the Buddhist tradition, among other ways, in terms of the concept of "skilful means."[7] Verbal statements (and other forms of expression) which are imperfect to the extent of being false are the only means at our disposal to point towards a greater "truth" or value. Thus they have to be both articulated and deconstructed. Understanding this process and taking part in it is itself a religious path. In such a perspective all religious discourse may be understood as a provisional construct which will eventually disappear. At the same time it is necessary for it to be continually appraised with respect to its viability and value. While this orientation is itself thought, at least by myself, to be consistent with a scientific theory of religion, it is possible that other religious orientations also are. That is a matter for independent perusal.

This position leaves open the question about what the traditional discipline of "philosophy of religion" should be concerned with today, if anything. The development of a theory of religion(s) is not to be equated with "philosophy," which has various tasks of which the study of religions is not one. Theorists of religion(s) do not need to solve general problems of epistemology, for example, which are the task of philosophers. They should not be side-tracked by questions such as "How does anybody know anything?" or about the general possibility of knowledge of other minds.

Even less is it the task of theories of religion(s) to introduce the notion of some special kind of "irrationality" just for religion. While there is still a tendency to hagiographise Rudolf Otto in some quarters, his work on "the holy" (rather than "the idea of the holy," as the title of his work *Das Heilige* was translated into English) may be regarded as a last desperate attempt to find a theoretical focus for the study of religion(s) which could plausibly coordinate the irrationality of some religion with Kantian modernity. Whatever their historical interest, those days really have passed now. Indeed they had already passed at the time, as can be seen in the very worthwhile essay by Ernst Troeltsch entitled "Das Wesen der Religion und der Religionswissenschaft," first published in 1906.[8] The above statement by no means ignores that irrationality may be important for religious people in their systems. Rudolf Otto was himself a religious person and irrationality was significant for him. Irrationality is important not only in the specialised experience of mystics but also in quite different religious attitudes such as fundamentalism. The fundamentalist believer lives partly by his or her disjunction from reason. So did Pascal. On the other hand a presumed consistency with general rationality is also important for a large number of religious people. Ernst Troeltsch, regarded by religious critics as a dangerous relativist, was in fact a rational and religious person. By contrast with all these options within the range of religious systems, the rationality of a scientific theory of religion(s) is itself independent of the rationality or the irrationality of any religious system.

A theory of religion(s), at the most elementary level, merely needs to be rational in the general sense that it can be expressed in words and/or numbers, and that it is itself internally coherent. That is, when stated it should not collapse into a sea of disorganised ink or jumbled bytes as in: "saltion a shiwith speciereferceando spectacles, saunan seura." A typical statement might, on the other hand, be: religious innovation takes place both in the context of existing traditions and, independently of these, in the form of new religious movements. If further investigation showed that this theoretical generalisation could not be maintained then it would have to be abandoned as inadequate. However it would have been rational. Attempts to remove the aspect of rationality from scientific studies and in particular from scientific theories of religion are simply doomed to self-destruction.

In this a scientific theory of religion is different from religious theories of religions, of which a significant number can be documented. Religious theories of religions are linked to whatever view of "reason" is held within whatever religious system advances the "theory." It is possible to conceive of a religious theory of religions which is consistent with a scientific theory of religion(s), but these are rare, and it is not the task of a scientific theory of religion to produce this consistency. This is not so much a question of academic territories, though institutional positions are important for the well-being of any discipline; rather, it is a question of achieving the necessary intellectual independence and clarity for theories of religion to be plausible, and instructive in the preparation of future investigations.

General conclusions

While any of the detailed formulations used above could no doubt be improved upon, it has been shown that it is not much more difficult to delineate the field, the appropriate methods and the procedure of theory development with respect to the scientific study of religions than it is in other areas of scientific endeavour. Naturally, nobody is compelled to engage in this discipline, and if they prefer to pursue problems in philosophy, theology, politics, ethics, or any other contexts where interesting and in some cases urgent matters seem to require attention, then they may do so. At the same time it is not at all helpful if these contexts are simply confused with the field of religions as an area for scientific research in its own right.

At the same time the general story or history of the development of theories of religion needs to be retold in various respects, in relation to Europe and North America, in relation to East Asia, and in relation to the interculturality of today's world. This will help to clarify further the main features of thought which have contributed to the development of the discipline. However we already know enough to be able to assert that the general features of theory formation with respect to religion are only in an extremely limited sense culture-bound. "Westernism" should be unmasked for what it is, namely an illusion. The main intellectual features necessary for the development of the scientific study of religions can be documented in the intellectual history of more than one major cultural area, and they continue to be relevant world-wide.

Notes

1. On these matters see further my paper "Methodological integration in the study of religions," presented at the 1997 methodology conference of the International Association for the History of Religions (IAHR) held at Turku, Finland, the proceedings of which have now been published under the editorship of Tore Ahlbäck (1999).
2. Presented at a special conference of the IAHR held in Brno, Czech Republic, in August 1999, and now in the press. This most interesting conference was devoted to an exploration of the history of the study of religions, east and west, during the Cold War period.
3. C.f. also "occidentalism" as discussed in my paper "Modern Japan and the science of religions," forthcoming in the proceedings of a conference held at Leiden in 1997.
4. This point was argued in detail in my critique of Troeltsch's de facto Eurocentrism entitled "The end of the problem about 'other religions'" (Pye 1976, c.f. also 1979). In that context the argument was addressed to Christian theologians who were thereby invited simply to give up the notion of "other religions" and work out their theology on the basis of prior knowledge that religions are in fact plural in number.
5. "Reification" has been regarded very critically by Wilfred Cantwell Smith, Robert Baird and others, and yet it seems to be a characteristic of at least one phase in the emergence of any historical view of religions, in East Asia as well as in the western world. Significantly, therefore, it is not just some kind of western disease.

6. For the present writer's extended statement of this fundamental point see "Religion: shape and shadow" (Pye 1994).
7. C.f. Pye 1979, 1986, 1990, 1998.
8. English translation under the title "Religion and the science of religion" (Morgan and Pye 1977). C.f. also my article of appraisal entitled "Troeltsch and the science of religion" in the same volume (pp. 234-252).

References

Almond, Philip C. 1988. *The British Discovery of Buddhism*. Cambridge, Cambridge University Press.

Amstutz, Galen 1997. *Interpreting Amida. History and Orientalism in the Study of Pure Land Buddhism*. New York, State University of New York Press.

Baird, Robert D. 1971, 1991. *Category Formation and the History of Religions*. The Hague (2nd. edition Berlin, New York), Mouton de Gruyter.

Brear, Douglas 1975. Early assumptions in western Buddhist studies. *Religion*. 5: 136-159.

de Vries, Jan 1961. *Godsdienstgeschiedenis in Vogelvlucht*. Utrecht, Het Spectrum.

de Vries, Jan 1967. *The Study of Religion. A Historical Approach*. New York, Harcourt, Brace and World, Inc.

Despland, Michel, Ed. 1991. *La Tradition Française en Sciences Religieuses. Pages d'Histoire*. Cahiers de recherche en sciences de religion.

Evans-Pritchard, E. E. 1965. *Theories of Primitive Religion*. London.

Girardot, N. J. 1999. "'Finding the way': James Legge and the Victorian Invention of Taoism." *Religion* 29(2): 107-121.

Kuper, Adam 1973. *Anthropologists and Anthropology. The British School 1922-1972*. Harmondsworth, Penguin Books.

McCutcheon, Russell T. 1997. *Manufacturing Religion. The Discourse on Sui Generis Religion and the Politics of Nostalgia*. New York, Oxford, Oxford University Press.

Morgan, Robert and Michael Pye, Eds. 1977. *Ernst Troeltsch: Writings on Theology and Religion*. London, Duckworth.

Preus, J. Samuel 1987. *Explaining Religion: Criticism and Theory from Bodin to Freud*. New Haven, Yale University Press.

Preus, J. Samuel 1998. "The Bible and religion in the century of genius. Part I: Religion on the Margins: Conversos and collegiants." *Religion* 28(1): 3-14.

Pye, Michael 1972. *Comparative Religion. An Introduction through Source Materials*. Newton Abbot (England UK) / New York, David and Charles / Harper and Row.

Pye, Michael 1976. The end of the problem about other religions. *Ernst Troeltsch and the Future of Theology*. J. Clayton. Cambridge, CUP: 172-195.

Pye, Michael 1977. Troeltsch and the science of religion. *Ernst Troeltsch: Writings on Theology and Religion*. Robert Morgan and Michael Pye. London and Atlanta, Duckworth/John Knox: 234-252.

Pye, Michael 1978. Diversions in the interpretation of Shinto. *Proceedings of the British Association for Japanese Studies (Volume Two: 1977, Part Two: Social Sciences).* D.W. (ed.) Anthony. Sheffield: 77-92.

Pye, Michael 1979. Theologie im Kontext des religiösen Pluralismus. *Christus allein – allein das Christentum? (Vorträge der vierten theologischen Konferenz zwischen Vertretern der Evangelischen Kirche in Deutschland und der Kirche von England).* Klaus Kremkau. Frankfurt am Main, Verlag Otto Lembeck: 11-25.

Pye, Michael 1982. The study of religion as an autonomous discipline. *Religion.* 12: 67-76.

Pye, Michael 1982. Diversions in the interpretation of Shinto. *Religion.* 11: 61-74.

Pye, Michael (trans.), Ed. 1990. *Emerging from Meditation (Tominaga Nakamoto).* London / Honolulu, Duckworth / University of Hawaii Press.

Pye, Michael 1994. Religion: shape and shadow. *Numen.* 41: 51-75.

Pye, Michael 1997. Reflecting on the plurality of religions (full text). *Marburg Journal of Religion.* 2: virtual pages.

Pye, Michael 1999. Methodological integration in the study of religions. *Approaching Religion.* Tore Ahlbäck. Åbo, Finland, Donner Institute for Research in Religious and Cultural History. 1: 188-205.

Robinson, Richard H. 1967. *Early Madhyamika in India and China.* Madison (Milwaukee) and London, University of Wisconsin Press.

Sharpe, Eric 1975. *Comparative Religion. A History.* London, Duckworth.

Smart, Ninian 1958. *Reasons and Faiths.* London, Routledge and Kegan Paul.

Strenski, Ivan 1987. *Four Theories of Myth in Twentieth Century History.* Iowa City, University of Iowa Press.

Urban, Hugh B. 1999. "The extreme Orient: The construction of 'Tantrism' as a category in the Orientalist imagination." *Religion* 29(2): 123-146.

Waardenburg, Jacques 1973. *Classical Approaches to the Study of Religions: Aims, Methods and Theories of Research.* The Hague, Mouton.

Some Reflections on Approaches and Methodologies in the Study of Religions

Kurt Rudolph

Professor, Fachgebiet Religionsgeschichte
Philipps-Universität, Marburg, Germany

A secular or profane treatment of the human endeavour that we usually demarcate and designate with the term "religion" – and not just in Europe or America – is very old. It dates from the time when human beings first began to think about religious matters, and above all from the time when they began to think about religious matters that were foreign to them, as did, for example, the ancient Greek historians and philosophers. Nevertheless, a definite break occurred when, in the wake of the so-called Enlightenment of the seventeenth and eighteenth centuries, a secular consciousness was established in Europe, independent of the requirements of Jewish and Christian tradition. The modern study of religions (in German: *Religionswissenschaft*) takes its rise from that break, rather than from the nineteenth century. In addition, one should carefully specify what one means by a critical "treatment" of religion, for such a treatment is not necessarily secular or profane. It is possible to treat religion critically from a standpoint that is itself religious, that is more or less anchored in a religious tradition, its horizon of meaning, and its cognitive and moral cosmos, as has been customary among Jewish, Christian, and Muslim theologians. Any theory that results from such a standpoint certainly does not provide a secular or profane view of religion. Such religious critical theories often divide religion into two parts: an external world of visible phenomena, and a metaphysical or metapsychological reality that is the "essence" of religion, the entity that manifests itself in the phenomena. In the context of describing or defining religion in general, the terms for this essence will be familiar from theology: revelation, God, the holy – and thus hierophany, the infinite, and so on. In earlier times the study of religions was also an influential advocate of such a conception of religion; recall the works of Friedrich Max Müller, Rudolf Otto, Gerardus van der Leeuw, Friedrich Heiler, and Mircea Eliade. In actual fact, in these works "religion" is conceived and interpreted "religiously". That is, in order to understand religious things these works invoke a religious mode of explanation, whether Christian, Jewish, or Muslim, the very terms for which are embedded in a religious framework. Despite this embeddedness we often use these terms unthinkingly still today. Scholars of the history of the study of religions have long known that in this discourse many different "religious" and religio-philosophical or rather theological theories have played a part. One may call these theories "phenomenological", since for them religious phenomena only constitute the gateway to the Holy in and of itself, to which religion can at any time be reduced. In other words, all religions ultimately merge into an undifferentiated, final unity. As a result, mysticism acquires a singular prominence in these theories. It provides the criterion for "genuine" religion and thus a "tried and true" way of approaching all religions. In such treatments religion is interpreted in terms of the religion of the (mystical) observer, who thereby often feels called upon to purify religion and who provides a playground where his or her own religiosity can amuse itself. Consider Rudolf Otto and Friedrich Heiler.

Distinct from this tradition is another one: a secular or profane treatment and analysis of religion. This tradition does not seek to "understand" "religion" in terms of patterns of religious or theological meanings or as an independent "reality" that stands beyond history, society, and human activity or behaviour. Furthermore, this point of view is not unitary, for it employs different kinds of explanation and considers things from different points of view: historical, philological, linguistic, sociological, psychological, geographical, ethnological, and biological. It follows an approach that lies on this side of religious assertions and meanings, inasmuch as these are merely self-referential. The concern of this approach, which is quite prevalent in the study of religions today, is not to repeat what the "religions" and their advocates say and do; that certainly does not require the study of religions. Rather, this approach seeks both to understand and to explain religious assertions and phenomena in terms of their profane sources or causes. In this way a secular theory of religion aims primarily at explanation, and it uses the tools of the contemporary cultural and social sciences.

At first this approach was only pursued sporadically, within as well as outside the study of religions. As a result, we do not yet have a generally accepted profane theory of religion, if we ever will. Instead, we have a whole series of theories, some older, some more recent, that have appeared to be of some applicability in the study of religions but have not been universally accepted, either because of traditional prejudices or improper use. The older theories include Marxist analysis, which was widely used until 1989, the psychoanalytic theories of Freud and Jung, the "communicative" theory of Emile Durkheim and his school, the "purposive" theory of Max Weber and its adaptations (e.g., Peter Berger), and functionalism (Bronislaw Malinowski). Among more recent theories we might note the cultural anthropological (Ralph Linton, E. E. Evans-Pritchard), the structuralist (Claude Levi-Strauss), the semasiological (Clifford Geertz), the ethological (Konrad Lorenz, Walter Burkert), the systems-theoretical (Niklas Luhmann), the cultural-critical (Hans G. Kippenberg), and the ideological-critical (see below). As this volume shows, there is considerable interest at present in developing a generally valid theory of religion, but so far as I can see that goal is a mirage, since neither the object itself not the method required to study it are unitary. One can illustrate this interest, perhaps, by pointing to Joachim Wach's *The Comparative Study of Religion* (1958), which conceives of religion in terms of a "religious experience" that manifests itself in terms of thought, action, and fellowship. So far as it goes, Wach's observation is correct, although it only describes religion phenomenologically and psychologically ("religious experience"). His account does not limit religion to the entity "religious experience" but relates that experience to three other areas of life, just as his earlier *Sociology of Religion* (1944) had related two independent entities, "religion" and "society". At the same time, Wach overlooks the continual relations between "religion" as an entity in itself and other areas of life that also constitute *homo religiosus* (merely an abstraction), because *homo religiosus* is at the same time *homo faber*, *sociologus*, and *oeconomicus*. For Wach, religion remains in the end an abstraction that manifests itself in different ways, without being bound from the start in the dynamics of historical and social processes, whether as an independent, dependent, or co-dependent variable. This is the difficult challenge that we face: to examine these processes in the past and the present and to formulate some general conclusions for a theory of religion.

My thoughts on the standpoint that such a theory must adopt are shaped by specific principles that must direct the role of the study of religion and that require this study to occupy a strict position between the critique of religion and the critique of ideology. The following remarks are devoted to these principles.[1]

"That which those sciences concerned with religion regard as the *Object* of Religion is, for Religion itself, the active and primary Agent in the situation or, in this sense of the term, the *Subject*." This is how Gerardus van der Leeuw begins his *Religionsphänomenologie:*[2] "In other words, the religious man perceives that with which his religion deals as primal, as originative or causal; and only to reflective thought does this become the Object of the experience that is contemplated. For Religion, then, God is the active Agent in relation to man, while the sciences in question can concern themselves only with the activity of man in his relation to God; of the acts of God Himself they can give no account whatever." I do not want to comment now on the problematic concepts and assertions in this passage, such as God (most religions worship gods, not God), experience and its role in religion, or the remarkable claim that religion is a matter of God's action, not human action.[3] Let me just note that in one respect Van der Leeuw is absolutely correct: that the study of religion approaches religions and religious data in a way that is completely different from the approach of religion and its faithful advocates. In what follows, I want to draw out some of the consequences of this different approach that van der Leeuw ignored. I do so by drawing on what I have already said elsewhere, without, however, simply repeating myself.

For all their multiplicity the methods of the study of religion are bound to the same rational presuppositions that undergird any scientific study: they must be critical, analytical, objective, interpretative, explanatory, and so on.[4] Theologians themselves, such as Helmut Gollwitzer and Rudolf Bultmann, have seen as the foundation of science – correctly, I think – a "methodological atheism,"[5] distinguished as a worldview from "dogmatic atheism". Ninian Smart has used instead the terms "methodological agnosticism" and "methodological neutrality."[6] To be absolutely clear, one should add that for the study of religions "God" or "the divine" or "the numinous" does not constitute an object of study. Instead, this study examines the manifold evidence and multiple data for human belief and action which appear in this realm and which one still encounters in living, changing form today, either through personal experience or through reading and study. To some extent, the history of religions is at heart really a history of faith (*Glaubensgeschichte*). Unfortunately, this terminology was somewhat discredited when during the National-Socialist period in Germany the history of religions, was to some degree transformed into a racist history of faith.[7] The search for God or for some transcendent being as a religious object is not historical but philosophical or theological; as a result, it lies entirely outside the study of religion, as does the question of whether atheism is correct. The study of religions, or rather the history of religions, is in principle incapable of providing any evidence about God, even though earlier practitioners of the discipline, such as Nathan Söderblom, Rudolf Otto, Friedrich Heiler, and even van der Leeuw, tried repeatedly to address such questions.[8]

Several consequences follow from adopting this stance toward traditions of faith and religious activity as objects of study. One of them is a necessary distance and neutrality toward religious judgements about the world, humanity, and human society, regardless of whether one employs philological, sociological, psychological, geographical, or some other methods. These religious evaluations and convictions are, as for example Van der Leeuw himself says, "bracketed".[9] They are from the start irrelevant to the scholar of religion insofar as they do not primarily concern that study's rational and scientific approach to such matters. Certainly they can be a theme of its work, but then only in a manner separated from their claims to submit oneself to them or to "believe" them. There is in these matters no direct transition from the scholar of religions to the faithful adherent of a religion, despite all assertions to the contrary. Either one engages in scholarship (*Wissenschaft*) or in worship. As a result, any attempt to unite both movements in a single act is, to my mind, bound to fail; it necessarily violates the distance between observation and object. From this point of view I once claimed, in a very radical formulation, that for the scholar of religions there is, strictly speaking, nothing "holy" or "sacred" that would occasion him or her to abandon the rational methods of the study of religions.[10] If that happens, one is no longer engaged in the study of religion but is in fact practising religion, which has happened repeatedly in the study of religions.[11] As that study has developed in Germany, it has been irrationalism above all that has overstepped the boundaries between an irrational interpretation and a personal acceptance of religion. This move has been made – and continues to be made – by that form of the study of religions that, under the strong influence of theology, talks about the "pure idea of religion".[12]

The rational or naturalistic understanding of the study of religion that I have briefly described has an ideological-critical impetus that is often overlooked. As long ago as 1978 I commented on the ideological-critical function of the study of religions.[13] In doing so, I sought to open up a debate within the field that had long been underway in fields such as sociology, history, and German studies. To what extent that occurred cannot be clearly answered. On the one hand, there seems to have been a certain reluctance to take up the theme, or else it seems that my remarks disrupted too much the traditional image of the discipline, so that people were upset – which is understandable, given the history of the field in Germany.[14] When I discussed the same theme in my Haskell Lectures at the University of Chicago in 1983-1984, I detected varied reactions.[15] The true disciples of Mircea Eliade vehemently rejected my thesis, as one would expect, for it sounded more or less "heretical" to them. Others thought that the theme was either unnecessary or had been surpassed by other problems that deserved more attention–this despite the fact that in the USA the difference between theology and the study of religions is a disputed question, although the debate is pursued more actively at some times than at others.[16] (Note that in America the so-called "scientific study of religions" is basically sociological and generally very narrow.)[17] Here I will develop my conception from a different point of view, and one that leads to a double-sided critique of ideologies in the study of religion: an internal critique and an external one.

One way to understand the term "ideology" is purely mental: as a concern with the origin and history of ideas. This was the understanding of the actual founders of this research, the French "ideologues" of the eighteenth and early nineteenth centuries.[18] On this understanding, the critique of ideologies in the study of religions, as I have described it, is identical with the analysis of the specific facts of religion, namely, the content of the ideas that serve to "explain, regulate, and assure" in the areas of religion.[19] In the process, however, one also encounters the various modes of religious activity. – ritual acts and daily life – without which religion could not exist and which I discussed in more detail in 1978 in opposition to Marxist-Leninist dogma.[20] The ideological-critical impetus of the study of religions concerns, therefore, both sides of religion, ideology and praxis or activity. It is, therefore, situated "internally" to the object of the study of religions, and it then has to establish its conclusions within the field of the critique of religions, which I have yet to describe.

There is also a second way to understand the term ideology: in a negative sense as a false, concealing, corrupting imagining in the realm of political, social, and also religious or confessional debates.[21] I do not know whether that kind of ideology is universal. What is certain is that it is found world-wide and quite frequently: the imagining of truth through an unthought out, uncritical construction of ideas, whether done consciously or unconsciously, in order to become dominant, exercise power, and suppress, but also intentionally to befuddle. This conception of ideology is also related to work in the study of religions; indeed, it relates to that work insofar as its descriptions and critical analyses, whether historical, sociological, psychological, or of some other sort, not only treat the religious field as such but also the "ideological" standpoint of researchers. Since this last task can only take place through a sort of double reflection, it has only developed relatively recently, at least as a conscious theoretical pursuit. I am thinking here of the investigations, inaugurated in the last several years by H. G. Kippenberg and members of his circle, into the cultural and religion-critical statements of earlier scholars of religions, such as Gerardus van der Leeuw.[22] In this way, the study of religions produces a contemporary critique of traditional views of the world, culture, and religion, as well as of the longing for a romantic, medieval or non-European world, devoid of corruption – including a longing for specific religious traditions, which in the world of the scholar-seeker can no longer be found or can only be encountered in fragmentary form. This appearance of a hidden or even of an open critique of ideologies directed at contemporary forms of European life and faith as they are found in the accounts and expressions of historians of religions is also a result of research in the study of religions, which reveals notable aspects of the history of the field and in doing so opens up a perspective on its various standpoints.[23] We can designate this form of ideological criticism implicit in the study of religions the "external" form. It, too, is a result of critical analysis in correlation with the critique of contemporary styles of life and thought. In the present this characteristic can be seen in the growing insight into the Eurocentric perspective and orientation of the traditional study of religions, including the terminology that we use without thinking. What is required is a two-fold reflection on the study of religions: that over against the object and that over against scholars and their methods.[24] The basis for both is reflective reason, that is, the rational-critical perspective on the methods and objects of the study of religions.

The critique of ideologies, as sketched above, makes a step in the direction of a critique of religions, for the two are closely related. In the critique of religions, too, one must naturally distinguish two sides: first, the religio-critical results of value-neutral, distancing, rational work in the study of religions, and second, the self-critical consequences for the researcher and the study, which one can also call "faith-critical consequences."[25] In every case, the objects of the study of religions are disrupted by its treatment, inasmuch as the explanation of religion often goes hand in hand with its critique.[26] This can be observed very well in the effects of the so-called biblical and tradition criticism within European Christianity from the nineteenth century, in parallel with the search that has been going on since Schleiermacher for an undisturbed (*sturmfrei*) idea of religion, which sought to escape the consequences of that criticism.[27] One of the few theologians who clearly saw the consequences of this for contemporary theology was Franz Overbeck, whose works are being issued in a complete critical edition.[28] That the study of religions has never completely realized its religio-critical potential is demonstrated by all the attempts from the time of its founding to grasp religion as an elite, mystical contemplation. Other points of view were seldom represented, as I have noted in "Die religionskritischen Traditionen in der Religionswissenschaft."[29] Now it is absolutely clear, and I would be the last to dispute, that the study of religions ought not to permit itself to propagate in any way either a religion or theology or an atheistic worldview. My experiences in Leipzig (former East Germany) were formative for me in this regard, as were my experiences in the United States and Marburg. The study of religions must in this regard be neutral, even if it will occasionally be involved in a dialogue with religions, whether intentionally or not.

Having established these points, we can now raise the question of the effects of the study of religions on the scholars themselves. How does working rationally and critically in this area affect those who are engaged in it? First, the investigator's own consciousness will without doubt be shaped by the investigation. This can be traced quite well in the history of the study of religions, since in this regard, too, cultural-critical and religio-critical insights "speak meaningfully." This is already quite apparent in the works of the founder of the field, Friedrich Max Müller. Not only did he

238

search for a romantic insight into the infinite within the various religions; he also came to the correct insight that whoever knows one religion knows none. Adolf von Harnack is supposed to have reversed that statement at the beginning of the twentieth century and thereby to have established the superfluity of the study of religions for theologians.[30] But there is no doubt that, when it comes to firm religious convictions, work in the study of religions has "ideological-critical consequences."[31] One of these ought to be tolerance for other beliefs. Another is the relativization of one's own convictions and positions. It remains for individual researchers themselves to draw specific consequences for their own thought and practice, but there is no question in my mind that they will inevitably do so. Knowledge is empirically a consciousness-changing power. "We free ourselves from the taboo [scil. of a tradition]," writes Karl Popper, "if we think about it, and if we ask ourselves whether we should accept it or reject it."[32] In one way or another, knowledge of the history of religions inevitably alters the religious consciousness of the researcher and of the perceptive reader of his or her work.

Related to the consequences of research in the study of religions or the history of religions is another much discussed question: What are the presuppositions of such work? First comes the question of whether a special sensitivity for religion or religious experiences is necessary to study religions. The old debate about this problem has today become almost completely obsolete, for the often repeated argument that such a sensitivity guarantees solid work in the study of religions is no longer persuasive. It has become increasingly evident that this is not the case. Indeed, such a sensitivity can be a disadvantage, for one will not always reflect logically upon the framework of prejudices, if one thinks that the "religious spirit" is so universal that one can "understand" everything; as a result one will prefer a religious explanation, even when others are available.[33] The studies of Max Weber, who admitted to being "unmusical" in matters of religion,[34] were surely more fruitful than those of specialists who were more "attuned" to religion, such as Rudolf Otto.[35] The measure that we must apply in the study of religions derives instead from the scholarly, critical-analytical, and historical-philological or sociological nexus. Just as a musicologist or historian of music is not required to be a musician, and just as an art historian or art theorist is not required to be an artist, so a scholar of religion or historian of religions is not required to be pious or to practice religion. It is certainly possible for a scholar of religion to be religious, but no one has to be pious in order to work productively in the field of the study of religions. In these matters the criterion of truth and falsehood does not lie on the plane of religion or faith, as some still claim, but on the plane of secular rationality and scientific judgement. As a result, the self-understanding of religious people is also excluded as a criterion for truth and falsehood in the study of religions. The ways religious people see and understand themselves certainly need to be taken into account as valuable religious data. But no religion is unitary in its outlook;[36] instead, all religions are pluralistic and varied, and in any case there is no bridge over which one can cross from the insider's perspective to the outsider's and back again. Thus, a religion's self-interpretation provides only a necessary aid to understanding, never a normative approach. The scholar of religion does not – at least should not – foster any religious undertaking through his or her scholarship, but rather is concerned with that segment of human life that we designate with the metalinguistic category "religion."

The foregoing touches upon a broader theme addressed by the 1990 Congress of the IAHR: the problem of "religion" as a category for comparative work in the study of religions. The addresses were published in 1994 and provide a glimpse of the difficulties that surround this umbrella term.[37] My own position paper was devoted to considering the extent to which the term "religion" is Eurocentric.[38] In origin and history, of course, this term is quite Eurocentric. But to my mind the study of religions has helped to free it from its ethnocentric limitations, so that today it is used all over the world. The uncritical use of the term "religion" is dangerous, especially when one does not at the same time pay attention to the terms that are used for this area of life in other languages and cultures.[39] To be sure, the logic of linguistic analysis demands that the meta-linguistic (scholarly) term mark out the semasiological field of investigation without taking into consideration the object-language data (i.e. the language or terminology of the object of our study), but above and beyond that logic the historical and philological approach of the study of religions requires an attempt somehow to relate the unavoidable general terms, without which comparative work is impossible, to the objects of study and to their demonstrable linguistic peculiarities. For it remains beyond doubt that all "umbrella terms" derive from some language that is an object of our study, whether biblical or European. I would not say, therefore, that "religion" is a European invention, as is sometimes said, but rather that it is a means of expression or a sign that derives from Latin, and one that makes it possible for us to approach scientifically, on regional and universal levels, an important set of cultural phenomena for which the languages spoken by the peoples being studied have many different designations. The adoption of the word "religion" into almost every language shows that we are already confronting a term that is used universally.[40] So far as I can see, this process is irreversible. Suggested replacements, such as the terms "culture" and "worldview," quickly lead to the same problems. A careful consideration of such problems in the study of religions as well as in other humanistic fields is absolutely necessary and characterises critical, self-reflective scholarship. As Ugo Bianchi once said, the term "religion" is *in fieri*.[41]

It remains to make a few remarks on the topic of the study of religions and public life. In Germany this is a difficult issue. In the years after the second world war the field has been much more fully developed, but neither federal not state officials take much notice of it, and it does not play much of a role in political life. This ignorance is so widespread that at times people use the plural, *Religionswissenschaften*, "studies of religions," to denote both the study of religions (*Religionswissenschaft*) and theology.[42] The dominance of both Catholic and Protestant theology, bound by law to two public corporations, that is, the churches, makes it difficult for the study of religions to express itself officially from the point of view of a non-religious, cultural or human science, on relevant social questions that touch upon religion. Precisely because the study of religions (*Religionswissenschaft*) must in principle be value-neutral and as objective as possible, it can and should speak significantly about the present-day marketplace of religious goods. But because the study of religions is not joined to any specific institution beside the academy and the international community of discourse sometimes referred to as "the republic of the learned," the field has no lobby. As a result, in Germany questions of religion are always church questions! Thus, in matters pertaining to the so-called sects and special religious communities one primarily consults the ecclesiastical or theological authorities or their institutionalised embodiments, who then naturally enough issue statements that correspond to their prejudices, whether these are hidden or admitted openly.[43] My own impressions are usually quite contrary to the judgements that are passed on other religions and religious communities, especially the smaller ones, above all when the mass media have manipulated these judgements ahead of time. One very seldom encounters a standpoint that is really tolerant, value-neutral, pluralistic, anti-Eurocentric, and non-ecclesiastical or non-Christian. But the study of religions has never completely lost the connection with tolerance and humanity that it inherited from the Enlightenment. For scholars of religions, human rights are not part of a creed that one merely recites without conviction. Furthermore, despite the value-neutrality of work in the field human rights should not be left at the door when one is required to take stances on public issues.[44] Here belongs the impetus to ideological criticism that I have described, as well as its various effects, whose potential contribution to public life must be emphasized more strongly than ever. In 1989 REMID, "The Information and Media Service of the Study of Religion, (*Religionswissenschaftlicher Medien- und Informationsdienst e.V.*)," was founded in Marburg, Germany. As stated in § 2 of its charter, the goal of the organisation is "to further and deepen in the general public knowledge about religion and religious movements. It does so from the point of view of the study of religions (*Religionswissenschaft*). This study examines a religion or religious community empirically, historically, and scientifically, and presents its conclusions in a manner that is independent of all religious views and convictions. The knowledge obtained in this way is to be communicated and thereby made useful to society in order to foster a peaceful and tolerant coexistence of people and of the various religions and to facilitate mutual understanding and respect." It is remarkable that in the USA Jacob Neusner has ascribed a similar task to the "Academic Study of Religion."[45] Neusner emphasises the great role of comparison in the study of the history of religions: on the one hand, it makes differences clear; on the other, it discovers similarities or communalities "in the human situation and in the shared challenges of social order, that religions exhibits." "Ours is a privileged field of learning for when we devote our lives to the academic study of religion, the nature of the documents that we examine and the ideas that we try to understand changes our work, transforming facts into insight and insight into wisdom ... Ours is the field of learning that offers students a most remarkable vision of what we are and what we can become. As a believer anashamed to say so, I may add, our subject promises also a vision of how God sees us."

Whether or not the scholar of religion practices a religion, he or she needs to be concerned now more than ever with fostering a climate of tolerance toward "the Other" in academic and public life. At the same time, he or she is not allowed to abandon the insight that religions are cultural and social institutions, characterised by their own strengths and weaknesses, just as every human creation is. As Immanuel Kant put it: human beings are made of bent wood, but they walk upright. Religions are not good in themselves. Like everything human, they can be harmful as well beneficial. Religions have both provoked wars and brought about peace – indeed, we experience both of these aspects of religion daily in international politics. Without openness, tolerance, and attention to human rights contemporary religious convictions also lose their value.

Translated from German by Gregory D. Alles

Notes and References

1. A German version of the following remarks is published in: G.M. Klinkhammer, S. Rink, T. Frick (eds.), *Kritik der Religionen*, Marburg 1997: 67-76.
2. *Phänomenologie der Religion*, Tübingen 1933, (2) 1956: 3; ET: *Religion in Essence and Manifestation*. Transl. by J. E. Turner with appendices incorporating the additions to the second German editions by H. H. Penner, Princeton 1964, Pb. 1986: 23.
3. Van der Leeuw entitled part I of his earlier *Einführung in die Phänomenologie der Religion* "God" and he entitled chapter 3 "The Object of Religion. Mana." In his larger work *Phänomenologie der Religion* of 1933, (2) 1956, he entitles ch. 1 simply "Power" (*Macht*). As is well known, Van der Leeuw drew upon the pre-animistic theory of *Mana* or "Dynamism".
4. Cf. J. S. Jensen/L. H. Martin (ed.), *Rationality and the study of Religion*, Aarhus 1997 (Acta Jutlandica LXXII: 1. Theol. Ser. 19).
5. R. Bultmann, "Protestant Theology and Atheism" in: *JR* 52 (1972), 331-335, esp. 332; K. Rudolph, *Geschichte und Probleme der Religionswissenschaft*, Leiden 1992, 90 with note 25a.
6. *The Science of Religion and the Sociology of Knowledge*, Princeton 1973: 2, 1977: 22f., 38f., 43, 57-57, 63, 67, 158-160, esp. 159.
7. Cf. Van der Leeuw, *Phänomenologie der Religion*, (2) 1956: 795 (not included in the ET!); *Religion in Essence*, 595 (on racial typology); J. W. Hauer, *Glaubensgeschichte der Indogermanen*, München 1943. On the German Study of Religions (*Religionswissenschaft*) during the NS-rule s. U. Nanko, "Deutsche Gottschau,1934", in: P. Antes/D. Pahnke (ed.), *Die Religion von Oberschichten*, Marburg 1989: 165-179; R. Flasche, "Gab es Versuche einer Ideologisierung der Religionswissenschaft während des 3. Reiches?" in: H. Preißler /H. Seiwert (eds.), *Gnosisforschung und Religionsgeschichte. Festschrift für K. Rudolph*, Marburg 1994: 413-420; H. Junginger, "Ein Kapitel Religionswissenschaft während der NS-Zeit: H.-A. Winkler (1900-1945)", in: *ZfR* 3 (1995), 137-162; F. Heinrich, "Das Religionswissenschaftliche

Institut der Ernst Moritz Arndt- Universiät Greifswald 1944/45" in: *ZfR* 5 (1997), 203-230. H. Junginger, *Von der philologischen zur völkischen Religionswissenschaft*, Stuttgart 1999.

8. J. Neusner writes correctly: "Historical facts have no bearing on the theological truth, not because theology requires us to believe what is not true, but because theology makes statements that rest on facts of an other-than-historical order" (*Bull.for Biblical Research* 6, 1996: 168, from "Judaism: Practice and Belief 63 B.C.E.- 66 C.E. A Review of Recent Works by E. P. Sanders", 167-178).

9. *Religion in Essence*, 645f., 675, 683, although the author does not follow this principle at all.

10. Cf. Rudolph, *Geschichte und Probleme*, 32f.; *Historical Fundamentals and the Study of Religions*, New York/London 1985: 40. The essay was originally published in *Kairos* 9 (1967), 22-42. Cf. now R.T. McCutcheon (ed.), *The Insider/Outsider Problem in the Study of Religion*, New York 1999 (an anthology of texts).

11. Cf. R. Flasche, "Religiöse Entwürfe und religiöse Wirkungen von Religionswissenschaftlern", in: P. Antes/D. Pahnke, *Die Religion von Oberschichten*, 203-218; "Der Irrationalismus in der Religionswissenschaft und dessen Begründung in der Zeit zwischen den beiden Weltkriegen", in: H.G. Kippenberg/B. Luchesi (eds.), *Religionswissenschaft und Kulturkritik*, Marburg 1991: 243-295; "Religiosität und Frömmigkeit in der neueren Religionswissenschaft", in: B. Jaspert (ed.), *Frömmigkeit. Gelebte Religion als Forschungsaufgabe*, Paderborn 1995: 11-19; B. Gladigow, "Religionswissenschaft. Historisches, Systematisches und Aktuelles zum Stand der Disziplin", in: *Berliner Theol. Ztschr.* 13 (1996), pp. 200-213, esp. 201f., 205ff. (on F. Max Müller). The entire *Phenomenology of Religion* by G. van der Leeuw is the document of "a modern Christian seeking God" (Rudolph, *Historical Fundamentals*, 36; cf. esp. *Religion in Essence*, ch. 88 and 100). On J. W. Hauer and his disastrous initiation of a racist "German Religion" (*Deutsche Gottschau*) s. U. Nanko, *Deutsche Gottschau, 1934* (s. note 6); *Die Deutsche Glaubensbewegung*, Marburg 1993.

12. Here the "*Religionsgeschichtliche Schule*" of German Protestant theology has been very influential, mainly through the works of W. Bousset (*Das Wesen der Religion*, 1903), R. Otto (*Das Heilige*, 1917), and E. Troeltsch. Troeltsch tried to transform Theology into *Religionswissenschaft* but without giving up the theological aims of the discipline. Cf. on this Rudolph, *Die Religionsgeschichte an der Leipziger Universität und die Entwicklung der Religionswissenschaft*. Sitzungsberichte d. Sächs. Akad. d. Wiss., Philol.-hist. Kl. 107:1, Berlin 1962: 52ff.; *Historical Fundamentals*, 74: 83ff.; *Geschichte und Probleme*, 125f., 303ff., 412ff.; U. Berner, "Religionswissenschaft und Theologie. Das Programm der Religionsgeschichtlichen Schule", in: H. Zinser (ed.), *Religionswissenschaft. Eine Einführung*, Berlin 1988: 216-238.

13. In: *NUMEN* 25 (1978), pp. 17-39; revised in: *Geschichte und Probleme*, pp. 81-103.

14. Only J. Waardenburg mentioned and discussed the essay; cf. his *Religion und Religionen*, Berlin 1986: 64-66. See further C. Colpe, *Theologie, Ideologie Religionswissenschaft*, München 1980: 131f.

15. "The History of Religions and the Critique of Ideologies", in: *Historical Fundamentals*, pp. 59-78.

16. Cf. G. D. Alles and J. M. Kitagawa, "The Dialectic of the Parts and the Whole: Reflections on the Past, Present, and Future of the History of Religions", in: J. M. Kitagawa (ed.), *The History of Religions. Retrospect and Prospect*, New York 1985: 145-181, and "The Santa Bar-

bara Colloquy: Religion within the Limits of Reason Alone", in: *Soundings. An Interdisciplinary Journal*, Vol. LXXI, No. 2/3 (Summer/Fall 1988). Further the Review-Article by Catherine Bell, "Modernism and Postmodernism in the Study of Religion", in: *RSR* 22 (1996), pp. 179-190 (with literature).

17. Cf. my critical remarks in *Historical Fundamentals*, 32f.
18. Cf. *Geschichte und Probleme*, p. 82ff., *Historical Fundamentals*, p. 62ff., H.-J. Lieber, *Ideologie*, Paderborn 1985: 33ff.
19. Cf. Hans Albert, *Kritik der reinen Hermeneutik*, Tübingen 1994: 227f.
20. *Geschichte und Probleme*, 86; *Historical Fundamentals*, p. 65f.
21. Cf. on this *Geschichte und Probleme*, 86ff.; *Historical Fundamentals*, p. 65ff.; H.-J. Lieber, *Ideologie*, p. 35ff., p. 66ff.; R. Boudon, *Ideologie. Geschichte und Kritik eines Begriffs*, Reinbek 1988 (French publication: Paris 1986).
22. H.G. Kippenberg/B. Luchesi (eds.), *Religionswissenschaft und Kulturkritik,* Marburg 1991; H.G. Kippenberg, "Die Relativierung der eigenen Kultur in der Vergleichenden Religionswissenschaft", in: J. Matthes (ed.), *Soziale Welt*. Sonderband 8 (1992), pp. 103-114.; *Die Entdeckung der Religionsgeschichte*, München 1997.
23. Cf. the essays by B. Gladigow, "Pantheismus und Naturmystik", in: R. Bubner et al.(ed.), *Die Trennung von Natur und Geist*, München 1990: 119-143; "Pantheismus als 'Religion' von Naturwissenschaftlern", in: P. Antes/D. Pahnke, *Die Religion von Oberschichten*, 219-239 (with literature); *"Religionswissenschaft "* (s. note 10), pp. 205ff. (on F. Max. Müller).
24. In general ethnocentrism (e.g. eurocentrism) is widespread and, often connected with xenophobia. For example in India which was idealised by many of the former historian of religions; cf. H. von Skyhawk, "Hinduism und Hindutva", in: *ZDMG* 146 (1996) pp. 112-127. On ethnocentrism s. now the collection of contributions ed. by M. Brocker & H. H. Nau, *Ethnozentrismus. Möglichkeiten und Grenzen des interkulturellen Dialogs*, Darmstadt 1997. I might also mention the wellknown and continous debate on "Orientalism" in oriental studies.
25. Cf. Albert, *Kritik*, p. 225.
26. *Ibid.*, p. 217
27. *Ibid.* p. 224ff. In my view the only modern theologian who attempted to combine both the modern subjectivity and the traditional religious basis of the European culture is Ernst Troeltsch (1865-1923). As a result, his ideas becoming increasingly important. Thus, the first French translation of his collected works began to appear in 1996 (published by Les Édition du Cerf, Paris, and Labor et Fides, Genève); H.-G. Drescher, *Ernst Troeltsch. Leben und Werk*, Göttingen 1991.
28. *Werke und Nachlaß*, since 1994 publ. by J. B. Metzler, Stuttgart: Vol. 1-6/2 until now. Especially noteworthy is the so called "Kirchenlexikon", completely edited for the first time by B. von Reibnitz (Vol. 4-6), which contains penetrating remarks on the state of modern Theology and *Religionswissenschaft*. C. A. Bernoully published excerpts from this material in 1919 under the title *Christentum und Kultur*, but although this volume became well known, its selections are very ideosyncratic.
29. In Kippenberg/Luchesi, *Religionswissenschaft und Kulturkritik*, pp. 149-156.
30. About this s. my *Religionsgeschichte an der Leipziger Universität*, 61ff., and C. Colpe, *Theologie, Ideologie, Religionswissenschaft*, pp. 18-39.

31. Cf. Albert, *Kritik*, p. 218

32. "Versuch einer rationalistischen Theorie der Tradition" in: *Vermutungen und Widerlegungen I*, Tübingen 1994: 178. Original: *Conjections and Refutations: The Growth of Scientific Knowledge*, New York 1962: 122.

33. Cf. Albert, *Kritik*, p. 218ff., and the articles by R. Flasche mentioned above in note 9.

34. Cf. *Soziologie, Universalgeschichtliche Analysen, Politik*. Ed. by J. Winckelmann, Stuttgart 5th ed. (Kröner Taschenbuch 229), p. 395, also p. 426 and p. 432. P. Allheit, *Das 'Areligiöse" im Denken Max Webers. Eine religionsphilosophische Studie um Probleme der Ethik bei M. Weber*, Diss. Marburg 1971. Marianne Weber, *Max Weber. Ein Lebensbild*, Tübingen 1984: 339 (letter of 19.2.1909); W. Hennis, *Max Webers Wissenschaft vom Menschen*, Tübingen 1996: 183ff., 213.

35. One of the best example of this kind of religious misinterpretation is G.van der Leeuw. In his influential *Phenomonology of Religion* (ET: *Religion in Essence and Manifestation*) he combines his own interest in collective forms of "primitive religions" with the outdated ethnological theory of preanimism (dynamism) and his personal religiosity with its concern for experience (*Erfahrung*) and feeling (*Gefühl*) which has a long tradition in the earlier study of religions, mainly in Germany. Cf. "Epilogomena" in *Religion in Essency*, p. 671ff.

36. This is observed correctly by Van der Leeuw, *Religion in Essence*, 610: "Every historic religion, therefore, is not one, but several; not of course as being the sum of different forms, but in the sense that diverse forms had approximated to its own form and had amalgamated with this". The same is true with his remarks on the different individual receptions of religious traditions and behaviours (*ibid.* p. 592f.)

37. *The Notion of 'Religion' in Comparative Research. Selected Proceedings of the XVIth Congress of the IAHR Rome 3rd-8th Sept. 1990*. Ed. by Ugo Bianchi, Rome 1994. Recently Ernst Feil has written a new monograph on the history of the term religion *Religio. I. Die Geschichte eines neuzeitlichen Grundbegriffs vom Frühchristentum bis zur Reformation*, Göttingen 1986; *II. Die Geschichte eines neuzeitlichen Grundbegriffs zwischen Reformation und Rationalismus (ca. 1540-1620)*, Göttingen 1997. See further the extensive discussion of the term in: *Streitforum für Erwägenskultur. Ethik und Sozialwissenschaften (EuS)* 6, Heft 4, (1995) pp. 441-514.

38. *The Notion of 'Religion'*, pp. 131-139. Now: "Schwierigkeiten der Verwendung des Begriffs 'Religion' und Möglichkeiten zu ihrer Lösung", in: H.-M. Haußig/B. Scherer (ed.), *Religion – eine europäische Erfindung?* (to be published by Syndikat, Berlin, in 2000).

39. On this s. B. Schmitz, *"Religion" und seine Entsprechungen im interkulturellen Bereich*, Marburg 1996; "'Religion' – oder: Eine Gleichung mit (zu) vielen Unbekannten", in: *EuS* 6 (1995), pp. 487-489 (cf. note 36). H.-M. Haussig, *Der Religionsbegriff in den Religionen*, Berlin 1999.

40. This can be seen clearly from the dissertation of B. Schmitz (note 38).

41. *Problems and Methods of the History of Religions*. Ed. by U. Bianchi, C. J. Bleeker, A. Bausani, Leiden 1972: 33. Cf. now R.T. McCutcheon, *Manufacturing Religion: The Discourse on sui generis Religion and the Politics of Nostalgia*, New York 1997.

42. S. my remarks in: H. Zinser (ed.), *Religionswissenschaft*, Berlin 1988: 38f.

43. Cf. the excellent introduction by H. Seiwert "Das 'Sektenproblem'. Öffentliche Meinung, Wissenschaftler und der Staat" to M. Introvigne, *Schluß mit den Sekten*, Marburg 1998: 9-

38. Further: M. Baumann, "Die Ausgrenzung der Religionswissenschaft aus der bundesdeutschen Kontroverse um neue Religionen", in: *ZfR* 3 (1995), pp. 111-136.

44. A case in point is the current dispute on female circumcision in some countries of Africa and the Near East. Here the objective, impartial, and neutral observation and description, explanation and "understanding" of a religious tradition or behaviour contradicts with the personal attitude of the scholar who accepts the Human Rights of the inviolability of the individual. Cf. on this Ursula Spuler-Stegemann, "Mädchenbeschneidung", in: *Kritik der Religionen* (s. note 1), pp. 207-219, and the panel-discussion after the lectures (ibid. pp. 221-248). There are many forms of power and oppression initiated or legitimated by religious ideas, rules and traditions. Cf. e.g. René Girard, *La violence et le sacré*, Paris 1972; *Le Bouc émissaire*, Paris 1982; G. Baudler, *Töten oder Lieben. Gewalt und Gewaltlosigkeit in Religion und Christentum*, München 1994.

45. "Scholarship, Teaching, Learning: Three Theses for the Academic Study of Religion", in: *Religious Studies News*, Sept. 1997: 21f.

Making the Gender-Critical Turn

Randi R. Warne

Professor & Chair, Department of Religious Studies
Mount St. Vincent University, Halifax, NS, Canada

My approach to the academic study of religion begins with the presumption that religion is a complex cultural phenomenon, a multifaceted artifact of human culture which has organized much of human life and understanding. In this it parallels gender, the cultural project of making humans into "women" and "men."[1] Much of my academic work has centred on the intersections between these cultural phenomena, and upon the ways one might go about generating more reliable knowledge in both areas than is currently available.

Despite significant resonances between the study of religion and the study of gender[2] there has been insufficient attention paid to how they might inform each other, methodologically and theoretically.[3] In my view, any adequate study of religion must be gender-critical, that is, it must employ gender as a key analytical category for how we think about religion, what we consider to be data, and what questions we bring to our studies. Gendering is a key component of world-building, arguably religion's central project. That gender-critical thinking does not characterize religious studies overall, and the implications of that reality for the academic study of religion, will be explored more fully below.

Academic perspectives are foundationally informed by the scholar's preparation and training. Unlike many (perhaps most – a salient fact in itself) religious studies scholars, all my academic training has been specifically in that field.[4] Many of my colleagues and certainly the majority of my teachers came to religious studies from other areas, primarily from Christian theological studies, and/or religious professions. Many of those who took the turn to non-confessional approaches to the academic study of religion seem to have a heightened sense of the importance of boundary maintenance between ("secular, scientific") Religious Studies and ("personal, committed, incommensurable") theology.[5] This is not to suggest an ad hominem argument here, or some deep psychological dysfunction which impairs academic judgement; rather, the point is that a line of demarcation has been established between appropriate and inappropriate stances to the subject matter of religion which masks other forms of embeddedness, and obscures how foundationally they are operating at the level of theory construction and methodological application. Specifically, insufficient (usually no) attention is paid by male religious studies scholars to their own gender-embeddedness, and how that embeddedness shapes the assumptions which they bring to their scholarship. At the very least it might nuance the advocacy of "objective and uncommitted" scholarship which puts religious studies scholars in the rather bizarre position of claiming the most reliable scholarship is that which has no investment in its subject matter.[6]

Failure/refusal to acknowledge male gender-embeddedness has had a number of practical effects on the knowledge-making practices of the academy. As Dale Spender and Cheris Kramarae have documented at length,[7] there has been a virtual explosion of analytical work in and amongst the disciplines on the subject of gender over the last quarter century. Initially that work tended to focus on those whose received cultural gender script was female: how they were depicted in tradition and theory, where they were ignored when in fact they were present, and how they might be understood as full human beings. This process generated a wide range of issues, both theoretical and methodological, including a shift of focus from "women and women's experiences" to gender as a complex cultural category in which all humans are implicated. However, the majority of those studying gender are still those who were/are studying "women," and indeed are women themselves.[8]

In effect, a two-tiered system has been created which is particularly visible in the academic study of religion: male/mainstream scholarship and the feminist scholarship of the margins. The latter has gained greater tolerance over the last two decades, but according to Carol Christ it has not decentred the androcentrism of the mainstream tradition an iota.[9]

This ghettoization is problematic for a number of reasons, not the least being its deleterious effect on the adequacy of religious studies scholarship. There are other concerns, of course. For those with justice concerns, it may seem inappropriate that a sole focus on one gender in scholarship is considered "serious" while focus on the other, or the disruption of the category of gender altogether is perceived to be a "special interest." Those with concerns about logical coherence might be similarly disturbed by this imbalance. Persons on the job market are keenly aware of which schools hire in what areas, and exactly how much one has to participate in the presumptions of the status quo to be accepted by the most prestigious institutions. But as scholars, we have an obligation to pursue knowledge which is reliable, despite our investment in our own reputations for expertise. As Elizabeth Minnich notes, the current situation in which gender-critical studies are tolerated on the margins but have not been integrated as foundational to academic inquiry makes no logical sense. As she puts it:

> *knowledge that is claimed to be inclusive – claimed to be both about and signific- ant for all humankind – but that is in fact exclusive must be transformed, not just corrected or supplemented.* Discoveries indicating that the world is round do not merely supplement knowledge shaped by and supportive of the theory that the world is flat.[10]

Specifically, Minnich argues that the knowledge-making practices of the Euro-North American academy (alternately, the western intellectual tradition) are build upon, and issue out of, a view of normative humanity which is also held up as the human ideal, setting both the standard by which all humanity is judged, and the goal towards which it ought strive. However, this norm and ideal has not been an inclusive one, but instead has been gendered male.[11] It involves tremendous intellectual effort, and a good deal of practice, to decentre maleness as the human norm and ideal which informs our imaginations.[12] It is easier, in my experience, to imagine, for example, that the imperial legacy of the 19th century has skewed our understandings of the religions of India, or western assessments of Islam. That is, it is easier to adopt a post-colonial perspective now that the overt cultural dominance of European empire has waned. Male gender dominance remains much more ubiquitous world-wide, and is obviously more immediately personal in that we are all gendered one way or another. Transforming gender relations implicates all of us, not just in our scholarship but in our daily lives.

The remainder of Minnich's analysis explores this partial knowledge base which takes as the pivot of its study of humanity a very particular, located male embodiment and universalizes it as the human norm and ideal. Key to the process is circular reasoning, assuming what needs to be proved. These particularly permeate "mystified concepts" like gender, woman, man, excellence, judgement, and reason which in turn serve as further strategies by which this system is created and maintained.[13] While I find Minnich the most useful and concise treatment of the androcentric construction of the dominant western intellectual tradition, the last twenty years of feminist epistemological explorations provide a rich and ongoing resource for rethinking a world that is human-centred rather than male-centred.[14]

One of the difficulties I have encountered in trying to make the case for more sustained conversation between the academic study of religion and admittedly located knowledge positions like feminist scholarship is an intense resistance to modifying the strong version of "objectivity" which undergirds much religious studies scholarship. As indicated by my use of scare quotes, I find the term problematic, at least in the sense in which it is often employed in religious studies discussions. To be more explicit, as noted above, a dominant theme of method and theory discussions in religious studies is the extent to which religious studies is different from "theology." From its inception in the 19th century, with Max Muller's call for a comparative, "scientific" Religionswissenchaft, the academic study of religion has been marked by this impulse. Where "theology" is characterized by "advocacy," the advancement of the values and viewpoints of a particular religious system by which all other systems are judged, religious studies is to be "objective." Where theology is normative, religious studies is descriptive, where theology is the viewpoint of the "insider", religious studies scholars are the "outsiders," garnering from their disengagement an assurance of, if not Truth, then certainly relatively provable truths. The appropriate stance for the religious studies scholar in this construction is that of the informed, observant outsider whose analytical categories supersede those of their data (religious folks and their beliefs and practices), because those categories have been generated out of comparative study which allows local conditions and horizons to be transcended. Unlike the theologian, whose admitted investments in a particular tradition mark intellectual investigation, the religious studies scholar has no tradition to advocate, and is therefore guaranteed an "objectivity" which the theologian, by definition, must lack. Or so goes the argument.

However, there is more than one form of normativity. As the discussion thus far contends, androcentrism is one such norm. Until and unless scholarship becomes intentionally gender-critical, it will remain enmeshed in the thoroughgoing androcentrism which marks the dominant western intellectual tradition. That is, it will enter into its investigations working from a range of unexamined assumptions which privilege/centre male experience in the generation of analytical categories, and the answers which will be seen as reasonable to the questions asked out of them. Yet as Minnich and others have demonstrated, bringing male gender-embeddedness to consciousness is a fraught and difficult process. Relinquishing the (illusion of the) "god's-eye-view" is a serious sacrifice in a profession marked by competition and peer evaluation, to give but one practical example. In contrast, women and other Others are always marked by their group identity, often explicitly with adjectives before their profession (e.g., "woman scholar") and certainly in the dominant imagination of the academy.

The fact that academic life and inquiry have been predominantly constructed and maintained by and for a very particular race/class/gender cohort is not irrelevant to its standards and practices. Because the assumption of androcentrism is shared so widely amongst academic practitioners, any pursuit of knowledge which does not replicate those assumptions is seen as invested, a special interest, rather than as an example of a different area or agenda of investment. Thus, the traditional academy, and religious studies within it, has been able to represent itself as value-neutral, rational, and reliable, over against admittedly located constructions of knowledge which are then dismissable as "advocacy." Indeed, it has been this characterization which has allowed otherwise serious male/mainstream scholars to remain almost completely ignorant of the intellectual specifics of feminist scholarship, despite the incredible vitality and significance of that work – *without scholarly penalty*.

Not to name names, but in my experience few expect senior (or even junior) male scholars seem to be familiar with feminist discourses, either contemporary or historical, but androcentric discourses are simply presumed as the necessary knowledge base for everyone. Nor is it acceptable to argue that western tradition has been androcentric, and therefore all the "greats" are likely to be male. Over two decades of feminist scholarship have demonstrated that even within the canonical standards of western tradition, women have contested their subordinating conditions throughout history, producing works of art and scholarship which were well known in their times, if not foregrounded in androcentric tradition.[15]

In any case, this argument begs the question of the construction of the canon itself, hardly a neutral process, all the appeals to the "self-evidence" of "excellence" notwithstanding.[16] Here too the circularity noted by Minnich continues to operate, as those with pre-existing cultural authority determine who might be its worthy recipients, not surprisingly finding it most meritoriously represented in those like themselves. It is important here to emphasize that the issue is not one of individual meanness or bad behaviour on the part of male scholars. Rather,

> *The principles that require and justify the exclusion of women, and the results of those principles appearing throughout the complex artifices of knowledge and culture, are so locked into the dominant meaning system that it has for a very long time utterly irrelevant whether or not any particular person intended to exclude women.*[17]

Given the complexity and enmeshment of the material and intellectual structures of knowledge production, the invisibility of their operations is understandable. However, once one has started to see what was previously masked, some lacunae come startlingly into view. In the remainder of this discussion I will illustrate the phenomenon in relation to the issue of secularization.

In her 1993 H. Paul Douglass Lecture, "Telling Congregational Stories," Nancy Ammerman describes the secularization story this way:

> *Once upon a time all of life was full of the sacred. Whatever could not be explained was chalked up to divine action. Eventually all this sacred power was drawn together into offices and institutions that defined the moral, political, and social life of a people.*
>
> *Religious officials stood at the center of the society, either wielding governmental power directly or defining the boundaries within which others could wield such power. Whether or no any given ordinary individual had strong religious sensibilities didn't matter because the whole culture carried the meaning and mores of religion. But then the evil beast of modernity arrived. [Or, alternative reading: Then the great white knight of enlightenment rode into view.] Slowly the sacred disappeared from view, taking refuge in the tiny crevices of the "private sphere." The*

> *authority of the religious leaders was usurped by the scientists, and might and right were defined by political leaders and technocrats. "Public" life was disenchanted and, despite periodic rumblings from the " private" sphere, religion was forever robbed of its power.*[18]

The academic study of religion has its origins in this process of secularization in its Enlightenment version, and its dynamics have played out throughout the discipline, notably in relation to tension between theology and religious studies discussed above. However, closer examination reveals that this is a gendered story as well.[19] The 19th century was marked not only by the "science/religion" debate occasioned by Darwinian thought and its consequences, but also by two corresponding social developments, the demarcation of human community into "public" and "private" spheres with the rise of the industrial state, and the ideological gendering of those arenas in the prescriptive doctrine of "separate spheres." Briefly, "separate spheres" ideology presumes that men and women are profoundly different sorts of creatures, biologically, morally, intellectually, and spiritually. Men are held to be by nature proper denizens of the public sphere: like their genitalia they are external, and their activities properly reside in the competitive worlds of commerce, government, and the intellectual life. Women, on the other hand, are inherently nurturant and maternal, emotional rather than analytical, and properly attend to the sensitive demands of morality and religion. The decline of religion, so the story goes, results from its "feminization"; indeed, movements like "muscular Christianity" were encouraged in the late 19th century to "save" Christianity from extinction.

Some things need to be noted here. First, the gender script of separate spheres was a *prescriptive ideology*, not a neutral description. It was class and race specific, and culturally located in Europe and North America, although the agents of empire were quick to export it along with other forms of domination. It was also *contested*, as the heated debate on the so-called "Woman Question" throughout the 19th century confirms. "Woman's True Place" is only an issue if women don't or won't stay there. The sixty-odd year struggle for woman suffrage was only one manifestation of these social dynamics, as women demanded recognition of their place in the public world. Women were *in* the so-called public sphere, working in factories and increasingly in professions, however much they contravened

255

ideological norms by doing so. Given the intensity and widespread character of this debate it is all the more remarkable that from its inception the academic study of religion – the "rational," "descriptive," "uninvested" analysis of religion as a human cultural artifact – operated from the naturalized and ontologized notions of gender marked by the ideology of separate spheres. Moreover, it has continued to do so. Consider a basic in the field, world religions textbooks. Even now, if women's religious lives are depicted at all, they are set aside in a page or subsection on "women and ...". That is, they are marked as an exception to the general case, which is formal religion, conducted by men. From the time of Max Muller, comparative religion has been the hallmark of the academic, nonconfessional study of religion, a sign of its rationality and reliability borne out of its non-investment in particular religious agendas. Yet it has reproduced in its assumptions and categories, and hence in its theories and methods, a gendered prescription for the organization of human culture which itself is thoroughly invested in male centrality and concomitant cultural authority.

But what happens when we disrupt this construction, and begin from a position which does not presume that men preeminently define the human? Ann Braude explores precisely this question in "Women's History Is American Religious History." After outlining the three most influential motifs that have been used to structure the narrative of American religious history, namely declension, feminization, and secularization, she makes the startling assertion that, whatever their explanatory appeal for historians, "from an empirical perspective, they never happened."[20] That is,

> Churches did not decline in Puritan New England; they did not experience a new female majority in the nineteenth century; nor did they disappear in the twentieth. All three fictions result from the assumption that the public influence of the Protestant clergy is the most important measure of the role of religion in American society.[21]

Further, "female majorities are the norm in American religious groups, so the perception that they constitute a "declension" is a normative assertion about the superior value of male church membership [not] an empirical observation."[22] The reality is that "per capita church membership in the United States increased steadily throughout the nineteenth century, beginning at less than 10 percent and reaching stunningly high rates (67-76 percent) that have persisted throughout the twentieth century."[23] Once the normative assumptions of androcentrism and male gender privilege are decentred, the narrative changes. Rather than a decline of religion's social power in the face of technology, "rationality" and industrial advance, "secularization" might be better understood as a discourse issuing out of anxiety about the relocation of social power and authority from one male group to another (e.g, from male clergy to male scientists, the "new priesthood") rather than having anything much to do with religious beliefs and practices. When women are placed at the centre of the study, what Braude finds is:

> the colonial period saw an increase in the spiritual status and role of women; the nineteenth saw a vast increase in the activities and influence of the female laity; and the twentieth century ... has witnessed the rise of female clergy and a reorientation of liturgy and theology based on women's experience.[24]

When androcentrism is relinquished, the world we see changes. The questions we ask, the information we accumulate, the knowledges we generate, all are transformed, and transformed not in the direction of "advocacy" but of *greater adequacy*. Androcentrism is a prescriptive ideological stance which is untenable on logical grounds. It is certainly indefensible in an academic, non-confessional scholarship on religion which seeks to distinguish itself by rigorous criteria of intellectual coherence, rational argumentation, and comprehensive analysis of human social data. Once our categories of analysis are seen through a gender-critical lens, the circularity of their construction (e.g., men are the public sphere; the public sphere is preeminent; why? because men are in it) is made plain.

As for the religion scholar as public intellectual, this too is a gendered discourse. As Bruce Lincoln has adeptly demonstrated, the processes of conferring public authority are complex and always shifting, but they must involve some identity which is being acknowledged and confirmed.[25] It is clear that public discourses are invested discourses, and religion scholars would be more believable, in my view, if we adopted a stance of acknowledging our own cultural enmeshments and assumptions, while articulating the values which inform any analysis of the social world which we may make. Culturally, religion scholars just don't have the war-

257

rant that scientists are still often granted, that of the assumed neutrality of expertise – and given the volatility and engagement of our subject matter of religion, it is unlikely it will be conferred on us any time in the near future.

I also believe we need to offer constructive alternatives, not just ostensibly disinterested critique, although critical analysis is a valuable contribution which religion scholars are well prepared to make. In both these projects, I am convinced that making the gender-critical turn is essential, not only for the intellectual integrity of our project, but for our plausibility and usefulness as public intellectuals. Making the gender-critical turn as a discipline could take us to the cutting edge of cultural analysis as the gendered dynamics of power and meaning are (re)inscribed across the globe.

Notes and References

1. My sex/gender analysis follows that of French materialist feminists Christine Delphy and Nicole-Claude Mathieu, and is most economically described as "radical constructivist." For a good introduction to this perspective see *Sex in Question: French Materialist Feminism*, ed. Diana Leonard & Lisa Adkins (London: Taylor and Francis, 1996).

2. See Randi R. Warne, "Religious Studies and Women's Studies: Resonances, Reactions and Future Possibilities," *Religious Studies: Issues, Prospects and Proposals*, ed. Klaus K. Klostermaier & Larry W. Hurtado, Atlanta: Scholars Press, 1991: 347-360.

3. On this point see Randi R. Warne, "Towards a Brave New Paradigm: The Impact of Women's Studies on Religious Studies," *Religious Studies and Theology in Alberta*, Vol. 9, 2 & 3, 1989: 35-46.

4. My undergraduate degree was in religion and literature (Winnipeg), my master's in philosophy of religion (Toronto) and my Ph. D. in religion and culture (Toronto). My doctoral qualifying exams were in philosophical and textual approaches to religions (specifically western philosophy of religion since the Enlightenment); social-scientific approaches (Freud, Jung, Eriksson, Weber, Durkheim and Marx); religion in Canada (with an historical focus); Christian tradition; and Judaism since the Enlightenment. This rather over-prescribed course of study was due to the then Dean of the Graduate School's concern that religious studies scholars distinguish themselves from those doing what he called "armchair theology." Since my primary source language was English rather than, say, Ugaritic, I was required to develop competence in an additional method, in my case, the social-scientific approach to religion described above.

5. For example, one of the most influential contributors to the discussion of "incommensurability" of theology and religious studies is Donald Wiebe, himself a former Mennonite evangelical. See Donald Wiebe, *The Irony of Theology and the Nature of Religious Thought*, Montreal and Kingston: McGill-Queen's University Press, 1991.

6. The Enlightenment ideal of the unconditioned, acontextual knower who operates with what has been called variously the "god's-eye-view" or "the view from nowhere" has come under serious critique over the last two decades, particularly in feminist, postmodernist, and/or post-colonial scholarship. For an interesting treatment of the issue from the perspective of ethics, see Sandra Harding, "The Curious Coincidence of Feminine and African Moralities: Challenges for Feminist Theory," in *Women and Moral Theory* ed. Eva Feder Kittay & Diana T. Meyers, Totowa, N. J.: Rowman and Littlefield, 1987: 296-315.

7. See *The Knowledge Explosion*, ed. Cheris Kramarae & Dale Spender (New York: Teachers College Press, 1992).

8. An exception to this pattern is *Que(e)rying Religion: A Critical Anthology*, ed. Gary David Comstock & Susan E. Henking (New York: Continuum, 1997), which positions itself at the intersection of religious studies and lesbian/gay/queer studies.

9. Carol Christ, "Feminists – Sojourners in the Field of Religious Studies," *The Knowledge Explosion*, pp. 82-88.

10. Elizabeth Karmark Minnich, *Transforming Knowledge* (Philadelphia: Temple, 1990). For a succinct treatment of this issue which is deeply indebted to Minnich, see my "(En)gendering Religious Studies, *Studies in Religion/sciences religieuses*, Vol. 27, 4, 1998: 427-436.

11. The slippage between universality and spcificity is evident in the debate in English over inclusive language, and the now-widespread rejection of the term "Man" to designate humanity.

12. That gender categories are themselves nuanced by considerations of race, class, ethnicity, and other social markers is axiomatic. Indeed, some scholars find gender so unstable a construction as to be illusory. For a pointed discussion on this see the exchange between Joan Wallach Scott and Laura Lee Downs in *Comparative Studies in History and Society*, vol. 35 (1993). Downs' article, "If 'Woman' is Such an Empty Category, Then Why Am I Afraid to Walk Alone at Night? Identity Politics Meets the Postmodern Subject," pp. 414-437 provoked Scott to accuse her of both misrepresentation and ignorance, a signal of the heated character of this debate. Joan Wallach Scott, "The Tip of the Volcano: A Reply to Laura Lee Downs," *Comparative Studies in History and Society*, vol. 35: 438-443. As noted above, my own position is consistent with French materialist feminism, in which sex/gender is a construct which organizes experience such that persons in particular groups may have differing perspectives which are consistent within group membership, but that these differences are neither natural nor ontologically required. For an overview of predominant sex/gender theories, see my entry on "Gender" in the *Guide to the Study of Religion*, ed. Willi Braun & Russell T. McCutcheon (London: Cassell, 2000: 140-154).

13. Minnich, *Transforming Knowledge*, pp. 82-147.

14. The work of Lorraine Code is particulatly important in thie regard. See for example, Lorraine Code, *What Can She Know? Feminist Theory and the Construction of Knowledge* (Ithaca: Cornell, 1991).

15. See for example Dale Spender, *Women of Ideas and What Men Have Done to Them* (London: Ark Paperbacks, 1983).

16. See Minnich, passim; also Henry Louis Gates, *Loose Canons: Notes on the Culture Wars* (New York: Methuen, 1984).

17. Minnich, p. 32. Emphasis in original.

18. Nancy Ammerman, "Telling Congregational Stories," *Review of Religious Research*, vol. 35, 4 (June 1994), pp. 289-90.
19. Note the normative character of Euro-North American (Protestant) Christianity in this theoretical construction as well. It would be a very interesting study to investigate how the theory would hold up if, for example, Taoism, or Shinto, were understood to be the "religion" implied, rather than Christianity.
20. Ann Braude, "Women's History 'Is' American Religious History," *Retelling U.S. Religious History*, ed. Thomas Tweed (Berkely: University of California Press, 1997), p. 87.
21. Ibid., pp. 92-93.
22. Ibid., p. 93.
23. Ibid., p. 95.
24. Ibid., p. 97.
25. Bruce Lincoln, *Authority: Construction and Corrosion* (Chicago: University of Chicago Press, 1994). Lincoln's text is marred by his naturalized assumption that women lack cultural authority, rather than problematizing and analyzing the phenomenon.

Suggested Readings

Kramarae, Cheris & Spender, Dale, *The Knowledge Explosion: Generations of Feminist Scholarship* (New York: Teachers College Press, 1992).
Minnich, Elizabeth, *Transforming Knowledge* (Philadelphia: Temple, 1990).

'Why the Academic Study of Religion?'
Motive and Method in The Study of Religion*

Donald Wiebe

Professor, Trinity College
University of Toronto, Toronto, Canada

I

The methodological implications of the motives that underlie the study of religion and, more particularly, the academic study of religion have not, I think, received the attention they deserve. They are of the utmost importance, however, for the differences of motivation between the study of religion legitimated by the modern university and the scholarly study of religion that antedates it, sponsor radically different, if not mutually exclusive, approaches to its study. In asking why the study of religion is undertaken as an *academic* exercise – which is, after all, a comparatively recent development – I shall be attempting to delineate, to some extent, the relation of motive to method in what has come to be called Religious Studies.[1] In clarifying that relation I hope also to show that Religious Studies – that is, the academic study of religion – must be a vocation in very much the same sense that Max Weber speaks of science as a vocation[2] and, therefore, that such study must take as merely preliminary a 'religious studies' that is concerned only to 'understand' rather than to explain the phenomenon of Religion.[3]

II

The scholarly study of religion, as is well known, has a very long history.[4] Much, if not all, of that study was religiously motivated; it was – and for many still is – a religious exercise designed for, or directed to, the betterment of the individual concerned and, ultimately, is concerned with 'salvation'. The ultimate goal of salvation is not, however, the only motivating

261

factor to be found as justification of this enterprise. There were (are) other lesser, but in some sense contributory, goals that have implicitly grounded or been consciously invoked as justification for such study. Such motivations are not easily discerned, however, for they are not always consciously and explicitly espoused.

Recognition of the psychological, cultural and political roles religion has played in society and of its continuing importance in those respects in our own context seems for many to imply that the study of religion ought to be undertaken as support to religion in its manifold tasks – that is, that it ought to complement religion. Religion has been, and still is, absolutely necessary, it is argued, for personality integration and contributes significantly to human personal development. Not only has religion provided individual identity, it has been the 'glue', so to speak, that has provided the cohesiveness necessary to social/societal existence. And a study of religion that fails to recognize these values and the truth of religion upon which they rest, it is then maintained, is obviously misdirected; it is at best but wasted effort if not, in fact, destructive. This implies, of course, that the study of religion is *not* understood as an exercise undertaken in and for itself but rather that it is to be seen as an instrument for the preservation of religion and its presumed beneficial effects. The purpose for the study, that is, lies outside itself, being found only in 'the truth of religion', however that phrase is interpreted. And it should be noted that such aims for the study characterise not only the individual engaged in that work but also the institutional structures that make the scholarly study of religion possible.

Such argument provides an answer to the question 'Why the study of religion?' but not, I suggest, to the question why one might, more specifically, undertake the *academic* (or scientific) study of religion as established within the university curriculum. Neither is it the only answer possible, nor the most persuasive. Indeed, even though it gives some indication of the pragmatic value the study of religion might have, the argument does not really answer the question satisfactorily since it seems to involve a non-sequitur of sorts. It is quite possible, that is, for religion to be of benefit to individual and society without being true; the benefits of religion do not necessarily rest upon the cognitive truth of religion's claims even though they may depend upon the belief by the devotees that those claims are (cognitively) true.[5] It is clear, that is, that the benefits religion has conferred, or now confers, upon individual and/or society may be achieved in other, and possibly better, ways. To assume that the study of religion ought to be the ally of religion is not immediately obvious and therefore hardly the only grounds on which to base the study of religion. It must be recognized that knowledge of the falsity of religion – should that be the case – would also make the study of religion of pragmatic value since it would permit its manipulation for the benefit of individual and society, or its replacement for the benefit of individual and society, or its replacement with superior 'social mechanisms' for the fulfillment of such psychological or social needs. It seems that exactly that kind of argument is raised, for example, with regard to the study of magical and astrological systems of belief. The effects of such beliefs on numerous societies have not been invoked as indicative of the truth of the claims made, exept by the faithful, nor that a study of those claims ought to be involved in promoting the results achieved through such systems of belief. There is no assumption here, that is, of the *sui generis* character of such systems of experience and belief and consequently no argument for the recognition of, say, *Magiewissenschaft* as a new discipline or call for the establishment of departments of magic or astrology. (As I recall, Brian Magee once raised the question 'If departments of religion why not departments of Magic?' on the BBC and, I think, quite rightly so). The postulation of the *sui generis* character of religion but not of magic, it appears, rests on the uncritical assumption that religion, in some fundamental sense, is True while magic (astrology, etc.) is not. Indeed, if this is not the assumption that implicitly grounds that postulation, the explicitly acknowledged grounds for establishing departments of religion referred to above, namely religion's profound impact upon individuals and society, constitute adequate grounds for the creation of departments of magic – that is, for academically legitimating what we might analogously refer to as 'Magical Studies'.

Concern for the practical value of religion, therefore, is not the same as the concern for the truth of religion in any cognitive sense. Indeed, understanding how religion has functioned in various societies constitutes knowledge about religion that is wholly independent of knowledge as to the truth or falsity of religious claims. Moreover, such mundane, objective knowledge is the only ground on which the pragmatic value of Religious Studies could be predicated short of presuming that the discipline can provide one with the insights of the religious experience itself. Furthermore, its pragmatic value would then be a matter of 'political' action based on the knowledge gained and not intrinsic to the study itself. It may motivate the individual to undertake the study of religion but does not constitute the *raison d'etre* of the discipline itself. And it is the failure to recognize this that has been the bane of the *academic* study of religion which, like other academic enterprises, sees itself as a scientific and not a 'political' vocation.

III

I have in the preceding discussion made reference to Religious Studies as a vocation. I have done so deliberately for it seems to me that much that Max Weber had to say of 'science as a vocation' is applicable to the academic study of religion. Even his discussion of vocation in 'the material sense of the term' – that is, to put it bluntly, with respect to the job prospects of the scholar – has a direct bearing on the religion graduate although I do not wish to focus attention on those matters here. What is pertinent, rather, is his discussion of 'the *inward* calling for science' which is inextricably bound up with what Weber refers to as the disenchantment of the world – with a recognition that meaning is the product of human creativity. Weber maintains that discussion of 'the *inward* calling for science' is of no assistance in answering the question as to the value or meaning of science within the total life of humanity, nor with ascertaining how one ought to live. Such questions are of a logically different order. Indeed, vocation in the sense of an inward calling for science presumes science is not directed toward answering such questions – that such questions, to rephrase the point, are not scientific questions. Rather, science 'presupposes that what is yielded by scientific work is important in the sense that it is "worth being known"', although Weber admits that this presupposition itself cannot be proved by scientific means.[6] It is simply a matter of historical fact that aims such as these have emerged in the development of Western culture.[7] The emergence of the desire for objective knowledge of 'the world', that is, constitutes the introduction of a radically new value into human culture. Weber then proceeds to show, moreover, that where personal or societal value judgements are introduced into a scientific endeavour there full understanding of the facts ceases and the inward calling for science is dissipated and science destroyed. Science is a vocation, then, in the exclusive service of, as Weber puts it, the self-clarification of ideas and knowledge of interrelated facts. 'It is not', he writes, 'the gift of grace of seers and prophets dispensing sarced values and revelations, nor does it partake of contemplation of sages and philosophers about the meaning of the universe.[8] It is simply a human activity with a peculiar – recent – intentionality, so to speak. And what he has to say of the natural sciences applies, *mutatis mutandis*, to the social sciences including those focused on religious phenomena. He writes of the former:

> The natural sciences, for instance physics, chemistry, and astronomy, presuppose as self-evident that it is worth while to know the ultimate laws of cosmic events as far as science can construe them. This is the case not only because with such knowledge one can attain technical results but for its own sake, if the quest for such knowledge is to be a 'vocation'. Yet this presupposition can by no means be proved. And still less can it be proved that the existence of the world which these sciences describe is worth while; that it has any 'meaning', or that it makes sense to live in such a world. Science does not ask for answers to such questions.[9]

The academic or scientific study of religion is, I would argue, simply one of several special areas into which the scientific vocation of which Weber speaks is organized and that, like the others, it seeks self-clarification and knowledge of interrelated facts. What I shall attempt to do in the remainder of this essay, therefore, is to give a precise formulation of the aim of the study of religion *qua* study and to explicate the implications this has for the method of that study and how the subject ought to be taught in the academic/university setting.[10]

IV

To put the matter somewhat tautologically, the academic study of religion must be undertaken for academic – that is, purely intellectual/scientific – reasons and not as instrumental in the achievement of religious, cultural, political or other ends. This means, quite simply, that the academic/scientific study of religion must aim only at understanding religion where 'understanding' is mediated through an intersubjectively testable set of statements about religious phenomena and religious traditions. As with any other scientific enterprise, therefore, the academic study of religion aims at public knowledge of public facts; and religions are important public facts. It is subject first and foremost to 'the authority of the fact', although not thereby positivistically enslaved, so to speak, to 'a cult of the fact' as my comments below on the role of theory in that study will clearly demonstrate. Religion, it must be recognized, is a form of human activity and therefore like any other form of human activity can become the object of human reflection.

This does not, of course, imply that persons who are religiously committed cannot be scientific students of religion or, for that matter, that Marxist atheists ought to be excluded from departments of Religious Studies. What it does imply, however, is that the value systems by which such individuals may be personally motivated to undertake the study of religion not be allowed to determine the results of their research. What is at issue here is the matter of what we might call 'the institutional commitment' that characterises the academic study of religion – that is, the commitment to achieve intersubjectively testable knowledge about religion(s) free of the influence of personal idiosyncratic bias or extraneous social/political aims.

That 'institutional commitment' is a kind of epistemic morality – a commitment to what can reasonably be called 'the morality of scientific knowledge'.[11] 'Morality' here does not refer to the moral effects scientific knowledge may or may not have – the uses to which scientific knowledge may be put – as important as that may be, but rather the 'behaviour' required for the achievement of the goal of 'public knowledge of public facts'. It concerns, in effect, the 'internal morality of knowledge' rather than the morality of the external effects of knowledge and the way knowledge is put to use. And like Kant's perception that action undertaken for any reason except as an act of a virtuous will constitutes not a moral but rather a prudential act, so also an act of 'scientific discovery' undertaken for extrascientific reasons produces ideology and not knowledge. That the scientific enterprise has extra-scientific significance is no surprise, but the suggestion that that extra-scientific value should determine the shape of the scientific enterprise is. It is, I would argue, an attempt to return from 'the open' to 'the closed' society.[12]

The goal of the academic study of religion, therefore, to riterate, is an understanding of the phenomena/phenomenon of religion 'contained in' scientifically warrantable claims about religion and religious traditions. Without intersubjectively testable statements about religions both at the level of particular descriptive accounts of the data *and* at the level of generalizations with respect to the data, no scientific understanding can be achieved.

At the simplest logical level the student of religion functions somewhat like the scientific naturalist with a concern 'to collect', describe and classify the phenomena observed. (Being aware all the while, of course, that a mere accumulation of data does not in itself constitute a science).[13] The range of data, obviously, is enormous, involving rites, rituals beliefs, practices, art, architecture, music, and so on. Some depth of perspective in the descriptive accounts is provided in relating it to the field of events and structures of which it is a part; in comparing it to similar phenomena in other cultural and social contexts; and in providing at least a narrative account of its emergence and historical development. This work is carried out primarily within the framework of the positive historical and philological disciplines but does not exhaust the task of description.

The work of the phenomenologist, the hermeneut, and the 'historian of religions' (in the broad sense of that phrase) in their concern for the *meaning* they think religious behaviour – beliefs, practice, rites, rituals, etc. – has *for the devotee* who participates in the tradition adds something new to the surface description of that tradition. Such 'thick description' as it has been called,[14] increases understanding of overt actions seen without reference to how they are 'taken' by the participant; ('seen' from the participant's point of view). The work of such students of religion is, as one might expect, much more of an imaginative activity than that of the positive historian or philologist. The results of their work is much less exact. The act of interpretation is in some sense the imposition of an external construction and therefore never likely to replicate exactly the participant's understanding of the phenomenon concerned. It will, consequently, be intrinsically incomplete and open to debate, although not on that account totally without merit, for such 'constructions' are not simply arbitrary but rather controlled by the context of information provided by the more positive sciences. That it does not allow the same degree of certitude that is to be found in the surface and depth descriptions of the other disciplines does not imply that that question of meaning can simply be ignored but rather that the student here will have to be satisfied with the more probable and plausible constructions and be willing to entertain alternatives to those constructions without overmuch fuss.[15]

It needs to be emphasized here that this concern with meaning and 'thick description' has nothing to do with speculative or intuitive insight as to the 'real meaning' or truth of Religion – its ultimate meaning that comes from a knowledge of the ultimate ontological status of the 'religious realities' as known by the participant within the tradition. Nor has it any kinship with direct, intuitive insight of the religiously perceptive student of religion. The meaning that holds the interest of the *academic* student of religion, rather, is a psychological matter; it involves overtones and undertones of actions, utterances, and events as well as an attempt to understand the psychological and emotional state or condition of the devotee who claims to know such ultimate mysteries. This kind of meaning, although not obvious at the surface level of religious phenomena, is not, as I have indicated, wholly beyond the reach of reason and scientific research.

Though knowledge of religion at the descriptive level is richly informative it is not primarily that for which the student of religion strives. Indeed, an increasing flow of such information soon inundates the individual for it is simply not possible for any one person to know all the particulars of the world's religious traditions. Like the other sciences, the study of religion seeks explanatory frameworks – theories – that account for the particulars; frameworks that permit an understanding of the multiplicity of particulars in terms of relatively few axioms and principles that can easily be held in mind. That thrust towards explanation and theory is implicit already in the descriptive and taxonomic levels that reduce 'individuals' to classes of things, persons, occurrences and events.

While explanations and theories transcend description they are nevertheless also dependent upon the descriptive level of activity of the student of religion. The data that accumulates as the result of the labours of the historian and phenomenologist are, in a sense, the substance for theoretical reflection in that they are what the theorist tries to provide a coherent account of. Moreover, the theories constructed to account for the data can only be properly adjudicated over against *new* observational data beyond that upon which theoretical reflection has been focused.

If these are the aims of the *academic* study of religion then that study is structurally indistinguishable from other scientific undertakings. The *academic* study of religion is, then, a positive science and not a religious or metaphysical enterprise in that it concerns itself with religion as a public fact and not a divine mystery. This does not mean that such a study must be limited to discussion of only the empirically obervable behaviour of religious persons and communities – that it adopt, for example, the positivistic empiricism of a Skinnerian behaviourism.[16] It merely implies that there not be 'privileged access' for some to the 'data'; that whatever does lie 'beyond' the empirically observable – whether that be the interior experience of the devotee or the 'intentional object' of that experience – be somehow 'intersubjectively available' for scrutiny and analysis. And that, it seems to me, presents no problems given that the empirically available religious traditions are considered by the devotees to be *expressions* of their faith, which faith is constituted by their religious experience and the truth of that 'encounter' with 'the ultimate', however it may be referred to in the various traditions. Thorough scrutiny of all aspects of the tradition, therefore, cannot but provide us *some* undertanding as to the nature of the 'faith' although, quite obviously, not with the experiential quality and emotional forcefulness with which the devotee will claim to understand it.[17] Thus, although there is an interior and esoteric aspect to religion, it is not wholly inaccessible to the 'outsider' for it can be approached from 'the outside in'. Moreover, should the devotee claim a superior understanding where a conflict of claims arises and do so on the basis of her/his direct personal experience of 'the Ultimate', the claim will be overruled on the grounds that it resorts to the use of 'information' to which s/he has 'privileged access'. To allow such a claim to stand would be to place all understanding of religion in jeopardy (and not merely the scientific understanding of religion) since such grounds would then also be acceptable for the settling of intra-religious (and even intra-traditional) conflict of claims as well. It is obvious, therefore, that the settlement of disputes would be achieved on highly idiosyncratic personal grounds – that is, on the basis of private religious experience – in which each and every disputant would be wholly successful. It would, in the final analysis, then, commit us to a radical relativism that precludes all possibility of transpersonal truth-claims and with it, all possibility of a scientific (i.e., academic) study of religion. What one could then know of religion would be that which one could know of 'faith' and that is only known *by* faith and the direct encounter of 'the Ultimate'. To know that the essence of religion is 'faith' would be to know that it cannot be scientifically understood.[18]

This, unfortunately, is too seldom noticed by students of religion. They fail to see that such reasoning makes the study of religion possible only from within the circle of the devotee/participant and therefore a religious rather than a scientific enterprise. The study of religion that appropriately finds its place within the university curriculum is rather that which I have sketched above. It is a critical study of a human cultural phenomenon and not a quest for some ultimate meaning or truth. It seeks 'objective' knowledge of a particular aspect of human culture. It is, therefore, essentially a positive, (*not* positivistic) social scientific endeavour that, although not necessarily behaviouristic is nevertheless *behaviouralist* in its approach to religion in that it attempts to provide a public rather than a private knowledge.[19]

V

If the foregoing discussion is anywhere near being sound it is obvious that the academic study of religion is, in Weber's sense, a scientific vocation. It is the search for 'objective' knowledge gained – free of presuppositions – for its own sake alone. It is true, as Weber points out, that every science presupposes rules of logic and method but such presuppositions are not of great consequence since they are the general foundation of orientation to the world for everyone – scientist and non-scientist alike. That scientific knowledge is 'worth searching for' is also a presupposition of science, but obviously not one that can be proved scientifically for it is that which itself establishes the enterprise. It simply is one of many values to have emerged in the growth and development of human culture. This presupposition can be interpreted with reference to its 'ultimate meaning' via-a-vis the ultimate position one takes up towards life as a whole but that is something that lies beyond the boundaries of the scientific undertaking itself, including the academic study of religion. Desire for finding such 'ultimate meaning' in the study of religious phenomena may in fact motivate many, if not most, of those who enter upon this field. This is *not* extraordinary and constitutes no problem for the academic study of religion unless one attempts to make that personal aim or intention an integral and essential element of the discipline as a whole. That would be, very simply, the introduction of 'confession' into science, thereby distorting the essential aims of science *qua* science and, therefore,

270

would be the destruction of it. Care is needed, consequently, to see that neither the rights of the individual are lost within the framework of scientific understanding nor that science is distorted beyond all recognition by personal or societal aspirations. This can be achieved by keeping clearly distinct what ought, structurally and institutionally, to characterize the study of religion that is *academically* housed and legitimated from what is permissible on the level of the individual scholar's extra-disciplinary (extra-scientific) aims and intentions for the results of that research. Weber's point that to analyze political structures and party positions is one thing but that to take a practical political stand quite another, is *apropo* here. To propagate one's faith is not the analysis of religious phenomena. The lecture-rooms of the university are wholly inappropriate for the propagation of either one's political or religious agendas. It is simply outrageous as Weber points out, to use the power of the lecture-room with its captive audience for such purposes. He writes:

> Now one cannot demonstrate scientifically what the duty of an academic teacher is. One can only demand of the teacher that he have the intellectual integrity to see that it is one thing to state facts, to determine mathematical or logical relations or the internal structure of cultural values, while it is another thing to answer questions of the *value* of culture and its individual contents and the question of how one should act in the cultural community and in political associations. These are quite heterogeneous problems. If he asks further why he should not deal with both types of problems in the lecture-room, the answer is: because the prophet and the demagogue do not belong on the academic platform.[20]

Similarly, the student entering upon the *academic* study of religion ought not to seek from the professors what the professors ought not to give. They should not, that is, crave leaders, but rather teachers.

I radically disagree, therefore, with the theologian H. Cox who puts bluntly the position so widely espoused by students of religion in the Anglo-American university setting today by insisting that 'the inner logic of the strictly academic approach to religious pluralism is leading it out of the academy and into the grimy world',[21] although in doing so, I do not mean to deny the value the 'product' of the academy may have in the 'grimy world'. The 'inner logic' of that study is that which makes it a

271

search for objective knowledge and as such a part of the academy. That knowledge, as Kurt Rudolph has so clearly pointed out, can make more than a merely intellectual and cognitive contribution. Although himself a champion of the study of religion as a positive historical science, he also notes the value of that study in the enterprise of ideology-critique which is something other than the study of religion pure and simple.[22] But to discuss that sense of the vocation of Religious Studies is a matter for discussion on some other occasion.

The task I set for myself in this essay was to delineate the nature of the study of religion as an academic exercise in the modern university. The aim of such a study, I have shown here, is to gain knowledge about religions and religion. Clearly, therefore, it is a scientific rather than a personal, social, or political undertaking. This is not to deny, as I have acknowledged in this essay, that the scientific study of religion may possess extra-scientific significance, but only that whatever that significance is, it falls outside the enterprise *qua* academic discipline.

*

I did not discuss the extra-academic aspects of the study of religion when this article was first published (1988), but I shall use the occasion of its reprinting to comment briefly on the broader value of the study of religion to society and on the broader social role (if any) of the scientific student of religion, *qua* scientific student of religion. I do so because of mounting pressure within the field to demonstrate social and cultural relevance and to incite the student of religion to assume the role of "public intellectual."

What is arguably of greater significance about modern science is its culture-transcending style of thought whereby knowledge of the world is gained by freeing thinkers from social, political, and cultural constraints. And while its success in matters of cognition is incontrovertible, its value as a tool for addressing human problems is open to question. As Ernest Gellner (1998) has recently pointed out, for example, science is of little help in providing a sense of belonging, or a basis of obligation and co-operation in society, or for consoling the afflicted. Gellner consequently concedes that science's "defectiveness in these respects is as distinctive and conspicuous as is its superiority in the spheres of cognition and production" (p. 184), and he acknowledges that modern science has not had great success in theorizing "the sphere of social and human phenomena" (p. 191). But these defects do not provide grounds for an epistemology in which knowledge is gained by means of immersion in the "wisdom" of cultural systems. What is at stake in the social sciences is not wisdom, value, or meaning, but knowledge, as it is in the natural sciences. The few successful extensions of science's cognitive style into the realm of human behaviour justifies continued support for the development of an explanatory social science which may provide knowledge relevant to the resolution of human problems. But the linkage between the social sciences and human problems will be of the same order as that between the natural sciences and engineering.

In *Can Modernity Survive?* (1990), Agnes Heller provides some interesting suggestions about how we might provide the link Gellner and others insist we find between our modern way of knowing the world and our modern values and way of life. Heller, moreover, is less pessimistic than Gellner about the extension of the new cognitive style into the social sphere and just as tenacious in advocating the scientific character of the knowledge sought by the social sciences. For Heller, extension of science to the social sphere does not entail the assumption that science is the only – or the highest – value for human society. Modernity, she argues, is characterized by "core values," but she does not attempt to provide a "single model of a supreme way of life" (p. 9), for the modern mind involves neither commitment to everything that is modern nor rejection of everything that is not. And science as quest for knowledge rather than for Truth and Meaning, embodies one such core value. "Truth [core values other than science] and true [scientific] knowledge are simply different in kind" (p. 14), she writes, even though the two may be closely connected. True (scientific) knowledge "cannot become Truth [Meaning] simply by presenting itself as true knowledge" (p. 14), she argues along Weberian lines, and scientists must not seek insight into the meaning of life in their scientific pursuits. The "culture sphere" of science (over against other cultural spheres such as the political, legal, aesthetic, economic, religious) stands alone, with norms and rules intrinsic to itself (p. 13): "[It] must be chosen as a vocation and not as a path leading to Truth. To offer insight into Truth through the pursuit of true [scientific] knowledge is to make a false promise, one that the social sciences have no authority to keep" (p. 15). For Heller, then, science is "core knowledge" compared to what she calls "ring knowledge" gained through particular personal and/or cultural interests and experiences, and concerned with existential matters – "meaning" and "value." Heller argues that these two kinds of knowledge can be combined in what might be called *Gesamtwissenschaft* (all-embracing science) that connects (scientific) knowledge with existential concerns. She warns, however, that if the "ring knowledge" is too thick (subjective) the project will amount to a work of fiction or of ideology, and if it is too thin (objective) the "core knowledge" will be informative but of little significance to anyone (p. 20). And she reiterates her main concern with respect to scientific knowledge, claiming that "as long as a genre remains social science, to the extent that it does so, the constitution or the 'unconcealment' of Truth cannot be either intended or pretended by it ... [T]he quest for true [scientific] knowledge has a different ambition" (p. 21). *Gesamtwissenschaft*, therefore, cannot transform the character of science, nor does it rival science; in fact, it is a different undertaking which, although involving science, must also be constrained by science. The work of the *Gesamtwissenschaftler* is a peculiar undertaking that, even though it involves familiarity with how the sciences might impinge upon other culture spheres and be used to advance their aims, is clearly distinguishable from science. And the *Gesamtwissenschaftler* – a person who makes use of science in taking up broader human cocerns – is also distinguishable from the public intellectual who, by all accounts, it seems, must always be engaged in social and political commentary and activity.

There is no doubt that the study of religion, like the natural and social sciences and humanities generally, bears some relevance to public issues and concerns, but it is important to recognize that this does not oblige the student of religion, *qua* student of religion, to become either a *Gesamtwissenschaftler* or a public intellectual – that is, to be directly and deeply involved in the shaping of culture or in competition for moral or political leadership in society. Playing a major role in public affairs of that kind is not part of "religious studies" training. So that to expand the portfolio of the student of religion beyond the search for knowledge about religion and explanation of religious phenomena to a concern for political action would clearly subvert the notion of "religious studies" as a scholarly, scientific undertaking concerned with empirical, explanatory, and theoretical analyses of religion.

Literary scholars have recently raised similar objections to the notion of the literary scholar as public intellectual and I think a brief look at Stanley Fish's response to the issue there is an appropriate guide to the issue for the student of religion. In response to literary critics who lament their invisibility within the larger community, wishing to expand the range of their disciplinary responsibilities, Fish points out that "... if the category of 'academic work' were enlarged to the point that it included almost anything an academic did – whether in the classroom, the jury box, or the town hall – the category would have no context because it would contain everything" (1995: 87). His advice, therefore, to those who want "to get beyond the current professionalization of literary studies to something else" (p. 43) – and who "want to send a message that will be heard beyond the academy" (p. 2) – is to get out of the academy. For such a mandate, although compatible with Gramsci's organic intellectual is not that of the literary critic (1). As he puts it, "a practice acquires identity [...] by not being other practices, by presenting itself not as doing everything but as doing one thing in such a way as to have society look to it for specific performance" (pp. 79-80). Engagement as an organic intellectual, moreover, requires expertise within a broad public context not provided by the confines of a university laboratory or classroom; as Fish points out, there are "no well-established routes by which literary criticism is first brought to the attention of those who inhabit the centers of power and then presented to them in a way that ties it to their concerns" (p. 52). He concludes, therefore, that "the [...] academic who goes public successfully will have done so not by extending his professional literary skills, but by learning the skills of another profession" (p. 125). For him, "public intellectual" is a job description and he justifiably insists that "it is not a job for which academics, *as* academics, are particularly qualified" (p. 125).[23]

This advice clearly holds for all humanists and social scientists, including the student of religion. And to complain, as does Richard Rorty (1998: 135), that the professionalization or academicization of university disciplines has left us with nothing but a lot of dismal social sciences that favour "a talent for analysis and problem-solving over imagination" and "replace enthusiasm with dry, sardonic knowingness" is to ask for a transformation of the humanities and social sciences amounting ultimately to their subversion. As John Ellis argues (1997), the adoption of social agendas by literary critics in the university has amounted to nothing less than "the corruption of the humanities," because politically orientated research,

even if "politically useful in the short run [,... will] crowd out more fundamental thought" (p. 140); this must be so for it is not possible to be committed to the cause of knowledge and to political and social causes at the
same time. And if students of religion find their scientific research boring
and dismal, they ought to heed the advice meted out by Fish and Ellis to
similarly placed literary critics and leave the university for a job more to
their liking.

Notes

*   This article (Wiebe 1988) is reprinted with the permission of the author and publisher.
The commentary pp. 272-276 has been added for this version.

1. I use the capitalized phrase 'Religious Studies' to disignate the political reality of academic
departments, schools, centres, institutes, etc. and not to characterize the style or approach
of the study untertaken.

2. Max Weber, 'Science as a Vocation' in H. H. Gerth and C. Wright Mills (eds.), *From Max
Weber: Essays in Sociology* (New York: Oxford University Press, 1946: 129-156). It was originally published in *Gesammelte Aufsaetze zur Wissenschaftslehre* (Tübingen, 1922: 524-
555). I use the notion of 'vocation' not, obviously, in its religious sense but rather to
emphasize the stark contrast in aims and intentions between a 'religious calling' and a 'scientific career'.

3. I have given brief attention to this contrast in my 'Explanation and the Scientific study of
religion', *Religion*, v (1975) and 'Theory and the Study of Religion', *Religion*, xiii (1983).
The position espoused is the precise opposite to that of D. L. Dougherty in 'Is Religious
Studies Possible?' in *Religious Studies*, xvii (1981: 295-309, especially p. 308).

4. The scholarly study of religion has a rather long history and it should be clearly distinguished from the narrower, more academic interest in religious phenomena that emerged
in, roughly, the last quarter of the nineteenth century. See, e.g., Erik J. Sharpe's *Comparative Religion: A History* (London: Duckworth, 1975), or Jan de Vries's *The Study of Religion:
A Historical Approach* (New York: Harcourt, Brace and World, 1967).

5. Important here is Peter Munz's distinction between 'catechismic' and 'cognitive' beliefs.
Beliefs, that is, function not only cognitively but socially (i.e., non-cognitively). Beliefs
have often survived falsification, he points out, because they constituted a catechism that
served as a social bond amongst members of the group. Indeed, the catechismic function of
beliefs depends upon the *incorrectness* of the beliefs: 'To form small groups distinct from
other small groups of the same biological species – to form pseudo-species – it was necessary to use propositional knowledge which differed essentially from propositional knowledge similarly used by another group. Only 'false' knowledge can, in this sense, be sufficiently exclusive of beings which belong to the same biological species. 'Correct' knowledge would not have been able to provide a criterion of exclusion, for correct knowledge
could be shared by members of other societies'. (*Our Knowledge of the Growth of Knowledge*, London: Routledge, Kegan Paul, 1985: 300) Membership of such a society, that is,

depends on members being able to give not the correct answer to a genuinely cognitive question but rather the 'correct' answer to a catechismis question.

6. Max Weber, *op. cit.* p. 143.

7. The desire for 'objective knowledge' – what we might refer to as 'cognitive intentionality' – first emerges in Presocratic Greece. Belief/knowledge, that is, was for the first time released from the non-cognitive/social function it had until then fulfilled in the structuring of a cohesive group. Changes in the economic, political and social complex of ancient Greek society provided opportunity for a truly cognitive apparatus to develop. Alternative kinds of social bonding, however, had not emerged so that the cognitive and non-cognitive uses of belief operated side by side. Nevertheless, the emergence of the more purely cognitive intentionality is the emergence of a new value that, like life itself, is its own justification. I have argued this claim in some detail in my (as yet unpublished) 'In Two Minds: Religion and Philosophy in Ancient Greece.' G. Thomson catches the ambiguity that must have existed by noting that scientists and philosophers were only one section of the ruling class in Miletos and that they functioned in society at two distinct levels. Thus he writes: 'These Milesian nobles had outgrown superstition in their private lives, but there was no question of abandoning it [religion/theology] as an instrument of public policy. (*Aeschylus and Athens*, [London: Lawrence and Wishart, 1973/1941: 152].

8. Max Weber, *op. cit.* p. 152.

9. *Ibid.* pp. 143-4.

10. Although my concern here is primarily with research and teaching in this field in the university setting it seems to me that it applies, in all essentials, to 'the teaching of religion' at the primary and secondary levels as well, although I shall not argue that matter here.

11. The concept of an 'epistemic morality' or 'morality of scientific knowledge' is quite appropriate although I do not here provide justification for its use. I refer the reader here to the use of that notion in the philosophical literature. See references, e.g. in my 'Is Religious Belief Problematic?' *Christian Scholar's Review*, vii (1977) pp. 33-52; especially note 5, p. 25.

12. My use of these notions follows that of K. R. Popper in his two volume *The Open Society and Its Enemies*, (New York: Harper and Row, 1962) and in the essays in *Conjectures and Refutations*, (New York: Harper and Row, 1963). I am not unaware of that vast body of literature from the Frankfurt School and other 'hermeneutical' type enterprises that argues the contrary claim. To argue the weaknesses of those claims here, however, is not possible. A good hint as to how such an argument might be developed, however, can be found in B. Nelson's comments on Habermas in his 'On the Origins of Modernity: The Author's Point of View', in his *On the Roads to Modernity: Conscience, Science and Civilization*, T. E. Huff (ed.) (New York: Rowman and Littlefield, 1981).

13. See, for example, D. Sperber, *On Anthropological Knowledge* (Cambridge: Cambridge University Press, 1985: 11).

14. This notion is borrowed from C. Geertz's 'Thick Description: Toward an Interpretive Theory of Culture', in his *The Interpretation of Cultures* (New York: Basic Books, 1973: 3-30).

15. On this score I am very much in agreement with D. Sperber's discussion of the nature of interpretation in ethnology. Interpretations are a species of nondescriptive representation of a culture based on a subjective understanding by the researcher. They are, Sperber suggests, faithful to the meaning of the phenomenon rather than mirroring exactly its directly

observable character. They are not, therefore, in and of themselves adequate to the phenomenon concerned but neither are they wholly useless. They can be very helpful, he insists, when combined with 'descriptive comments' that allow for some intersubjective assessment of their adequacy to the phenomenon in question. See Sperber, *op. cit.*, especially chapter 1.

16. This is not, of course, to rule out all possibility of such a reductionism, although a reductionism somewhat less crude than such a behaviourism. I have touched on this matter in my 'The "Academic Naturalization" of Religious Studies: Intent or Pretence?' (in *Studies in Religion*, xv 1986) and will not, therefore, elaborate further here. On the general question of the possibility of such reductionist moves in the social sciences, however, see especially Alexander Rosenberg's *Sociobiology and the Preemption of Social Science* (Oxford: Basil Blackwell, 1980).

17. On this score I find myself in serious disagreement with a number of scholars in the field. Time does not permit counter-argument here. However, grounds for the disagreement can be found in my response to a similar argument put forward by W. C. Smith: 'The Role of Belief in the Study of Religion: A Response to W. C. Smith', *Numen*, xxvi (1979) pp. 534-549.

18. This is a fairly common argument from a purely religious/theological perspective that, it seems to me, has some merit. When it is the conclusion of an argument in support of an academically legitimated study of religion(s), however, it makes the argument in support of an academically legitimated study of religion(s), however, it makes the argument a *reductio*. On the former issue see, for example, Thomas J. J. Altizer's 'The Religious Meaning of Myth and Symbol' in Thomas J. J. Altizer *et al.* (eds.), *Truth, Myth, and Symbol* (Englewood Cliffs: Prentice-Hall, 1962) and on the latter see my 'Does Understanding Religion Require "Religious Understanding"?' in W. Tyloch (ed.), *Current Progress in the Methodology of the Science of Religion* (Warsaw: Polish Scientific Publishers, 1984/85).

19. For possibilities of developing the argument in this direction see W. Richard Comstock, 'A Behavioral Approach to the Sacred: Category Formation in Religious Studies'. *The Journal of the American Academy of Religion*, xlix (1981) pp. 625-643.

20. Max Weber, *op. cit*. p. 146.

21. H. Cox, *Religion in the Secular City: Towards a Post-modern Theology* (New York: Simon and Schuster, 1984: 229).

22. See, for example, his *Historical Fundamentals and the Study of Religions* (New York: Macmillan, 1985; especially chapter 4, 'The History of Religions and the Critique of Ideologies').

23. Fish maintains: " [...] if you want to speak to the public, there is no degree to be had, no accepted course of accreditation, no departments of Public Relevance" (p. 117) and so he claims that the public intellectual is not recognized as such until she has the public's attention (p. 118). He furthermore maintains that such attention cannot be gained from the stage of the academy, and that academics are therefore not candidates for the role. Scholars at Florida Atlantic University are in obvious disagreement with this notion for they have recently created a Ph.D. program in Comparative Studies billed as "the first interdisciplinary program to educate public intellectuals" (publicity brochure). The brochure continues: "The Latin word *docere* originally meant not simply to teach, but to lead. This dual meaning underpins this Ph.D. program. It is for those who want to change the social order

278

as well as understand it." [This claim leads to another set of problems since *ducere* means to lead whereas *docere* means only to teach, but that matter will not be taken up here.] Such a program, however, cannot guarantee its participants the attention of the public; and I think Fish is likely right to insist that that attention will not be commanded even by this kind of academic enterprise.

References

Ellis, John. 1997. *Literature Lost: Social Agendas and the Corruption of the Humanities.* New Haven: Yale University Press.

Fish, Stanley. 1995. *Professional Correctness: Literary Studies and Political Change.* Oxford: Clarendon Press.

Gellner, Ernest. 1998. *Language and Solitude: Wittgenstein, Malinowski and the Habsburg Dilemma.* Cambridge: Cambridge University Press.

Heller, Agnes. 1990. *Can Modernity Survive?.* Berkeley: University of California Press.

Rorty, Richard. 1998. *Achieving Our Country: Leftist Thought in Twentieth-Century America.* Cambridge, Mass: Harvard University Press.

Wiebe, Donald. 1988. "Why the Academic Study of Religion? Motive and Method in the Study of Religion." *Religious Studies* 24, pp. 403-413.